AF555915

INFLATIONARY TRENDS IN INDIA

INFLATIONARY TRENDS IN INDIA

Editors

APARNA BHARDWAJ
RAJESH KUMAR

REGAL PUBLICATIONS
New Delhi - 110 027

INFLATIONARY TRENDS IN INDIA

ISBN 978-81-8484-109-1

Typeset by
RAHUL COMPOSERS
358, Pocket-B, Phase-2, Sector-16 B, Dwarka, New Delhi - 110 075

Printed in India at
MAYUR ENTERPRISES
WZ Plot No. 3, Gujjar Market, Tihar Village, New Delhi - 110 018

Published by
REGAL PUBLICATIONS
F-159, Rajouri Garden, New Delhi - 110 027 • Phone : 45546396
E-mail : regalbookspub@yahoo.com

Contents

Preface ix

List of Contributors xi

Introduction xv

1. Inflation : 'An Iniquitous Tax' 1
Md. Quddus and *Rajendra Prasad Gupta*

2. Commodity Prices and Inflation in a Global Scenario with Special Reference to India 13
Dev Raj

3. Inflation, Recession, Financial Meltdown and the Indian Economy : An Analysis of Some Missing Roots 44
Paramanand Singh and *Shashi Bhushan Singh*

4. Inflation in India : A Result to the Excess Supply of Money 64
C.B. Sharma

5. Inflationary Trends in India 75
Anil Kumar Thakur and *Aparna Bhardwaj*

6. Role of Fiscal and Monetary Policies to Control Inflation 88
V.D. Sharma and *Brijesh Sharma*

7. Inflation in India : An Analysis 94
Shrawan Kumar Singh

8. Inflationary Trends in India : An Analysis 119
Dalip Kumar, Rekha Rani and *Bharti Kumari*

9. Inflation Pendulum Strikes After 20 Years—2008 135
Abha Mittal

10. Issues and Policy Options for Inflationary Trends in India 144
B.M. Jani

11. Determinants of Inflation in India : An Empirical Analysis 157
Zafar Ahmad Sultan and *Sharful Hoda*

12. Inflationary Trends and Measures Taken to Curb 173
S.P. Saha and *Bishnu Roy*

13. Inflation in India : Causes and Measures 181
Shailesh Kumar and *Ratnesh Kumar*

14. Inflationary Trends in India 201
Jagdish Prasad Sharma, Kanchan Prabha and *Vivek Kumar*

15. An Analysis of Inflationary Trends in India : Pre and Post-Reform Period 209
Sunil Kumar and *Sunil Kumar*

16. An Analysis of Inflationary Trends in India : With Special Reference to Foodgrains Prices 217
Kumari Rekha and *Vikash*

17. Global Inflation : Changing Dynamics and its Impact on Indian Economy 228
Sudha Ranjan Singh and *Ajit Kumar*

18. Inflationary Trend in India : During Five Year Plans 234
Syed Alay Mujtaba and *Pankaj Purushotam*

19. Inflation in India and Ways Out 247
Sadanand Jha and *Anil Kumar Jha*

20. Inflationary Trends in India Over-all : An Exclusive Truth 259
Priyatam Kumar

21. Growth and Inflation 264
Rina Chand

22. Review of Inflationary Control Measures : A Micro Analysis 270
Chandra Shekhar Ravi and *Badri Narayan Sah*

23. Recent Global Inflationary Trends and the Role of Central Banks in Developing Economy (India) 281
D.K. Bhattacharya and *Niyati Chakraborty*

24. Inflationary Trends in India 289
Mina Kumari and *Manoj Kumar Verma*

25. Inflation Trends During Pre and Post-Reform Era 295
Vivek Kumar, Manish Kumar and *Niranjay Kumar*

26. Global Economic Crisis and U.P.A. Government Policy to Counter it 308
Ravi Ranjan

27. Pros and Cons of Global Economic Crisis 318
Pushpa Kumari

28. The Global Economic Crisis and India 327
Sanjay Kumar

29. Monetary and Fiscal Policy to Control Inflation 336
Rahul Kumar Santosh

30. Impact of Global Economy on Price Movements in India 343
Surendra Kumar Bhagat and *D.N. Sah*

31. Recent Global Inflationary Trends and its Impact on Indian Economy 350
Chitranjan Ojha and *Uma Shankar Singh*

32. Agflation in India : A Paradoxical Situation 355
Shyam Sunder Singh Chauhan, Ravi Kant and *Manish Dev*

33. Price Inflation and its Economic Effects 364
D.C. Mishra, Md. Tahir Hussain and
Uma Shankar Bharati

Index 373

Preface

The current wave of inflation in India reminds us nine such episodes during the last 60 years. Double digit inflation lasting beyond twelve months occurred on five such occasions. The longest period of hyper inflation, triggered by sudden rise in oil prices, was during October 1972 to March 1975. The historic year of economic crisis, i.e. 1990-91 too witnesses the heat of inflation followed by high inflation for 15 months between March 1994 and May 1995. Despite these significant periods of high inflation of the order of double digit, India remained a country of moderate inflation. What is significant is that the average rate inflation has a declining trend. Monthly annual average inflation during 1956-57 to 2009-10 is 6.7 per cent and the same has dropped to 5.1 per cent during 2001-02 to 2009-10. A close analysis of inflationary trends during the last 60 years reveals that high inflation periods were coincided either with episodes of oil price surge or droughts/floods in food producing regions of the country.

The current surge in inflation has two peculiar things. One, the double digit inflation of food articles is lasting for over two years and hurting the poor most. Second, the monetary policy instruments have little impact on food inflation. Supply side constraints are making the situation beyond control.

The present book reviews various aspects of inflation in India and the world. The book examines various options of price control available with the government and the central bank and their impact. Some of the papers in the book gives a vivid view of current global meltdown and its impact on the price rise in India.

The book includes selected papers presented at the 12th Annual Conference of the Economic Association of Bihar held at T.M. Bhagalpur University, Bhagalpur, on 4-6 July, 2009. The papers are a part of presentation and discussion on the theme "Inflationary Trends in India", under the chairmanship of Dr. Shyam Sunder Singh Chauhan. We express our sincere thanks to all those who came to participate in the session on the above theme of the conference.

We express thanks and gratitude to Economic Association of Bihar in general and Dr. Bikrama Singh, The Executive President and Prof. T. Haque, the conference president in particular for giving this excellent opportunity to bring this book. All the contributors of this book deserve our sincere thanks for their efforts. We are also thankful to Regal Publications for bringing this book in an excellent manner.

APARNA BHARDWAJ
RAJESH KUMAR

List of Contributors

Abha Mittal, Reader in Economics, Maharaja Agrasen College, Delhi University, Delhi.

Ajit Kumar, Research Scholar, Magadh University, Bodh Gaya (Bihar).

Anil Kumar Jha, Lecturer in Commerce, Cooperative College, Jamshedpur, Jharkhand.

Anil Kumar Thakur, Post Graduate Department of Applied Economics and Commerce, College of Commerce, Patna under Magadh University, Bodh Gaya (Bihar).

Aparna Bhardwaj, A Brilliant Graduate from Magadh University, Bodh Gaya (Bihar).

B.M. Jani, Professor of Economics, Saurashtra University, Rajkot.

Badri Narayan Sah, Lecturer, Commerce, Rameshwar Yadav Manihari College, Manihari, B.N.M.U., Madhepura (Bihar).

Bharti Kumari, Research Associate, Research Institute for Rural Development, Hajipur, Vaishali.

Bishnu Roy, Department of L.S.W., A.S. College, Deoghar.

Brijesh Sharma, Sr. Student, D.B.E., P.U., J.N.P. (U.P.).

C.B. Sharma, Head, Department of Economics, S.S. College, Jehanabad.

Chandra Shekhar Ravi, Student, Tilkamanjhi Bhagalpur University, Bhagalpur (Bihar).

Chitranjan Ojha, P.G. Department of Commerce, Magadh University, Bodh Gaya (Bihar).

D.C. Mishra, Head, Department of IRPM, TNB College, Bhagalpur (Bihar).

D.K. Bhattacharya, Senior Lecturer, Department of Economics, H.D. Jain College, Ara (Bihar).

D.N. Sah, Department of Commerce, B.N. College, Bhagalpur (Bihar).

Dalip Kumar, National Council of Applied Economic Research, New Delhi.

Dev Raj, Professor (IB)-*cum*-Controller of Examinations, Sri Sharada Institute of Indian Management-Research, New Delhi.

Jagdish Prasad Sharma, Faculty of Commerce, T.M.B. University, Bhagalpur (Bihar).

Kanchan Prabha, Dr. Vikhe Patil Foundations, C.M.R.D., Pune (Maharashtra).

Kumari Rekha, Lecturer, Dr. R.M.L.S. College, Muzaffarpur (Bihar).

Manish Dev, Research Scholar, Department of Economics, Narain College, Shikohabad (U.P.).

Manish Kumar, Lecturer in Economics, Department of Economics, J.L.N. College, Chakardharpur, Ranchi University, Ranchi (Jharkhand).

Manoj Kumar Verma,

Md. Quddus, University Professor of Commerce, College of Commerce, Patna (Bihar).

Md. Tahir Hussain, University Department of Rural Economics & Co-operation, TMBU.

Mina Kumari, Teacher, Economics, MHS Inter School, Mainpura, Patna (Bihar).

Niranjay Kumar, Research Scholar, Department of Economics, J.L.N. College, Chakardharpur.

Niyati Chakraborty, Lecturer in Economics, Barahea Degree College, Munger (Bihar).

Pankaj Purushotam, Pankaj Purushotam Bakhra Lodge (East), Nayatola, Muzaffarpur (Bihar).

Paramanand Singh, HOD, Economics, BNM College, T.M. Bhagalpur University, Bhagalpur (Bihar).

Priyatam Kumar, Research Scholar, University Department of Rural Economics, T.M. Bhagalpur University, Bhagalpur (Bihar).

Pushpa Kumari, Department of Economics, P.K. Roy Memorial College, Dhanbad (Bihar).

Rahul Kumar Santosh, Lecturer, Department of Economics, Sahibganj College, Sahibganj, Sido-Kanhu Murmu University, Dumka (Jharkhand).

Rajendra Prasad Gupta, Lecturer in Commerce (MLC Bihar Legislative Council), College of Commerce, Patna (Bihar).

Rajesh Kumar, Department of LSW, Magadh University, Bodh Gaya (Bihar).

Ratnesh Kumar, Research Scholar, B.R.A. Bihar University, Muzaffarpur (Bihar).

Ravi Kant, Reader, Department of Economics, R.B.S. College, Agra (U.P.).

Ravi Ranjan, Lecturer (L.S.W), Allama Iqbal College, Bihar Sharif, Nalanda (Bihar).

Rekha Rani, Department of Economics, Patna University, Patna (Bihar).

Rina Chand, Department of Economics, MAM College, Nangachia.

S.P. Saha, Head, Department of Commerce, J.M.D.P.L. Mahila College, Madhubani (Bihar).

Sadanand Jha, Lecturer in Commerce, Sabour Collge, Sabour, Bhagalpur (Bihar).

Sanjay Kumar, S/o Kedar Pd. Singh Shivpuri (Chitkohra), Anisabad, Patna (Bihar).

Shailesh Kumar, Department of Economics, H.N.B. Govt. PG College, Kumaun University, Nainital.

Sharful Hoda, From Darbhanga (Bihar).

Shashi Bhushan Singh, HOD, Economics, C.M. College, L.N. Mithila University, Darbhanga (Bihar).

Shrawan Kumar Singh, Professor of Economics, IGNOU, (Retd.), B-2/71-A, Keshavpuram, Delhi.

Shyam Sunder Singh Chauhan, Reader and Head, Department of Economics, Government Girls P.G. College, Sirsaganj (Firozabad) (U.P.).

Sudha Ranjan Singh, Head, Department of Economics, Gaya College, Gaya (Bihar).

Sunil Kumar, Head, Department of Economics, S.N.S. College, Muzaffarpur (Bihar).

Sunil Kumar, Senior Lecturer, Department of Economics, L.S. College, Muzaffarpur (Bihar).

Surendra Kumar Bhagat, Lecturer, R. Lal College, Lakhisarai (Bihar).

Syed Alay Mujtaba, S. Villa, Moh. Chandwara Hall Compound, Muzaffarpur (Bihar).

Uma Shankar Bharati, University Department of Rural Economics & Co-operation, TMBU.

Uma Shankar Singh, Research Scholar, P.G. Department of Economics, L.N.M.U., Darbhanga (Bihar).

V.D. Sharma, Gandhian Thinker, Coordinator: C.G.S.H.R., Chief Editor : Gandhian Vision (International Journal), Sr. Fellow, Department of Business Economics (Faculty of Management Studies) Proctor, VBS Purvanchal University Jaunpur.

Vikash, Research Scholar, B.R.A. Bihar University, Muzaffarpur (Bihar).

Vivek Kumar, Bachelor of Engineering, Computer Science, Arya College of Engineering & IT, Rajasthan University, Jaipur (Rajasthan).

Vivek Kumar, Research Scholar, UGC NET-JRF, Post Graduate, Department of Economic, Bodh-Gaya, M.U. (Bihar).

Zafar Ahmad Sultan, Lecturer in the P.G. Department of Economics, L.S. College, Muzaffarpur, B.R. Ambedkar University, Muzaffarpur (Bihar).

Introduction

Inflationary Trends in India show a vide fluctuations during the last six decades with varied degree of ups and downs. The year 1964-65, 1973-74, and 1990-91 witnessed all time high inflation in India. The price rise during 1964-65 was the outcome of Chinese invasion and Indo-Pak conflict, while the galloping inflation during 1973-74 caused by price increase in the crude oil in the international market. High inflationary pressure during 1990-91 was the result of mismatch between the supply and demand.

The current wave of inflation in India is unique in the sense that despite negative inflation rate in June 2009, the prices of agricultural commodities were rising at a fast pace. Prior to the eruption of global meltdown, the global economy faced severe price rise of agricultural commodities during 2006-08 because of natural disasters such as droughts and cyclone, speculative activities in financial markets, failure of government to maintain required buffer stocks and changing consumption habits of consumers in major developing countries of the world.

India is the only country in the world which witnessed negative WPI-based inflation rate in June 2009. But, that was not a sign of depression or recession, as is generally associated with the fall in the prices, but was the result of decline in prices from a high base in June 2008. Another uniqueness in the price rise was the wide gap between the WPI-based inflation rates. CPI-RL-based inflation rate in June 2009 was more than twice of WPI-based inflation rate.

The raging inflation and rising prices of commodities, particularly of mass consumption, is a matter of concern for the policy-makers—Central Bank and Ministry of Finance—Galloping inflation severely hurts the common man whose real income decrease with every rise in prices of essential commodities. Moderate inflation rate between 4-6 per cent acts as catalyst for the growth of the economy. It encourages investors to expand the production base and reap the benefits of price rise.

In the present context of hyper inflation in India, Central Government seems to be in compromising position with the rising prices just to achieve 9 per cent plus growth rate of GDP so as to fullfil the wishes of Prime Minister Dr. Man Mohan Singh. Because of this thinking the government has left the responsibility of price control on the Central Bank. This has adopted a tight monetary policy in 2010. There is a pervasive belief that inflation can be reduced only at the cost of giving up growth, despite evidence to the contrary. A major determinant of results, as have been observed in many countries, is the policy mix and instruments used to reduce inflation and promote growth. Indian economy disapproved this theory during the entire period of Tenth Five Year Plan, which achieved 7.9 per cent growth rate in GNP at 1999-2000 prices along with the average WPI-based inflation rate of 4.47 per cent.

In this scenario of conflicting views on the required or a threshold level of Inflation in India, the root question is whether to adopt tough fiscal and monetary measures to control inflation and keep the growth rate achieved in its natural way, so as to protect the interests of common man. What should be the threshold limit of inflation? In the Indian context the Chakravarty Committee (RBI, 1985) first made a reference to 4 per cent level of inflation, which was regarded as the first influential fix on the threshold level of inflation in India. C. Rangarajan (1998), introduced the concept of "threshold inflation" to identify the level of inflation from which the adverse consequences begin to set in. Rangarajan regarded 6 per cent of inflation to be the outer limit. Tarapore

Committee recommended 3 per cent level of inflation rate. Thus the acceptable range of inflation rate in India lies between 3-7 per cent.

The current book consists of 33 research papers in all presented at 12th Conference of Economic Association of Bihar held at T.M. Bhagalpur University, Bhagalpur on 4-6 July 2009. These papers were presented under the theme "Inflationary Trends in India". The session chaired by Dr. Shyam Sunder Singh Chauhan, had a lively and fruitful discussion. The contributors have tried their best to present the subject matter in a vivid and coherent manner. They have discussed the problem of inflation in India from various angles. Nature and contents of these papers are varied. Some are analytical, and then some others are statistically significant. *Md. Quddus* and *Rajendra Prasad Gupta's* paper entitled "Inflation: An Iniquitous Tax" present a generalised view of inflation in India. The authors are of the view that the runaway inflation is unannounced and painful taxation on people. The paper entitled "Commodity Prices and Inflation in a Global Scenario" with special reference to India by *Dev Raj* emphasizes that the inflation confronted the policy-makers throughout the world in the form of dominant economic problem. The paper, purely of theoretical nature, presents the type of inflation and remedies to control it. According to author the present inflationary trend in India is profit inflation which is fueled basically by excess demand for a variety of goods, notably primary commodities, including food articles. *Paramanand Singh* and *Shashi Bhushan Singh* traces some missing roots of current global meltdown in their paper. "Inflation, Recession, Financial Meltdown and the Indian Economy: An Analysis of some Missing Roots". The authors present a historical view of policies of USA during the 20th century that resulted into inflation or recession from time to time. They, very categorically, make it clear that monopolistic hegemony of US and European economies with its gigantic productive potential, acts as obstacles in the way of making full use of resources and manpower of the third world countries in the interest of their common people, thus, fails to producing a counteracting force against accumulation and as a result world witnesses the weakening of investment of demand.

The paper "Inflation in India : A Result to the Excess Supply Money" by *C.B. Sharma* treats inflation as a monetary phenomena. The author is of the firm opinion that Indian policy-makers often acted beyond the norms of financial discipline in terms of money supply. Government and the corporate world often compromise with high inflation for a higher growth of GDP. The author seems agree with the monetarists that there is a trade-off between inflation and growth implying that a country has to suffer inflation in order to achieve higher growth. *Anil Kumar Thakur* and *Aparna Bhardwaj* emphasizes in their paper entitled "Inflationary Trends in India" that inflation is a global phenomenon in present-day time. There is hardly any country in the capitalists world today which is not affected by the specter of inflation. The paper analysis the effects of inflation on production and the distribution. The most serious effect of inflation is that it disrupts the smooth working of the price mechanism. It also losses the flexibility under the inflation forces, which results in the reduction of mobilization of productive resources. The author is of the firm view that hyper inflation adversely affects the wage earners and the common man but stimulates businessmen, traders, merchants and speculators which reap rich harvest on account of windfall profits accruing to them as a result of price rise.

Shrawan Kumar Singh's paper entitled "Inflation in India: An Analysis" makes an attempt to analyze some of the complications that cloud the perception of the link in the short-run and tries to show that policy-makers cannot escape theory when dealing with the short-run. According to Prof. Singh money is generalised purchasing power, hence the monetary policy is very much concerned with the general price level. Prof. Singh is highly critical about the existing measures used to gauge inflation at any point of time. There is no all-purpose, all-inclusive and universally valid index that can be used to measure the trends in price rise.

The paper "Inflationary Trends in India : An Analysis by *Dalip Kumar, Rekha Rani* and *Bharti Kumari* examines the causes and impact of inflation during 1995-96 to 2008-09 giving more emphasis on the period from January 2008 to February 2009. *Abha Mittal's* paper "Inflation Pendulum Strikes after 20 years 2008", observes that the hyper inflation during 2008 was due to supply side constraints. *B.M. Jani* examines various issues and policy options for inflation in India in his paper entitled "Issues and Policy Options for Inflationary Trends in India". The author is of the opinion that the current spate of inflation in India is an outcome of transmission of global inflation into India, rising oil prices in the international market, adverse balance of payment and finally the food inflation largely due to speculation in agricultural commodity exchange market.

Zafar Ahmad Sultan and *Sharful Hoda* present a theoretical view of the measurement of inflation in their paper entitled "Determinants of Inflation in India: An Empirical Analysis". The author says that in a closed economy, price level is generally influenced by domestic factors. When an economy is opened to the world economy, change in price level takes place even when domestic variables show normal trends they empirically proves that the world inflation and money supply have positive and significant relation with inflation in India. The papers by *S.P. Saha* and *Bishnu Roy, Shailesh Kumar* and *Kanchan Prabha* and *Vivek Kumar; Sunil Kumar* and *Sunil Kumar* deal with the causes and impact of inflation in India. The authors have suggested some specific measures to control the inflation because it affects the common man. *Sudha Ranjan Singh* and *Ajit Kumar's* paper entitled "Global Inflation: Changing Dynamics and its Impact on Indian Economy" states that most of the acceleration in inflation in India is due to global inflation which has driven the prices upward in India. The papers by *Syed Alay Mujtaba* and *Pankaj Purushottam* suggests that economy should capable of absorbing inflationary impact of development expenditure, should have agricultural growth fast enough to meet the requirements of growing industrial incomes. He says more emphatically that the monetarist anti-inflationary policy can get support only from an expanded structural stabilization policy because the price behaviour under the Indian conditions call for an attack on both the variables and it may effectively be tackled inflationary situation in the long-run perspective. The papers by *Sadanand Jha* and *Anil Kumar Jha; Priyatam Kumar;* deal with the inflation in generalized form while *Rina Chand* examines the issue of inflation in relation to growth. *Chandra Shekhar Ravi* and *Badri Narayan Sah* review inflationary control increases. *D.K. Bhattacharya* and *Niyati Chakraborty* discusses the role of Central Banks in developing economies to control inflation. The authors make it clear that inflation is the most regressive form of taxation as it affects the poor and vulnerable sections of society.

The papers by *Mina Kumari* and *Manoj Kumar Verma; Vivek Kumar, Manish Kumar* and *Niranjay Kumar* discusses the trends in inflation during pre and post-reform era. The *Ravi Ranjan's* paper "Global Economic Crisis and UPA Government Policy to counter it" discusses the policies of Central Government during the era of global recession during 2008-09. Likewise *Pushpa Kumari; Sanjay Kumar's* papers deal with the global financial crisis and its after effects on Indian Economy, *Rahul Kumar Santosh* suggests some monetary and fiscal measures to combat hyper inflation while *Surendra Kumar Bhagat* and *D.N. Sah* trace the impact of Global Economy on Price Movement in India. *Chitranjan Ojha* and *Uma Shankar Singh* also present the same view. The paper entitled "Agflation in India : A Paradoxical Situation" by *Shyam Sunder Singh Chauhan, Ravi Kant* and *Manish Dev* deals with the paradoxical situation of negative inflation rate based on UPI and a hyper inflation in agricultural commodities. Agflation, a term coined in early 2007 by analysts at Merril Lyunch, describes generalised inflation led by increase in prices of agricultural commodities, mainly the food articles. The term, developed during the global price rise in food articles, describes a situation under which external prices drive up core inflation rates. The authors analyse the situation that took unwarranted turn in the late 2005 when the prices of almost all food commodities increased extraordinarily. Wheat prices doubled and prices of almost every crop under sun—maize, oilseeds, pulses were at or near peak in real terms. Even in real terms prices had jumped by 75 per cent in just 6 months. According to authors price rise in agricultural commodities took ugly turn between the early 2007 to early 2008.

"Price Inflation and its Economic Effects", the paper by *D.C. Mishra, Md. Tahir Hussain* and *Uma Shankar Bharati* presents various indices used for the estimation of inflation.

CONCLUSION

Research papers presented in this book make significant contribution to understanding the theoretical concepts, types and nature of inflation that may cause havoc in the economy by bringing the sudden fall in the real income of common people. Although, a moderate level of inflation is a pre-condition to encourage investment, but at the same time hyper inflation creates problems before democratically elected government whose popularity eroded with every rise in prices. The current dose of policy mix at Government of India level seems in compromising mood with a higher side of inflation for a higher growth of the order of 9 per cent or more.

These seminal contributions cover the various dimensions of inflation in India and the world. Some of the papers had gone in deep to assess the effectiveness of monetary and fiscal policies to control the hyper inflation. The book will help policy planners to choose a right mix of policies for the proper balance in demand and supply of various commodities. The book will also be useful for researchers and students to understand various aspects of inflation.

APARNA BHARDWAJ
RAJESH KUMAR

1

Inflation
'An Iniquitous Tax'

MD. QUDDUS AND RAJENDRA PD. GUPTA

INTRODUCTION

In India, the rise in inflation is an effect of the financial crisis seen, globally. Thus, to put it differently, it is an imported one from the outside of the country. Though 13 years ago the inflation was an all time high close to 13 per cent, it has now come down remarkably very low. It is very likely to come a single digit in March 2009. However, economists are of the opinion that a low range of inflation is an inducing tonic to the developing economy. Hence some amounts of inflation are always welcomes, though not the highest one as was experienced in August 2008, when it was as high as 13 per cent. About inflation in India, the Prime Minister Dr. Manmohan Singh an economist of repute admits; "International factors beyond his Government's control" have laid to such a situation, this was bound to happen. The raging inflation and rising prices of commodities is worrying everybody and is a matter of grave concern. We should analyse the causes of inflation and think over it whether it can be tamed. In my view inflation can be tamed and there is nothing to be worried about. This situation is the outcome of the idea of mixed economy conceived, propagated and executed by Pt. Nehru, who established the public sectors. Pt. Nehru was of the view that the establishment of public sectors will strengthen the Indian economy. The nation waited for long 40 years for the growth of our economy, but we could not achieve what was expected in these four decades. At last in 1991 the then finance minister Dr. Manmohan Singh, who is today our Prime Minister implemented The New Economic Policy based on Liberalisation, Privatisation and Globalisation of Indian economy by privatisation of public sector and encouragement for establishment of private sector organisation. After review of the new economic policy the nation has been given to understand that whatever we have achieved during the last 15 years, we could not achieve in the previous 40 years.

Regardless of the degree of gains achieved consequent upon the all pervasive and remarkable changes in the economic policy there is hardly any dispute over the fact that the 1991 crisis was converted into an opportunity to change the direction of the Indian economy. It is a fact that after the failure of the concept of mixed economy, i.e. encouragement to public sector, LPG model of development was introduced with several major changes. In this model, the first step was to the area reserved for public sector were opened to private sector by liberalising the economy both domestic and foreign with a view to facilitate direct foreign investment and to make public sector more professional. The second step was to open up the economy to other countries to encourage more exports. That is why the new policy of development puts emphasis on a bigger role for the private sector. It envisages a much larger quantum of FDI to supplement our growth process in 1984. The then Prime Minister Rajiv Gandhi in his first broadcast to the nation said, "the public sector has spread into too many areas where it should not have been". Therefore, reforms of the reform process started by liberalising the economy from public sector to private sector which resulted into the reduced role of public

Inflation as on Jan. 19th, 2008 in Major Groups (%)

Commodities	Weight (%)	Variation (Apr.-Jan.)				Variation (Year on Year)			
		Cumulative Changed		Contribution		Inflation		Contribution	
		2007-08	2006-07	2007-08	2006-07	2007-08	2006-07	2007-08	2006-07
(1)	(2)	(3)	(4)	(5)	(6)	(7)	(8)	(9)	(10)
All Commodities	100.00	3.18	5.93	100.00	100.00	3.93	6.31	100.00	100.00
Primary Articles	22.3	3.20	11.02	22.68	40.10	3.82	10.22	22.3	35.35
Fuel Power, Lights and Lubricants	14.23	4.47	1.74	30.36	6.69	3.92	3.57	21.86	12.73
Manufactured Products	63.75	2.66	5.76	46.62	53.94	3.91	5.88	55.20	51.92

sector investment. Resultantly, idea generated a wave of entrepreneurial optimism, improved business confidence by transforming the reforms of investment climate. In contrast to the increase in savings, the increase in investment has been driven up by private investment which went up by 10.3 per cent of GDP over the 5 years of 10th plan period. There is an improvement from 5.4 per cent of GDP in 2001-02 to 14.5 per cent in 2006-07 due to heavy money supply, RBI expects 8.5 per cent GDP growth with inflation close to 5 per cent and targeted the monetary expansion in the range of 17-17.5 per cent and credit expansion in the range of 20-24 per cent as consistent with targeted growth and inflation as envisaged in the economy policy. The following shows the growth rate and inflation.

INFLATION

To understand about inflation in a broader sense it is said that "persistent increase in the general price level is known as inflation. It is a purely monetary phenomenon when currency of a country exceeds the production. Existence and availability of surplus currency raises the general price level and lowers the purchasing power of the currency." There are, at least two distinct views on the concept of inflation, to some economist (i) Inflation is a pure monetary phenomenon, and (ii) It is a post-full employment phenomenon. But in context of India it is well recognised that inflation in India is a structural as well as a monetary phenomenon, i.e. localised demand-supply imbalances in wage goods, often due to seasonal variations in production—coupled with market rigidities and regulatory failures have supported inflationary expectations that have resulted in a more widespread impact on the consumers than the initial inflationary impulse. It is a fact that the huge surge in capital inflows, the liquidity management with it's underlying implication for inflation has been a major challenge. If I go into perspective of the whole about inflation since 1951, I find the picture which is stated as that the objective of first plan was to combat inflationary pressure. During second plan period, there was a gradual and steady rise in prices by 20 per cent in 1964-65. The price position during third 5 year plan deteriorated badly (Due to the Chinese invasion and Indo-Pak conflict) resulted price position became really difficult because of the hoarding and black-marketing in foodgrains and other essential goods. Fourth plan was significant due to the rise in price between 7 point to 9 points and at the end of the plan prices rose by 19 points and 47 points respectively. During 1973-74 the position of inflation was galloping. This was aggravated by a sudden rise in crude oil prices and also rise the lack of public confidence in the ability of the government to manage the price situation. The picture was as under:

Price Trends During 1975 to 1979
(1961-62 = 100) and (1970-71=100)

	WPI of all commodities
September 1974	331
March 1975	309
March 1976	283
March 1977	183
January 1978	184
January 1979	185

The condition during 1979 were highly suitable continuance of price stability as stated in above table. But by January 1980 it had risen to 224. It is fact that the price rise was started in the beginning of 1990 which was almost engineered by Government itself. The average annual rates of inflation were quite high between 10 per cent and 14 per cent till 1994-95 also known as double digits inflation. The average rate of inflation since 1991 is shown as under :

Average Annual Inflation Rate

	All commodities	*Primary article*
1991-96	10.6	11.3
1996-01	5.1	5.4
2001-06	4.7	3.6

The above table shows the decline of inflation rate from 10.6 per cent to 4.7 per cent between 1991-2006.

Price Situation during the 10th Plan

	Annual rate of commodities	*Primary inflation of all commodities*
2002-03	3.4	3.3
2003-04	5.4	4.2
2004-05	6.4	3.7
2005-06	4.4	2.9
2006-07	6.5	11.7

It is clear from the above table that during the 10th plan period annual rate of inflation was around 4 per cent.

UNRELENTING INFLATION IN INDIA : CURRENT SCENE

The current inflation is an imported one fuelled by speculation, Rich countries are exporting inflation to us. They no longer wish to invest their money in manufacturing assets. Their idle funds are being used for speculation and for investing in commodities. The IMF has called upon developing countries to make the fight against inflation their top priority. The unabated rise in the inflation rate is now proving to be a nightmare, despite fierce fire fighting by Government. Every tried and tested recipe in the book has been deployed—monetary curbs, export curbs on essential items like cement and the suspension of futures trading in staple foods such as rice and wheat. Inflation is becoming progressively a major concern since the number has reached crazy heights and the more pessimistic ones are already likening this situation to the pre-forms crisis phase. Runaway inflation is unannounced and painful taxation on people. The rising rate of inflation and its trends is as under :

THE TRENDS OF INFLATION

Further it is projected by Global investment Banker Barclays Capital that inflation may surge to 17 per cent by Sept. 2008. On account of another hike in fuel prices in the same month. Inflation today is caused more by global rather than by domestic factors. Naturally, as the Indian economy undergoes structural changes.

CAUSES OF DOUBLE-DIGIT INFLATION IN INDIA (SINCE 1995)

Price rise gets out of hand and it may be a serious challenge to maintain the economic growth as estimated by the end of 11th plan period.

Price Trends on July 25, 2008
(Base : 1993-94 = 100)

	WPI	*Rate of Inflation*
July 14, 2007	213.6	4.76%
June 05, 2008	238.7	11.91%
July 12, 2008	239.0	11.89%

The rate of inflation eased marginally to 11.89 per cent for the week ended July 12 on account of fall in the prices of certain food items. This is a fact that the liberalisation of Indian economy from 1991 had resulted in the rich become richer and the poor, poorer. It means that the 13 years high since 1995 inflation affected "AAM ADMI" i.e. common man's consumption basket and in near future it is likelihood to come down inflation to single digits. It hurts the poor more than the rich.

The Effect

1. The dramatic rise in the price of crude oil by international oil companies to $ 145-150 expand per

barrel from the current $ 132 per barrel and it could be triggered for another round of increase in fuel prices. It was apprehended that the inflation increase to 19 per cent. Causing the Government to revised retail petroleum prices w.e.f. June 08 when petrol prices was increased by Rs. 5 a litre, diesel by Rs. 3 per litre and cooking gas by Rs. 50 per cylinder. This resulted in the inflation a double digit of 11.05 per cent for the weekend June 07, 2008.

2. Foreign Exchange inflows 20 plus per cent growth in money supply was driving inflation higher. The huge increase in forex reserves since 1990-91 has responded to both international and domestic condition. Despite cut in interest rate in India relatively higher Indian interest rate had attracted NRI investment to India, resulting consequent rise in forex resources, leads to increase in liquidity—kicked up inflation. Therefore, we have already built a Foreign Exchange reserve of $ 300 billion which is enough to meet our import needs for the next two years. This is to be understand that these inflows are not "wealth". They are liabilities some of the forex reserves, however may be regarded as hot money having entered India for stock market speculation. The twin causes—excessive liquidity due to under-valuation of various currencies (technical) and fear of the US dollar collapse leading to increased purchasing of various commodities to hedge against a fall in US dollar needs to tackle upfront if inflation has to be confronted globally. This incremental flows of forex into the country has resulted in an increased credit flow by our banks. Naturally this is another fuel for growth and crucial for inflation.

3. Rise in global food prices and shortage due to high demand prices go up. This is not a long-term problem. The catch is that higher food prices do not always reach the farmers, the middleman pocket it. The world-wide surge in food prices in 2008 reduction in purchasing power of the poor owing to the increasing gap between wages and food prices.

> The spurt rise in prices in 2007-08 is peculiar because the UPA-led Government has come to power by promising to promote the welfare of the common man, i.e. "AAM ADMI".

The present causes of inflation in India passing through has been mentioned above in detail. In addition to this there are certain other traditional causes of inflation too which has got relation with the present situation. These are as follows :

> There are mainly three approaches to explain the source of inflation: (1) Demand pull, (2) Cost push, and (3) Structural. These three factors or causes are said to be conventional as well as most widely held view about the proximate cause of inflation.

DEMAND PULL INFLATION

This is basically when the aggregate demand in an economy exceeds the aggregate supply. It also define as "too much money chasing too few goods". Mounting total expenditure of both centre and state implies a growing public demand for goods and services and consequent rise in price. Another reason is deficit financing and increase in money supply, increasing black money and growth of population which is responsible for the persistent gap between demand and supply.

COST PUSH INFLATION

The best example to describe cost push inflation is the oil stock in the 1970s. When OPEC was formed. It squeezed the supply of oil and this caused oil prices to rise contributing to higher inflation. This is similar to what has happened recently when the oil price hiked. In 1980, 130 per cent increase in all fuel prices by OPEC and second jump was in the year 1980. Of course the same in this year 2008 the price of oil product and fuel hiked. In the prevailing situation it is difficult to control price level.

STRUCTURAL AND OTHER FACTORS OF INFLATION

In this situation inflation caused by structural rigidities such as stickiness in wages and other bottlenecks prevailing in the economy. This is a difficult situation to remove in the short-run.

Way to deal with an outbreak of inflation?

There are two types of majors to control inflation:

Supply Side Measure

By open market sale of foodgrains and increasing of distribution system Government can prevent an undue increase in prices of essential commodities.

1. To eliminate the hoarders and speculators Government has to fixed the wholesale and retail prices of foodgrains, bringing wheat and wheat product under the purview of licensing and stock limit.
2. By introducing dual system of essential commodities like sugar, cement through fair price shops at controlled prices supplying to the poor peoples.
3. To increase in the supply of foodgrains and other essential goods in time of internal shortage through larger import for example, during 1995-96 one million tonnes of rice and 3.5 million tonnes of wheat were sold by FCI in the open market to check the price rise.
4. The steep rise in oil seeds and edible oils in 1990-95 and 2008 along with pulses were responsible for rise in general price level.

Demand-side Measures

Inflation management has always been a key policy concern of the Government. Traditionally it has been a structural issue. Fiscal and monetary measures are the main tools to maintain the general price level.

1. *Fiscal measure* : Government has to control its own expenditure and keeping in check both its revenue

deficit and fiscal deficit. Fiscal policy is a budgetary policy in relation to taxation, public borrowing, and public expenditure. Changes in the total expenditure can be effected by fiscal measures. To combat inflation, fiscal measures would involve increase in taxation and decrease in Government spending. It means Government expenditure is curtailed.

2. *Monetary measure* : In this measure the main thrust is to restrict bank credit against inflation. *Milton Friedman* once said, "Inflation is always and every where a monetary phenomenon". It means that inflation is always caused because of too much money in the system, i.e. supply of money is much greater than the demand for it. However, Prof. Friedman later changed that to "substantial inflation is always and everywhere a monetary phenomenon". RBI uses its monetary policy to achieve a judicious balance between the growth of production and control of general price level. RBI uses Bank Rate, CRR, SLR and Open Market Operation to check speculative activity in the period of inflation.

CONCLUSION

In my opinion the time has come to make yet another departure from conventional thinking. Because India has emerged as the world's 10th trillion-dollar economy. Its GDP growing at an annual rate of 8 per cent on a sustained basis. It is world's second fastest growing economy and expected to become the world's fifth largest consumer market by the year 2020 and third largest economy by 2035. But the unabated rise in inflation to a crazy height is highly uncomfortable and unwelcome. In this connection the Finance Minister said, "Fast growing economies like India will face such problem but the right attitude, patience and grift can help us not only face the problem but also tackle it." It is said that inflation in India is part of the larger global phenomenon and the government has taken several steps to ease the liquidity and increase the money supply to lowering down the rate of inflation.

References

Economic Survey, 2007-08.

Economic Survey, 2007-08.

Economic Survey, 1981-82 and RBI Bulletin (Various Issues).

Economic Survey, 2006-07.

ET Report, The Union Minister of State for Industry, Mr. Ashwini Kumar.

Indian Economy, Rudra Dutt and K.P.M. Sundram.

India Today, June 30, 2008.

K.B.L. Mathur, The Growth Rate Mystery.

N.K. Sinha, Money Banking and Finance.

The Hindu, 14.07.08.

The Hindu, 25.07.08.

The Hindu, June 23, 2008.

Commodity Prices and Inflation in a Global Scenario with Special Reference to India

DEV RAJ

INTRODUCTION

Inflation is one of the most critical macro-economic problem for many countries of the world. In the post-World War II period in almost every country in the world have been tormented by the vagaries of Inflation. Then prices have kept on rising year after year so much systematically that any temporary change in the direction of upward movement of prices is not easily and at once believed. Thus, inflation confronted the economic policy-makers throughout the world in the form of a dominant economic problem. Even those people who have no idea of the precise meaning of Inflation, feel that it is something which creates dis-equilibrium in the national economy and spells distress. Actually speaking, they are reminded of what happened in Germany and the countries of Central Europe after the Two World Wars. Let us now we may discuss in detail the meaning of Inflation. There are two theories of Inflation that have been developed by economists in connection with it. These are: (i) The Traditional Money Supply, and (ii) The Theory of Inflationary Gap, which depends upon the Income-expenditure approach, i.e. the Keynesian approach. As the Quantity Theory Approach being practically inadequate, Lord J.M. Keynes introduced Inflationary Gap theory, which depends upon the functional relation of expenditure to disposal income, the value of current output being the base, which in the considered opinion of monetary experts provides the starting point of Inflation. According to Prof. Roy Harrod, Keynes' Theory of Inflation is in essence a Demand Theory.

DEFINITION OF INFLATION

According to Whittlesey, Friedman and Herman, "Inflation mean an extra-high expansion of currency and credit beyond the legitimate requirements of trade, commerce and industry with the resultant effect of increasing, sometimes, sky-rocketing prices." While according to Milton Friedman, "Inflation is always and every where a monetary phenomenon...and can be produced only by a more rapid increase in the quantity of money than output." But the economists do not agree that money supply alone is the cause of Inflation. Mr. Geoffrey Crowther has defined Inflation as, "A stage in which the value of money is falling, i.e. prices are rising." While in the opinion of Prof. Kemmerer, "Inflation is too much money and deposit currency, i.e. too much currency in relation to the physical volume of business being done. Further, Mr. H.G. Johnson defines, "Inflation as a sustained rise" in prices. While according to Mr. F.S. Brooman, Inflation is, "a continuous increase in the general price level." Mr. Edward Shaprio defines Inflation in a similar vein, "as a persistent and appreciable rise in the general level of prices." While, R.G. Hawtrey associate Inflation with "the issue of too much currency". While, Prof. R.G. Hawtrey associated Inflation with, "the issue of too much currency." Dr. Paul Einzig and

Lord J.M. Keynnes, consider it desirable to note that the majority of the leading German Economists and Bankers were convinced during and after the First World War that Inflation did not exist in that country. While Lord J.M. Keynes have meant by Inflation an access of the aggregate demand over the aggregate supply at full employment and a given price level.

RESEARCH METHODOLOGY USED

In this article a careful critical inquiry in seeking facts or principles, diligent investigation in order to ascertain the facts about the Inflation has been made. A formal, systematic, intensive process for carrying on the analytical analysis of adequate data analysis has been made. Further, the relationship between the facts and theories has been made in a systematic manner. Moreover, when we talk about the research methodology, we not only talk of the research methods used, but also consider the logic behind the methods we use in the context of our study and explain the way we are using a particular method or technique and why are not using others to ensure that the results are capable of being evaluated properly. There is a constant and intricate relationship between facts and theory. Facts without theory or theory without facts lack significance. Facts take their significance from the theories which define, classify and predict them. Theories possess significance, when they are built upon, classified and tested by facts. Hence, all out efforts have been made to accumulate the facts and for the formulation of a new/broader approach of Inflationary trend in the Global scenario with special reference to the Indian Economy.

Types of Inflation: Let us now, we may illustrate the trend of prices in brief as under:

- *Creeping Inflation*: A sustained rise in prices of annual increases of less than 3 per cent is known as "Creeping Inflation".
- *Walking Inflation*: When the rate of rise in prices is in the range of 3 to 6 per cent P.A.
- *Running Inflation* : It is the sustained rise in prices is about 10 per cent P.A.

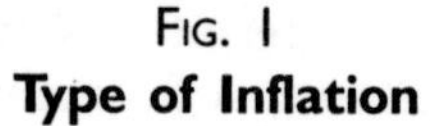
FIG. 1
Type of Inflation

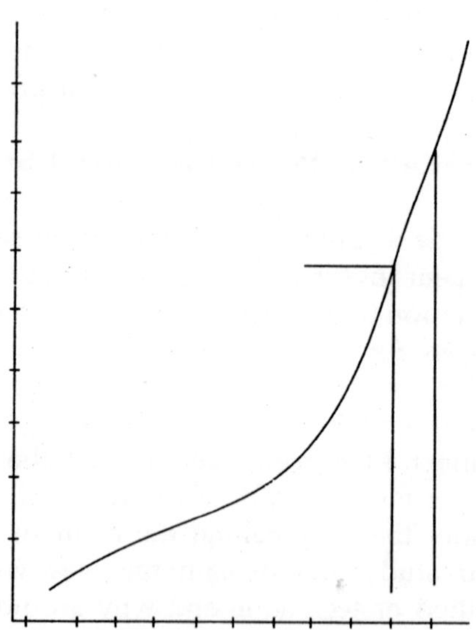

- *Jumping Inflation*: While, "Jumping or Hyper Inflation or galloping inflation" is the last stage which starts after the point of full employment has been reached. The monthly increases in prices is 20 per cent or more than that. Lord J.M. Keynes called this stage "full inflation" or "true inflation".

Further, it may be mentioned that Inflation is of different types. These different types may be considered by dividing them into different categories on the basis of different considerations. These criteria are:

(i) Full employment,
(ii) Causes on account of which Inflation has been caused,
(iii) Processes through which it is induced
(iv) Time Sphere,

(v) Government Regulations, and
(vi) Speed on rapidity with which prices increases.

DEMAND-PULL INFLATION

Demand-Pull or excess demand inflation is a situation often described as "too much money chasing too few goods." According to the concept of Demand-pull Inflation takes place because the demand for goods and services exceeds their supply at current prices. In other words, Inflation is created by fast-increasing demand. Its earliest explanation is to be found in the simple Quantity Theory of Money. The theory states that prices rise in proportion to the increase in the money supply. Given the full employment level of output, doubling the money supply will double the price level. When the money supply increases, it creates more demand for goods but the

FIG. 2

Demand-full Inflation or Monetary Theory of Inflation

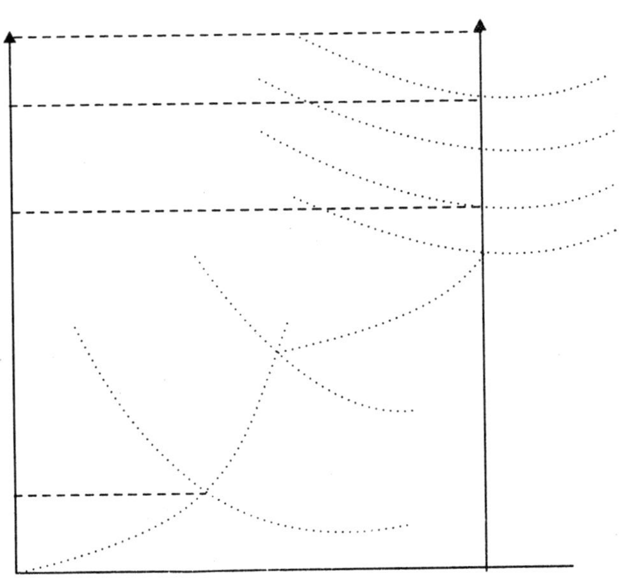

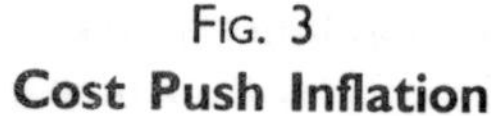

FIG. 3
Cost Push Inflation

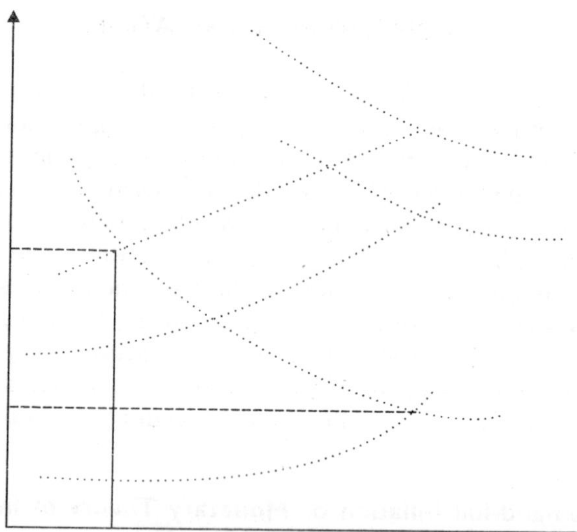

supply of goods cannot be increased due to the full employment of resources, which leads to rise in prices. It is a continuous and prolonged rise in the money supply

COST-PUSH INFLATION

The concept of Cost-push Inflation shows that inflation is caused by Supply or Cost function. This approach is sometimes called as the *New Inflation Theory;* but that is not correct. Cost-push Inflation is caused by wage increases enforced by Unions and profit increases by employers. This type of Inflation has not been a new phenomenon and was found even during the medieval period. But it was revived in the 1950s, and 1970s as the principal cause of inflation. In India it was also in the year 2007-08 and the current financial year 2008-09. It also came to be known as the "*New Inflation.*" Cost-push inflation is caused by wage-push and profit-push to prices.

HOW TO CONTROL THE STAGFLATION

We have observed that it is Inflation which leads to Stagflation. The experiences reveals that if stagflation is controlled either by restrictive or expansionary measures, it will increase. Suppose, the restrictive Demand Managed Monetary and Fiscal measures are adopted, they tend to lower aggregate demand so that the new Demand curve cuts the Supply curve at the old price level. This policy reduces the level of employment further and at the same time lowers the price level. Thus, such a policy tends to increase unemployment and reduces inflation. It fails to control Stagflation. On the other hand, if expansionary demand managed monetary and fiscal policies adopted, they will raise the aggregate demand so that the new demand curve D2 cuts the supply curve S1 at E2 at the old employment level ON.

FIG. 4

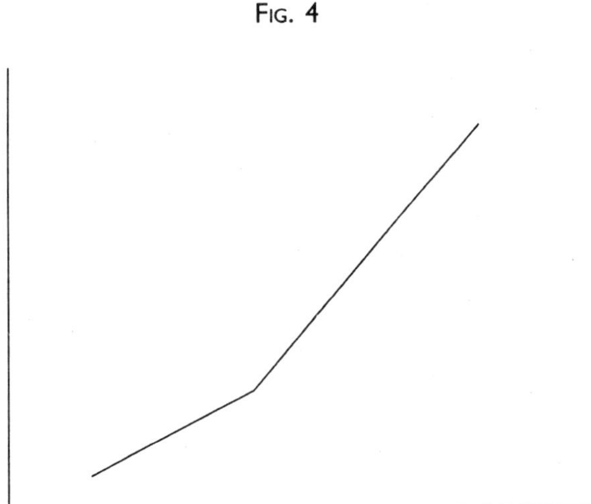

With this employment raises from ON1 to ON but increases the price level to OP2. It also fails to control stagflation because it generates more Inflation combined with higher employment. To slow down Inflation and maintain higher employment, Economists, therefore, suggest the following measures like:

(i) Minimum wages should not be raised;
(ii) Tax based Income policies should be started;
(iii) To introduce Income policies; and
(iv) To reduce personal and business taxes as they reduce labour costs and raise demand of labour.

PHILIPS CURVE AND INFLATION

The phenomenon of demand inflation is frequently controlled by restoring to the Instruments of Monetary and Fiscal Policies. According to the Classical Quantity Theory Approach, Demand Inflation can be controlled by resorting to an appropriate Monetary Policy so as to halt expansion of the Money Supply. While, according to the Monetarist explanation of Inflation, money does matter significantly in the occurrence of Inflation in the economy. While, according to the Keynesians, however, the Monetary Policy alone will not be able to check Inflation. Consequently, it is suggested to apply the restrictive Fiscal Policy instruments of curtailing unproductive expenditure and widening and deepening of the tax structure in the economy. The restrictive role of the Monetary and Fiscal Policies is not, however, so clearly appropriate in the matter of controlling the supply of Cost-push Inflation. The restrictive Monetary and Fiscal measures have their immediate impact on the aggregate demand in the form of restricting it, but Supply Inflation is not the result of the aggregate demand rising in excess of economy's full-employment output. An important difference between the demand and supply inflation is that unlike the former in the case of Supply Inflation price rise takes place well before the full employment output has been hit. While, the cost-push inflation is largely accounted for by rising costs, Supply Inflation can be controlled by maintaining wage-rate stability by preventing such wage increases which are not related to the increase in labour's productivity. Restrictive policy may check a wage-push inflation provided it reduces the aggregate demand and output sufficiently to create enough unemployment to prevent wage increases in excess of the increases in labour's productivity.

REMEDIES TO CONTROL INFLATION

Inflation is like toothpaste: once out, it is hard to push-back into the tube. Thus the challenge for economic policy-makers is to stop it rising in the first place. RBI Governor considers 4 per cent inflation as the 'threshold level' of inflation which will not impede growth in India. However, the actual rate of inflation has been far above this level. Corrective measures, therefore, need to be taken to control the inflation. As we have seen above many factors contribute to inflation. Corrective measures, thus, necessarily to have a broad sweep. They have to encompass different aspects of the economic policy, some of these are of immediate consequence, like monetary and fiscal policies, commercial policy, etc. Others have long-term well-conceived strategy. Let us analyse the basic components of these various measures. The Table 1 gives in brief the measures to control Inflation and the method of control to Inflation INFLATIONARY GAP.

TABLE I

Remedial Measures to Control Inflation

Sl. No.	*Measures to Control Inflation*	*Method of Control to Inflation*
1.	Monetary Measures	(i) Currency Contraction: Surplus money to be withdrawn from the circulation (ii) Credit Contraction: Credit squeeze and Bank Rate/Open Market Operations.
2.	Non-Monetary Measures	(a) Voluntary: (i) Deferred Pay Scheme, (ii) Increased Production (b) Compulsory: (i) Price Control, Rationing and Controlled allocation of Raw-materials, i.e. adjustment of Demand to Supply of essential commodities
3.	Fiscal Measures	(i) Public Borrowing, (ii) Increased Taxation, (iii) Under-valuation of currency, (iv) Higher Rate of Interest is a great inducement for saving deposits, (v) Postponement of Public Works Expenditure.

By Inflationary Gap, we mean that possession of more purchasing power which people can spend on goods than the value of those available goods at the pre-inflation prices. The gap between these two things has been defined by Prof. Kurihara as "an excess of anticipated expenditures over available output at base prices". In the opinion of Prof. Klein, "Inflationary gap is the difference between what the population will try to consume out of the income, which is determined by the interaction of the Consumption function and the level of government expenditure, and the amount available for consumption at pre-inflation prices." For example, the National Income of a certain country is Rs. 10,000 crores, out of which Rs. 1,000 crores have been collected from people in the form of various taxes by the government. The community has Rs. 9,000 crores to spend on Consumable goods. Further, suppose that the total value of the National Product at the pre-inflation rate is Rs. 8,000 crores. Thus, the Inflationary Gap is Rs. 9,000 crores – Rs. 8,000 crores = Rs. 1,000 crores. If the level of full employment has not been reached, the economy is not fully developed and if the production of consumption goods can be increased by Rs. 1,000 crores, Inflationary Gap would be nil. But in practice, production cannot be increased in a short-run. Even then, as the employment increases, people do not greatly feel slightly increasing prices. While on the other hand, if full employment level has already been attained, Inflationary Gap will have serious consequences on the economy concerned.

CAUSES OF INFLATION

The causes of inflation can be summed up as under in the following manner:

Table 3 gives in brief the evil effects of Inflation on the various sectors of Economy.

Good Effects of Inflation

The good effects of Inflation can be summed up as below:

- Debtor's gains
- Agriculturist's gain

TABLE 2

Causes of Inflation

Sl. No.	*Cause of Inflation*	*Method of Inflation*	*Effect of method on Inflation*
	(1)	(2)	(3)
1.	Deficit Financing	(i) Issue of more currency, (ii) Borrowing from Foreign countries,	Increased Supply of money in country and creates partial Inflation,
2.	Increase in Velocity of Circulation of Money	(i) Particularly in Boom MEC/ Reduction in Liquidity Preference or with an increase in Propensity to Consume.	Causes Price Spiral to shoot-up.
3.	Credit Expansion	(i) Reduction in Bank Rate by RBI, leads to expansion in Loans and Advances, (ii) Commercial Banks expand Credit by lowering their Cash Reserves it continues for long period of time.	Affects the Credit structure of the country.
4.	Imports	Increase in the Supply of Precious Metal	More Demand than Supply. Prices will go up.
5.	Natural Calamities	Floods, Earthquakes, Plague, etc.	Mis-match between Supply and Demand.
6.	Trade Union Activities	Demand for increased wages, Shorter hours of work and more Holidays and more pay.	Demand supply mis-match. More demand for goods.
7.	Industrial Development	Law of diminishing Return apply on production	Inflationary trend is created and prices start rising.
8.	War	Abnormal conditions in Economy and Expenditure on it increases	Prices start rising
9.	Rapid increase in Population	Output does not increase in the same proportion	Shortage of goods and prices starts rising rapidly.

TABLE 3

Evil Effects of Inflation on the Various Sectors of Economy

Sl. No.	*Category of Economy*	*Impact/Results*
1.	Wage earners and Salaried class people	Hard-hit
2.	Investors	The value of their Investments falls due to the depreciation of currency.
3.	Creditors	Lose because they lent out when the money was Dear, and is being paid back when it has become Cheap.
4.	On Tax Payers	To pay higher Taxes.
5.	Decline in Capital accumulation	Owing to increase in Expenses.
6.	Increase in Unemployment	Lead to unemployment and poverty.
7.	Economic Disequilibrium	Distorts saving habit, solvency of business, sakes the foundation of forward planning, which is essential for balanced growth.
8.	Moral Degeneration	It germinates among the Businessmen and officials.

- Exporters gains: as the exports are stimulated due to the depreciation of money.
- Manufacturers, Wholesalers and Retailers are placed in better position.

MONETARY POLICY AND CONTROL OF INFLATION

The basic task of monetary policy in a developing economy is to meet the credit needs of the growth sectors on the one hand, and to curb the supply of money meant to be used in non-productive activities like speculative dealings and hoarding, on the other. Monetary policy in India has been designed on the same principles and hence is known as the "policy of controlled monetary expansion." The Reserve Bank of India has been manipulating various quantitative and qualitative controls to make this policy effective. However, Monetary Policy is effective in controlling Inflation if it is of the demand pull type. The Central Bank can reduce the reserves of commercial banks by raising interest rates, selling securities, by raising margin requirements and controlling consumer credit. Thus, the monetary authority can control inflation by reducing the Money Supply and raising the cost of money to the borrowers. While, in a demand pull inflation, prices rise due to an overly rapid expansion of the aggregate demand. However, the following are the limitations of Monetary Policy in containing inflation:

1. *Increase in the Velocity of Money:* (i) This can be controlled by putting a check on the misuse of securities with them for credit expansion, (ii) Role of Non-Bank Financial Intermediaries
2. *Discriminatory:* A tight monetary policy is discriminatory in its effects on particular sectors of the economy.
3. *Time Lags:* Another important limitation on the effectiveness of monetary policy is the existence of time lag between the need of action and the recognition, decision and operation of actions. Friedman distinguishes among these three Basic lags namely:
   (i) The recognition lag, (ii) the decision or administrative lag; and (iii) the operation lag.

FISCAL POLICY

There is a need to curb fiscal deficits. A rise in fiscal deficit leads to higher government borrowings from the RBI and monetisation of the deficit through an expansion in the money supply exerts and upward pressure on prices. Public borrowings, through deflationary in the short-run, eventually become inflationary when repayments are made. They also add to the government's interest liabilities—which are already heavy—and cut into the resources for development and when the fiscal deficit is reduced through external borrowings, the result is worsening of the BOP situation. That is why containment of fiscal deficit at a reasonable level has been regarded as one of the key elements in the reform package.

Further, it has been observed that a reduction in the fiscal deficit by axing development expenditure can lead to recession and lower revenue yields. In fact, public expenditure on development, particularly on infrastructure, will need to be raised appreciably to revive industrial activity. On the other hand, there is limited scope to slash non-development expenditure. Any saving on this count may be offset by the increased requirements of funds for defence. What is required is that either or both of the followings must happen:

1. Government sharply reduces its expenditure by recognizing itself, improving its efficiency, reducing subsidies and other in fructuous expenditures;
2. Government is able to get much higher returns on its investments in the public enterprise system and other parts of the public sector; and
3. In addition to the above, the remedies to inflation have to be seen in :
   (i) Monetary Policy; (ii) Fiscal Policy, (iii) Distribution Policy, (iv) Administered Price Policy, (v) Production Policy, (vi) Commercial Policy, and (viii) Income Policy.

It has been observed that the inflation based on the WPI Index came down from the high level of 12.9 per cent last year. However, the inflation of primary articles, including food items, increased to 11.06 per cent. The sustained high prices of food articles is bound to become an electoral issue. Decline in WPI-based inflation would be little comfort to the vast majority of the Indian population—as 77 per cent of the country earns less than Rs. 20 a day—for whom the spiralling inflation last year meant that food prices rose at a fast pace. For this large section, the continued high food prices will have a great deal more significance than a decline in the overall inflation. Moreover, the pinch of high food prices is something that is not limited to the poor, the middle classes feels it as well.

The Table 4 given below gives the detail of WPI and CPI for Industrial Workers for selected years from 1950-51 to 2006-07:

TABLE 4

Sl. No.	*Year*	*WPI average (Base: 1993-94=100)*	*Consumer Price Index average for Industrial workers (Base 1982=100)*
1.	1950-51	6.8	17.0
2.	1960-61	7.9	21.0
3.	1970-71	14.3	38.0
4.	1980-81	36.8	81.0
5.	1990-91	73.7	193.0
6.	2000-01	155.7	444.0
7.	2002-03	166.8	482.0
8.	2003-04	175.9	500.0
9.	2004-05	187.3	520.0
10.	2005-06	195.6	542.0
11.	2006-07	206.2	125

Source : Economic Survey: 2007-08, Ministry of Finance, Government of India.

The details of the contribution of selected commodities groups to the month-wise Inflation for the years 2006-07 and 2007-08 (up to December, 2008) are given in the Table 5.

An upward movement in crude oil prices and the rising demand from the consumption markets such as India and China has been responsible for the continuing bull-run in the world vegetable oils market. This is despite the world witnessing higher edible oils output during the last few years. As regards dairy products, it appears that the high inflation of oil cakes has passed through to the prices of dairy products. The average inflation rate, period-on-period, of oil cakes during November 2007-July 2008 was 39.19 per cent, against 18.79 per cent recorded during the corresponding period of previous year. The high inflation of oil cakes is reflected in the average inflation, period-on-period, of dairy products of 9.25 per cent during November 2007 to July 2008, which is about 4 per cent higher than the figure during the corresponding periods during the year before.

TABLE 5

Contribution of Selected Commodity Groups to Inflation

(Per cent)

Month/ Year	Headline Inflation	Edible Oils	Food Articles	Mineral Oils	Chemicals	Cement	Metals	Machinery	Total
(1)	(2)	(3)	(4)	(5)	(6)	(7)	(8)	(9)	(10)
				2006-07					
April	3.9	-8.6	18.5	37.9	9.5	6.3	-3.4	5.4	65.7
May	4.7	-4.9	21.0	35.3	7.1	5.6	0.2	4.3	68.6
June	5.1	-3.7	24.9	39.0	8.6	5.3	0.7	4.6	79.3
July	4.8	-4.3	13.9	35.1	9.4	5.9	8.3	5.3	73.7
August	5.1	-2.1	15.9	36.1	6.8	5.7	8.7	5.3	76.3
September	5.4	0.1	25.7	18.3	6.8	5.0	9.1	4.8	69.8
October	5.5	1.3	24.6	13.1	4.9	4.9	11.2	6.3	66.3
November	5.5	6.2	21.3	11.0	4.8	5.3	12.8	7.7	69.1
December	5.7	13.4	23.8	7.3	5.2	5.3	14.1	8.4	77.5
January	6.4	15.2	23.0	7.0	4.8	4.2	20.9	7.8	83.0
February	6.4	17.3	24.8	3.5	4.8	3.7	22.6	7.9	84.6
March	6.6	18.7	23.6	2.1	5.8	3.8	22.0	8.0	83.9

				2007-08					
April	6.3	21.1	24.9	1.2	7.7	2.8	17.5	8.5	83.7
May	5.5	21.6	25.1	-0.6	10.5	2.9	17.1	10.2	86.7
June	4.5	26.3	18.4	-8.1	11.0	3.7	20.0	11.9	83.3
July	4.7	28.1	31'.8	-11.2	9.6	3.7	12.8	11.8	86.5
August	4.1	29.7	31.7	-15.0	13.5	4.2	11.6	12.8	88.5
September	3.5	33.9	22.8	-12.7	17.7	6.0	14.4	15.5	97.0
October	3.1	38.3	15.2	-7.2	20.6	6.2	12.8	14.7	100.5
November	3.3	34.5	12.7	4.6	19.5	5.3	10.9	13.5	101.0
December	3.6	27.6	13.1	15.7	17.3	4.9	7.8	10.3	96.8

Among the various reasons identified for the inflationary situation in India, soaring food prices have received considerable national attention. The rising prices of "food products" group have been the major factor responsible for high overall and food price inflation in India. Primary food articles, including the foodgrains, have little to do with the rise in food prices. Interestingly, a look at the trends in the past to years reveals that the current primary food articles inflation, year-on-year, is not as precarious as perceived by the public. Also among the primary articles, the non-food articles have caused moiré damage than food articles to overall inflation during the current price spiral. The three food products, namely, oil cakes, edible oils and dairy products have found to be the major contributors of the current food price spiral. This implies that the present food price inflation in India is the result of the higher prices of only a few food items. The root cause of the high inflation of edible oils has been larger edible oils imports since November 2007 at soaring international prices. Larger edible oils imports were necessitated due to the anticipated fall in domestic production of oilseeds in the rabi season of the oil year 2007-08. In case of diary products, the high inflation of oil cakes has fed into the prices of diary products.

Further, the Asian Development Outlook 2008 update offers a rich and insightful analysis of the growth and inflation experience in nine Asian countries of which India is one. In its analysis of the surge in food prices, however, it falls prey to a diagnosis of underlying factors that is not just simplistic but also misleading. In fact, in a subsequent chapter in part of this report, this analysis is abandoned and the focus is on the dynamics of food and oil prices and a different and more nuanced policy stance. The Outlook 2008 had projected inflation in Asia to rise to 7.8 per cent in 2008, up sharply from 4.3 per cent in 2007 and 3.3 per cent in 2006. The benign paradigm of strong growth and subdued inflation, it emphasizes, has ended.

PRICE STABILITY

On the inflation front, the period from 2003-04 to 2007-08

enjoyed relative price stability with the exception of some price spikes. Inflation measured by the Wholesale Price Index (WPI) was mild during the lower growth early years of the decade. It experienced a spurt in the summer of 2004, but then retreated to around 5 per cent and remained there till the end of calendar year 2006. While a sharp increase in the price of foodgrains, particularly of pulses, edible oils, caused WPI inflation to climb sharply in the first part of 2007, it settled down at slightly below 4 per cent by the end of the year as the price pressure from foodgrains eased. This stoked ill-advised comfort in same quarters, for domestic petroleum-based fuel prices were much below what they ought to have been and a storm was brewing across the broad commodity space. With average WPI and Consumer Price Index (CPI) inflation in the period 2003-04 to 2007-08 at about 5 per cent price stability was certainly a major contributor to conditions conducive for sustained growth, notwithstanding the couple of price spurts and the fact that inflation sky-rocked since March 2008.

In 2008, higher international prices across a range of Commodities especially petroleum and steel, resulted in manufactured goods turning more expensive. This pressure caused the rate of WPI inflation to climb into double digit levels by the summer of 2008. It is expected to peak at under 13 per cent and appears to be stabilising, even easing. The extent that it will ease through March 2009 is to some extent a function of how much further commodity and other prices soften in world markets. Consumer Price Inflation has broadly tracked the changes in the WPI inflation rate. A WPI inflation broke past 12 per cent in the summer of 2008, CPI inflation went past 9 per cent in August.

PRICES POSITION IN INDIAN ECONOMY

Inflation as reported by the weekly WPI soared unexpectedly in early 2008 on account of a very steep increase in iron ore and steel prices, taking the end-March 2008 inflation number upto 8 per cent, a big departure from earlier expectations that it would be between 4 to 5 per cent. In the meantime, World prices of crude petroleum, iron ore, steel, wheat, cotton, soyabean oil and other commodities continued

TABLE 6

Indian Economy : Broad Average Framework of Growth

Parameters	*1993-94 to 1996-97*	*1997-98 to -2002-03*	*2003-04*	*2004-05*	*2005-06*	*2006-07*	*2007-08*	*2008-09*
(1)	*(2)*	*(3)*	*(4)*	*(5)*	*(6)*	*(7)*	*(8)*	*(9)*
		GDP and Components						
Investment Rate	25.12	24.26	28.16	32.19	35.53	35.89	37.38	37.50
Saving Rate	23.92	29.84	29.81	31.77	34.28	34.77	37.15	35.50
GDP real growth (Market prices)	6.84	5.10	8.37	8.28	9.24	9.69	9.02	7.10
Coming from: (i) Capital formation	1.85	1.57	4.98	5.41	5.94	3.63	4.51	4.00
(ii) Govt. Consumption	0.55	0.73	0.29	0.59	0.37	0.63	0.68	0.80
GDP real growth (Factor cost) of which:	7.08	5.22	8.54	7.46	9.40	9.62	9.03	7.10
(i) Agriculture and Allied Sector	4.47	0.66	10.00	-0.17	5.92	3.76	4.55	3.30
(ii) Industry sector	8.53	4.85	7.38	10.34	10.15	10.99	8.55	5.70
(iii) Service sector	8.10	7.97	8.51	9.21	9.21	11.08	10.78	9.00
Per Capita Real GDP Growth	5.01	3.27	6.72	5.78	5.78	8.06	7.49	5.60

to rise to new record levels. Headline inflation in developed economies rose to levels far beyond what the comfort zone was. Inflation in India accelerated over the six months period, February-July 2008, possibly finding its peak in August, with revised figures for the first three weeks of August at around 12.8-12.9 per cent. The provisional estimates have shown an expected easing in line with the change in international commodity prices, bringing the headline number to 10.7 per cent for the week ending 18th October, 2008.

CPI are being recast. CPI inflation has increased alongside WPI inflation but, unlike WPI, it has stayed in single digits. It continued to rise till August 2008 when the CPI for industrial workers and CPI for urban non-manual employees touched 9.0 and 8.5 per cent, respectively. These indices should also ease broadly in the same manner as outlined for WPI. We know that the objectives of Monetary Policy in India have been the price stability and growth. The broad objectives of the Monetary Policy in India have been namely : (i) to maintain a reasonable degree of price stability; and (ii) to help to accelerate the rate of economic growth.

THRESHOLD LEVEL OF INFLATION

One way of reconciling the conflicting objectives of price stability and economic growth in the short-run is through the determination of the "threshold level of Inflations" beyond which inflation begins to affect growth. Below this level, monetary authorities can take into account. Other considerations such as growth; above it, however, control of inflation becomes the dominant concern. The Chakravarty Committee regarded 4 per cent as the acceptable rise in prices. Further, in the Indian context, an inflation rate of around 5-6 per cent may be more appropriate. However, this estimation was made at a time when the actual inflation was between 8 and 9 per cent. While econometric study can further help in determining the threshold level of inflation, some judgment is still involved in determining the rate. This approach can provide good guidance as to when policy should be tightened or loosened. In a highly integrated world, domestic monetary authorities also need to take into account the behaviour of inflation in the rest of the world, if domestic inflation remains above the average level of external inflation, it has implications for exchange rate management. The world has now come to accept a much lower order of inflation as most desirable.

The concept of threshold level of inflation leads to another critical issue that is being debated in many countries—whether countries should adopt inflation targeting as a goal of monetary policy. Inflation targets give greater precision to the idea of price stability as it would mean that the monetary authorities should reinsure that inflation remains within the target level. While low and stable inflation is the most desirable objective, it is not clear whether Central Banks should be forced to keep the inflation rate at, or below, a given level. It may be necessary to provide same flexibility to Central Banks in this regard, particularly in economies which are subject to frequent supply shock. Besides an appropriate level of inflation as a designed target has to be determined. This is not an easy task. Nevertheless, it goes without saying that the dominant objective of monetary policy should be the maintenance of price stability.

The term "price stability" needs some clarification. One issue that has assumed importance in the recent period is whether monetary authorities should also monitor asset prices. Normal price indices, whether retail or wholesale, do not take into account prices of assets such as stocks and houses. It is quite possible to conceive of a situation of rising asset prices and stable commodity prices. If Central Banks choose to ignore asset prices, the resultant "asset bubbles" can have a damaging effect on the economy. This is one lesson that can be drawn from the recent experience of the United States. From the point of view of stability, the need for monitoring asset prices along-with the prices of commodities and services has become imperative.

COMMODITY PRICES AND INFLATION IN DEVELOPING COUNTRIES

Strong growth in developing countries during the 1960s coincided with a low-inflation environment, while high inflation during the subsequent two decades coincided with low average growth. The recent sharp pick up in GDP growth occurred in an environment of low and stable inflation. Although the causality is always difficult to untangle, the potential adverse impact of high inflation on the ability to interpret price signals, on disciplined fiscal management, and on savings and investment are well understood. Inflationary pressures during the 1970s are well explained by a combination of commodity price increases by a combination of commodity price increases and persistence. However, during the 1990s many developing countries experienced high inflation unrelated to commodity prices. These increases in inflation were caused more by loose policy reactions to debt crises, especially in Latin America, and the transition toward market economies in Europe. While, in the recent period, inflation has actually remained lower than what was predicted, largely as a result of Institutional reforms, which made monetary policy more independent in many countries and inflation targeting more prevalent. Owing to these facts the inflation have been brought down sharply by the Institutional reforms. Moreover, increased competition in global markets, making it more difficult to pass through increases in the higher costs of production, is another explanation.

The additional low cost supply from developing countries, notably China, in global markets carried deflationary effects. Further, the share of commodities in world and trade has declined over time, as a result of which the impact of commodity price increases in now substantially less than during 1970s. Indeed, with the recent rise in commodity prices, the share of commodities in the global economy, and with that, their effects on the general price level, is increasing rapidly. Many fast growing developing countries have reached capacity constraints in infrastructure, energy, and other inputs to production, and the increase of low-cost goods in global markets is waning. With broader inflation rates rising, it becomes easier to pass through cost increases, and low inflation expectations might be revised upward quite quickly. These are serious challenges to be faced to prevent a re-emergence of high-inflation environment.

From the Table 7, it may be observed that the volatility did increase for almost all of the principal commodities in

2008, reflecting the rise in prices earlier in the year and their subsequent decline. In the Table 8 gives the details of Poverty effects of the changes in relative food prices.

TABLE 7

World Price Volatility : Average Monthly Per Cent Price Changes

Year	*Crude Oil*	*Copper*	*Aluminium*	*Coal*
2000-03	8.4	3.4	3.1	4.0
2004-07	6.9	6.2	4.6	5.7
2008	7.6	6.3	6.5	15.0
	Wheat	Corn	Rice	
200-06	4.5	5.0	2.9	
2007	7.9	6.1	1.8	
2008	9.5	9.4	18.3	

Source : The World Bank, "Global Economic Prospects: Commodities at the Crossroads" 2009, p. 101.

TABLE 8

Poverty Effects of the Changes in Relative Food Prices January 2005-December, 2007

Region	*Initial Level*		*Change in*	
	Poverty Headcount	*Income Gap Ratio*	*Poverty Headcount*	*Income Gap Ratio*
	(Per cent)		*(Percentage point)*	
(1)	*(2)*	*(3)*	*(4)*	*(5)*
	Urban Population			
East Asia and Pacific	13.2	20.3	6.3	2.7
Europe and Central Asia	2.5	8.7	0.0	0.2
Latin America and the Caribbean	3.7	37.6	0.1	-0.7
Middle East and North Africa	2.7	17.8	2.4	5.7

(Contd.)

TABLE 8 (Contd.)

(1)	(2)	(3)	(4)	(5)
South Asia	32.3	25.0	2.0	0.5
Sub-Saharan Africa	34.1	38.1	1.7	0.3
Developing World	15.3	27.1	2.9	0.5
	Rural Population			
East Asia and the Pacific	31.9	23.2	4.9	0.7
Europe and Central Asia	8.2	6.6	0.0	0.0
Latin America and the Caribbean	18.6	43.9	0.1	0.1
Middle East and North Africa	15.4	22.9	0.7	0.9
South Asia	43.3	24.0	0.8	0.3
Sub-Saharan Africa	54.9	41.5	0.3	0.0
Developing World	37.1	28.2	2.1	0.1

Source : The World Bank, "Global Economic Prospects : Commodities at the Crossroads : 2009", p. 120.

WHY INDIA SHOULD ADOPT INFLATION TARGETING?

The inflation targeting (IT) framework has been successfully implemented in several developed and developing countries. However, the success of IT system requires equal commitment from the government and the Central Bank. In the case of India, targeting inflation is politically sustainable given the over-whelming preference of the population for lower headline inflation. Inflation targeting involves a public announcement of a medium-term numerical target for forecasted inflation that the Central Bank is pre-committed to, based on its own assessment. However, in practice the Central Bank is assigned a socially optimal inflation target by the government to be achieved in the medium-term, while the bank has the freedom to choose its instruments. Lars E.O. Svensson in 1997 claims inflation forecast to be an ideal intermediate target as it is by definition the current variable that is most correlated with the goal. At the heart of the concept of the inflation targeting problem (14) is the following equation.

$$\Pi_t + 2/t - \Pi = -\phi \hat{y}_t + 1/t$$

Where:

Π = is the long-run unconditional and socially optimal Inflation target;

y_t^{Δ} = is the output gap (log actual relative to potential output);

Π_t = $P_t - P_{t-1}$ = Inflation Rate;

ϕ = is a positive parameter which is a function of the weight on output stabilization, discount factor of the inter-temporal objective function and supply function parameter of the output gap; and

P_t = is log price level.

The equation requires selecting the instrument such that deviation between the two-year conditional inflation forecast is ô time the negative of the one-year output-gap forecast. The above relationship is derived involving both inflation and output forecast and it implies:

(a) All else equal, lower—the expected inflation, lower will be the inflation today, and
(b) Lower the expected inflation the higher today's output gap can be without resulting in higher inflation today.

Thus, it is better for the Central Bank to keep expectations of the private sector towards lower future inflation. In a strict inflation targeting framework ô=0, which leads to the inflation targeting rule, and there is no consideration for output stabilization. On the other hand, in a more general form, the policy rule could include other goals such as exchange rate or interest rate smoothly. With inflation as the target of monetary policy, several countries have registered impressive success in reducing inflation or maintaining it at lower levels. After demonstrating considerable interest in the inflation targeting framework during the late 1990's, the Indian monetary authorities appeared to have abandoned this idea for sometime. However, since then the first phase of financial reforms are almost complete. Basel-I has been implemented and the RBI is fast moving on Basel-II. All these conditions are favourable to an inflation targeting framework. Moreover, in the light of the several issues that need to be taken care of before actual inflation targeting can be adopted in India and it is important to address the following issues sooner rather than late:

(i) The policy statements of the RBI invariably state that price stability is its main monetary policy objective, the same is not enshrined in law. The preamble of the RBI describes the basic function of RBI as under: ". . . to regulate the issue of Bank Notes and keeping of reserves with a view to securing monetary stability in India and generally to operate the currency and credit system of the country to its advantage".
The above objective means little to an IT framework. Hence, there is an urgent need to have a change in RBI-related laws essential to make it objectives consistent with recent development and practices of conducting monetary policy.

(ii) In India, inflation is not considered a monetary phenomenon. It is believed that inflationary pressures builds up from both the Supply as well as the Demand-side. Hence, a more cautious approach to inflation targeting in the Indian context would rely on both monetary and fiscal instruments and be closely coordinated with other instruments as such government buffer stock and other side Supply operations.

(iii) There has been little liberalization in the area of directed credit. Commercial Banks are required to direct 40 per cent of their commercial advances to the priority sector. The percentage of directed credit appears to be too high and needs to be brought down to highly focused areas.

(iv) Further, the combined fiscal deficit of Central land State governments hover around the range of 8-10 per cent of GDP. Under these circumstance, the role of Government in committing to the IT framework is no less than that of the RBI.

(v) Even, if it is a long way off from adopting IT, the RBI should without delay start publishing a full-fledged "Inflation Report" on the lines of "Inflation Targeting" Countries to bring in transparency in its operations leading to a smooth-transaction.

(vi) Further, the government should establish an inflation Committee comprising-the Ministry of Finance, exhaustive Inflation Report.

CONCLUSIONS

The recent past inflationary episode in India, there can be little doubt, is one of profit inflation, since it is fuelled basically by excess demand for a variety of goods, notably primary commodities, including food articles. Indeed, one can say that this was the first time since "economic liberalisation" was introduced in 1991 that we are witnessing an excess demand caused "profit inflation". This is because "liberalisation" typically keeps the level of demand deflated, through a variety of instruments, including fiscal responsibility legislation. The classic fall out of "neo-liberal" fiscal policy, by way of making the system demand constrained, was visible right until mid-2002 when the country has 63 million tonnes of foodgrains stocks and that too after more than a decade of declining per capita foodgrain output, together with unutilised capacity in most sectors. This situation marks a contrast to this entire period of demand deflation-based price stability, during which prices only rose either because world market price increases were "passed on", as in the case of oil, or due to administered cost increase caused by the curtailment of subsidies. Hence, the inflation in the years 2007-08 and part of the year 2008-09 too is accompanies by inflation in the world market, but can scarcely be attributed to the "passing on" of world market price increases. The transition to a demand pull inflation, affecting food prices in particular, is reminiscent of the pre-liberalisation period. The fact that it has recurred is often attributed in the popular press to an "overheating" of the economy, reflected in the high growth rates. But this "overheating" explanation cannot stand scrutiny. It camouflages the fact that the agricultural sector has actually been discriminated against. Its profitability has declined; rural development expenditure as a proportion of GDP has declined to a level must lower than in the Eighth Five Year Plan; per capita foodgrain output declined over a long period, and especially since the beginning of this century; public procurement operations were wound down and the procurement prices offered for foodgrains were simply not been remunerative enough; and so on. Further, Demand deflation characteristics of the era of neo-liberalism, meant that notwithstanding all this, foodgrains stocks were still piled up during the period under reference.

Owing to the adjustment to that situation since mid-2002, through the dumping of huge amounts of foodgrains on the world market and the whittling down of procurement operations, was so pronounced that it had carried the Indian Economy from an ex-ante excess supply to an ex ante demand situation. In brief, we can say that in a situation where both demand and supply were squeezed, if demand fell and supply were squeezed, and if demand was falling more rapidly than supply, the opposite happened was the case under reference. Now the basic feature of a profit inflation is that it is self-limiting, in the sense that leaving aside the elements of speculation, the "forced savings" that such inflation generates, eventually eliminate the *ex ante* demand that causes it. Even after prices have stopped increasing in terms of the wage unit, both prices and the wage may still continue to rise in nominal terms, and does not lead to any decline in real wages. The end of profit inflation, in short, does not mean the end of inflation in nominal wages and prices.

Further, protecting the poor against profit inflation means much more than simply the end of profit inflation; it means negating its effects on their living standards, by making them regain what they have lost through profit inflation. Even if augmentation of supplies through resorting to imports, as the government is doing in the foodgrains, succeeds in ending inflation in terms of the wage unit, there is still the need to put in additional purchasing power in the hands of the poor so that they regain their earlier real income. This year's Global Economic Prospects finds the global economy is at a crossroads, transitioning from a sustained period of very strong developing country-led growth to one of substantial uncertainty as a financial crisis rooted in high-income countries has shaken financial markets worldwide. Commodity markets too are at a crossroads with the very high prices of 2007 and early 2008 having fallen by more than half in many instances. Further, higher food prices are estimated to have increased global poverty by some 130-155 million people. Most of the countries responded to the food crisis by expanding existing social safety net programs, which made good sense given the profound and long-term consequences that increased malnutrition could generate. Now that food prices are declining, countries need to take steps to revamp their social welfare systems so that they are better targeted and that the next time a similar crisis comes along, additional spending will be more effective in limiting poverty impacts. Further, at the international level, steps need to be taken to prevent producing countries from exacerbating shortfalls by introducing export bans or by withholding stocks from the global market. An international scheme to share information about the private and public stocks and coordinate their management during times of crisis is worth pursuing. Similarly, funding for international food aid programs should be made more predictable, and agencies should be endowed with a line of credit that would allow them to respond rapidly to future food emergencies in a way they cannot at present.

It may be mentioned that the i*nflation hit a near seven year low of 3.03 per cent for the week to February 21, 2009, continuing its steady slide close to zero projected by the government/RBI, as prices of many food items and steels manufactured products such as metals and transport equipment fell sharply.* It is expected that the same will fall to sub-zero levels by end March, 2009. Retail inflation as measured by Consumer Price Index for the Industrial Workers hit a 11 year high of 10.45 per cent in

January 2009 from 9.7 per cent in December 2008. While, the Weekly Price Index-based inflation in food articles, which had been hovering around a 10 year high of 11.5 per cent in the first week of January, 2009, dropped marginally to 8.24 per cent in week to February 21, 2009, although the head-line inflation has fallen a lot more during the period under reference. Hence, the WPI-based inflation rate fell to its lowest level since October 2002 because of an overall drop in the prices of 435 articles that make-up the Index. Though the food Inflation Rate has dropped by more than a percentage point on a year-on-year basis, sugar prices have increased at an annual rate of 23 per cent in the reported week.

REFERENCES

Dev Raj, "Monetary Economics: Theory and Practice", 2004: Rajat Publications, New Delhi (India).

Edwin Walter Kemmerer, "The ABC of Inflation", p. 6.

Edward Shaprio, Solomon, E. and White, W.L., "Money and Banking," 1968, p. 14.

F.S. Brooman, "Macro-economics", 4th Edition, 1968, p. 285.

Geoffrey Crowther, "An Outline of Money", p. 107.

H.G. Jonhnson, "Essays in Monetary Economics.

K.K. Kurihara, "Monetary Theory and Public Policy", pp. 6-11 and "An Introduction to Keynesian.

Lars, E.O. Svensson, "Inflation Forecast Targeting: Implementing and Maintaining Inflation Targets", *European Economic Review*, 41:1111-48, 1997.

Lord, J.M. Keynes, "A Tract on Monetary Reform", pp. 44-45 and "How to Pay for the War", p. 69.

Milton Friedman, "Studies in the Quantity Theory of Money", p. 3.

Paul Einzig, "Inflation", pp. 17 and 22.

R.G. Hawtrey (1928), "Currency and Credit.

Roy Harrod, "Policy Against Inflation", p. 66.

The IMF, "World Economic Outlook", September 2005, pp. 176-77.

The World Bank, "Global Economic Prospects: Commodities at the Crossroads", 2009.

Various Issues of the Economic Survey : 2006-07 and 2007-08, Ministry of Finance, Government of India.

Whittlesey, Friedman and Herman, "Money, and Banking", 1964, p. 385.

3

Inflation, Recession, Financial Meltdown and the Indian Economy

An Analysis of Some Missing Roots

PARAMANAND SINGH AND SHASHI BHUSHAN SINGH

The present article attempts to analyse the present economic scenario prevailing in the world economy *vis-a-vis* India—where we are witnessing inherent inflationary trend side by side the recessionary environment in various sectors of the economy, agriculture, industry, manufacturing and even in trade and services. The financial boom witnessed in the banking and insurance sector has shown a meltdown symptom, thus creating a panic in the entire economic domain. Peoples are guessing that it will lead in worsening direction. The article analysis some of the basic fallacies in the analysis of such situation in the neo classical frame and points out the fact that the basic roots of ills lies in the analysis of global capitalism and therefore the remedies are some where else. It is not in the prescription of financial stimulus and thus worsening the system from these ills. The ills are inherent in the capitalism itself. It is in the D.N.A. of apitalism. Financial robustness lies in the quality of earning, be it individual or financial institution which directly stems from capability of the economy to utilize its natural and human resources. The bullish environment created by global economies of U.S. and European world in recent past has seem many companies across the globe to succumb to the temptation of stretching the earnings in order to maintain quarterly growth trend resulting in compromising governing norms of the financial institutions as well as multinationals. To credit where credit is due is a wrong policy. This led to collapse of global greats like Lehman brothers, Wachgovia, and Bear streams. The challenge has come from recessionary environment which streams from easy profit seeking motive with added pressure to sustain profits and thereby increase the temptation or greed to flout financial norms, ignoring long-term value to an organization and thus poor governance as a mechanism of value destroyer. Therefore, the test of time is to determine and decide good and bad genes of creating with value consciousness and thus making up an ideal D.N.A. for the system to float on with creative psychology for bigger-convas of self-condifence devoid of the temptation of any soft. The article runs in five sections—First, Introduction, Second, Theoretical explanation and historical background, Third, *Recession in global economies of the U.S., U.K. and its fallacious policy regime,* Fourth, the Indian scene and its policy fallouts and the last conclusion the wayout from the present crisis.

INTRODUCTION

Inflation is a situation of rising prices resulting from an increase in the supply of money and credit. This generic explanation of inflation does not capture the whole issue. Inflation may also arise because of increased effective demand for commodities. It sometimes comes into existence because of rising cost due to increase in wages and input prices. Thus inflation arises not only because of increase in the supply of money or credit which is generally understood but it comes into operation either because of pressing demand or pushed up production costs. It is, thus either demand pull or cost push.

Trade cycle theory explains upswings and down wings of the economy governed by market forces of demand and supply. We know that capitalism as a marked centric system is based on profit motive. The seekers of profit pressured entrepresnurs or innovators making commercial use of technology use it for their own profit motive. The seekers of profit observed get rich quick motive or psychology created a mad rush for accumulation ignoring value judement or norms. Thus madness thrushed the capitalist system, which has entered its financial phase, to undesirable direction which not even economically viables credit where credit due is a wrong policy.

The belief in the unlimited wants for additional capital goods have survived in this date in economics text book and popular protagonist of supply side theory, which provides the ideological rationalization for Reagan's administration's economic policies. According to this theory the malfunctioning of U.S. economy in recent years stems from too much spending and not enough saving, a combination which is supposed to have produced a low growth rate, with its attendants evils of stagnation, falling profits, rising unemployment and all the rest.

This vision of capitalism steems from the view that there was no need for a special theory of demand side of the investment process. The presence of unlimited demand for additional means for production could be taken for granted. The determination of actual rate of accumulation, was therefore, shifted ensirely to supply side of the equation. Marshal in 8th edition of his principles of economics in 1920, chapter entitled "The Growth of Wealth" has highlighted this issue, where he profounded that the growth of wealth depends much on the supply of saving and paid little attention to the demand for capital. Believing in the notion of unlimited demand for additional capital goods. But the history of economic thought is full with literature against this proposition of Marshall and followers of the Neoclassical frame of analysis. The forbidings of the classical economists beginning with Ricardo and Malthus earned therefore for this explanation a reputation of dismal science to economics. Ricardo argued on the basis of two presumed natural laws—law of diminishing returns and the Malthusian law of population, that accumulation of capital would eventually run-out of stream because wages and rent would so far eat into profits as to leave capitalists with neither the wherewithals nor the incentive to continue accumulating. This argument of Ricardo and Malthus has a very strong political and ideological element. This argument bolstered the case for free trade that Neoclassicals advocated. The result was abrogation of corn laws (agricultural protectionism) would effectively repeal the law of diminishing returns as far as England was concerned and thus liberate the accumulation process from its shackles. This goal was finallay achieved (the liberation goal) in 1846 after which economists stopped worrying about threats to future growth of capitalism. Since the capitalism saw a prolonged and sustained growth period and it passed from transitional period of adolescence to maturity and climaxed, by the First World War boom in the United States and by then the leading capitalist power in the world. The automobile boom and growth in related sectors of manufacturing, oil, rubber, glass, highway construction, sub-urban housing reflected some fundamental economic feature—(a) The bourgeonising of consumer credit, as booster to final demand for products of these leading industries and (b) The gradual down drift of the manufacturing capacity utilization rate after 1925.

There were clear signs that despite the injection of strong debt guaranteed demand for consumer durables, the rate of investment which powered the boom of 1920's was unsustainable. Thus came the crisis of 1929 which was nothing but church of investment demand and was arising out of over accumulation.

Keynes provided a practical framework to the over accumulation in a broader framework of public investment via public expenditure expansion in infrastructure building measures, with massive doses of deficit spending. But Keyesian tools or tricks failed to provide the solution for long. In its inner most sense capitalism has always been a process of capital accumulation and in no time in its history has this process been smooth or un-interrupted. Thus capital is subject to fluctuations and uneveness which is evident in the normal business cycle. Thus, the theory of business cycle most popularly known as trade cycle is now a Universally recognized phenomena in a market centred self regulating capitalism of today. All schools of economic thought accept this.

The manifestations of market forces fluctuotions used to be of varied nature. There may be longer waves of speeded up boom and slower rate of retarded growth for sometime. The cycles between 1789-1814 and 1814-96 and first half of the third wave 1896-1920. These are long waves of fluctuations and had been studied by economists as Kondratieff long cycles of some fifty years. The point here as Schumpter has pointed out is not whether capitalists development is uneven with periods of long expansionary waves, successed by periods of low or even no expansion or *vice versa*. The point referred to by Schumpter as Kondratiest long cycle is as long waves.

The other short-term waves are also in existence. Schumpeter calls this short wave cycles as kitchin Juglar cycles. These cycles are less than ten years duration. Where two basic phases of the cycles—expansion or contraction contain the seeds of its opposite.

There was a long debate between two protagonist of Keyne's view which says market can't be self-regulated. It is subject to fluctuations and stationary state is automatic out-come unless efforts are being made by the state via public investment to increase the income generating capability of the common man and increased effective demand as a result of it generating thereby adequate profitable investment opportunities.

But even this growth has its own limit. After the publication of Keynes general theory in 1937, as result of new deal, the unemployment rate was 14.3 per cent in America and it jumped by the end of the year, unemployment in 1939-40, 23.3 per cent in U.S. Economy resulting into lowered income and mass unemployment and chronic depression—a condition rummed up in terms of stagnation. The breaking out Second World War produced a boosting climate for speedy recovery. The war altered the givens of the world economic situation in ways that enormously strengthened the incentive to invest. Paul, M. sweezy listed the main factors responsible for incentive to invest are: (a) to make luartime damage, danger, (b) increased potential demand for goods and services, the production of which eliminated during the war (houses, automobiles, appliances etc.) (c) huge purchasing power accumulation by firms, individuals during war, which could be used to transform potential demand into effective demand, (d) Ltd. of U.S. global hegemony as result of war, (e) U.S. Dollar became the basis of the international monetary system, pre-War trade and currency blocks were dismantled, (f) Conditions of free capital movements were created—All of which served to fuel an enormous expansion of international trade, (g) Civilian spin-offs from military technology, especially electronics and Jet planes, (h) The building by U.S. of a huge peacetime armaments industry—which got spurred by Korean wars (1950-52s) and Vietnam (1960-64) was in Indo-China.

These changes reflected itself as a fundamental change in business climate. The post-war boom thus had much deeper roots than merely repairing the damages and losses of the war itself. The mood changed into long-term optimism resulting in great investment boom in all the essential industries of modern capitalist society was triggered : steel, autos, energy, ship building, heavy chemicals, and many more. Capacity was built up rapidly in all the leading capitalist countries and in a few of the more advanced countries of the third world like Mexico, Brazil, India and South Korea.

In 1970s there was again reemergence of stagnation. The process of building up new industries (including the peace time area industries) require a lot more investment than maintaining them. Expanding industrial capacity always ends up by creating over capacity. To put it differential strong incentive to invest produces a brust of investment which in turn undermines the incentive to invest. This is the secret of long post-war boom and of the return of stagnation in the 1970's. The monetarist explanation of Milton Friedman in 1976, advocating supply side explanation of the phonema, the boom began to peter out, stagnation was fought-off for some years by more and more debt creation, at both national and international levels, leading to more and more frantic speculation and more and more inflation. By now these palliatives have become more harmful than helpful and to the problem of stagnation added a rapidly deteriorating financial situation. To credit where credit is due is a wrong policy leading to stretching of income generating capability of financial institution and its turning into final collapse or meltdown or explosion.

THEORETICAL EXPLANATION AND THE BACKGROUND

There are two important explanations of this recessionary trend leading to a summered up expression in terms of stagnation. One is the theory of vanishing investment opportunities given by Alvin Hanson and the other is new deal theory of stagnation. According to Hanson modern developed capitalist economy has an enormous capacity to save, both because of its corporate structure and because of its very unequal distribution of personal income. But if adequate profitable investment opportunities are lacking, this saving potential translates into real capital formation and sustained growth. This sustained growth usually directed towards lowered income generation and mass unemployment and chronic depression—a condition summed up in the term stagnation. This Hanson's framework analysis is a derivation of keynes's general theory. Hanson gave an explanation of why there is lack of investment opportunities in 1930 as compared to earlier times. Hanson blamed this world crisis of 1930s to certain irreversible historical changes—which had begun to build up in earlier decades, but finally came to dominate the scene after.the crisis of 1929.

Hanson summed up these historical changes in a more simplistic way as follows:

(a) The end of geographical expansion. It is closing of frontiers, Hanson interpreted this phenomena in wider global scene;
(b) a decline in the rate of population growth; and
(c) a tendency on the part of new technologies to be less

capital using than in earlier stages of capitalist development.

In Hanson's view all these historical changes operated to restrict the demand for new capital investment and in this way transformed the system's greater capacity to save into a stagnation producing force rather than engine of rapid economic growth.

Schumpeter criticizes this explanation of Hanson of stagnation theory. In his two important treatises treaties in 1938—"full recovery or stagnation" ? and other in 1939 written in two volumes on "Business cycles". He saw little merit in Hanson's theory. Hanson's theory of stagnation not only denied the necessity for healthy capital formation to sustain growth and high employment. He even charges that Hanson's argument that the changes in real estate demand for capital transformed the system's great capacity to save into vanishing investment demand thus leading the system into a stagnation producing force rather than an engine of rapid growth. Thus, it is the demand of saving for real, that they would necessarity entail a weakening of the demand for new investment.

Schumpeter further sited the example of American economy to refuse Hanson's argument. The end of geography in the case of American economy came in the late nineteenth century. Why should it begin to have such an adverse economic effects three to four decades later. Further he critised Hansen's view that population growth does not stimulate investment.

It rather results into more unemployment, doubling up housing, and lower living standard and mal nourishment, poor health conditions, and object poverty out of these. He alleged that Hanson failed to prove the nature and changes in technological innovation, which is nothing but various commercial uses of the new technological spiral. It is this which causes growth in investment demand. The labour cost shift mechanism of technology enforces the investment demand for capital.

Thus opposed to Hanson' scheme Shumpeter put forward another theory of stagnation. Instead of asking what casued stagnation in 1930, he gave the explanation why the cyclical upswing which began after 1933 and why it came to end in just a far short time. What other assumed a normal situation at the end of prosperity phase of the cycle—fall employment, rising prices, tight credit etc. Schumpeter's classification of economic cycles into three—which after their earlier investigator, Kitchews very short or basically inventory cycle say of 40 weeks cycles usually happeneing in U.S. economy. Juglar's Business cycles is a short duration of 10 years and Kondratieffs cycle of some 50 years duration, which Schumpeter calls the very long cycles. To him 1930's experiences were a disappointing Jugler.

Opposed to Hanson Schumpeter advocated anti business climate—Which is a by product of capitalist development process. His new deal theory of stagnation was later on shared by all conservative political thinking. The heart of his explanation of stagnation lies not in the content of new deal legislation but in normal functioning of capitalism. What is termed as anti-business characteristics of New deal legislation in spirit in which they acted. It has a dampening repressive effect on entrepreneur's confidence and optimism, belighting their hopes for the future and in visiting their investment activities in the present.

With the above two classic explanationa of stagnation theory of capitalist fluctuation, the theory of business cycles in economics remained more or less in the realm of historical curiosities. By the end of mid-1970 the problem come back again with a new twist reflected in a new name "stagflation" when it reappeared again and become a subject of debate. In late 1950's also it appeared and the victim war acted as a temporary relief, which resulted in pospouing factor of the pohenomena of stagnation.

In early 1970's it again re appeared following Penn-Central Credit Crunch and Nixon's administration formal abandonment of the gold standard and his brief experiments with wage and price control and leading the economy to a direction of unlimited credit expansion.

Later on Reagan administration and successive five presidential regimes and their economic policies caused this new situation to emerge. What is happening these days in entire global capitalist world's not depression. It is a chronic state of employment and Industrial slack. The government caused it and the people are a victim of that. To credit where Indit is due is a wrong dictum. It results in out stretching of income both at individual as well as at the level of institution of finance thus resulting in extravagance, more expenditure and less income generation capacity, resulting into resource crunch, and the present melt down of financial institution, which is nothing but slow down effect of the growth process.

THE RECESSION IN AMERICA AND THE REGIME OF CAPITAL ACCUMULATION

The economic environment of war and post war situation created a situation which altered the givens of the world in ways that enormously strengthened the incentive in invest and as result of it we witnessed a prolonged development decades in capitalist history led by America. The contributory factors were the need to make good wartime damage, existence of vast potential demand for goods and services, the production of which were elimated or greatly reduced during the war (houses, automobiles, appliances, etc.) a huge pool of purchasing power accumulated during the war by firms and industry. Thus started the long period of post-war capitalist expansion. Much earlier Josef Steindle Valued book on *Maturity and Stagnation* American capitalism while working in Oxford institute of statistics, came in but it was ignored by the economics profession, and the problem of inherent process of stagnation of the system was released to historical curiosities.

In the mid-seventies the problems again came back with a new twist and in new name "staglation". It was in the late 1950's and it failed to reappear as a subject of debate because of the push factor created by Vietnam war in early seventies, the stagflation situation was created following the Penn-Central Credit Chrunch and Nixon's administration abandonment of the gold standard and with experiment of wage and price controls. But the real return of stagnation was dated in American economy since the recession of 1974-75. Thus, the second half of 1970's displayed phenomena of new forces of stagflation for all to see. It got worse since then. Because of two factors wide range of unemployment in the capitalist world and second in U.S. there has been two recessions in successive years, with the present one quite possibly degenerating into full scale depression. In this process it is continuing despite changing mode of financial capitalism is outstretching the income generation capability leading to consumer is and service sector growth as result of it, and not creating capacity for the common man by providing resources for the livelihood and capacity building measures, since here profit generating process is rather slow.

The performance of the American economy in recent years, a result of these policies has been much worse or as bad as it was in 1930s owing to three causes: (a) much greater role of government spending and government deficits, (b) the enormous growth of consumer debt, including residential mortgage debt, especially during the 1970's, (c) the ballooning of the financial sector of the economy which not only led to the growth of debt as such but also includes an explosion of speculation of all kinds, old and new. This excessive speculation in turn generate not merely a trickle down of purchasing power into the real economy, but mostly in the form of increased demand for luxury goods.

TABLE 1

Outstanding Debt in U.S. Economy Index 1965, Number 100

Borrower	*1965*	*1970*	*1975*	*1980*	*1985*
Government	100	123.1	182.4	284.5	585.8
Consumers	100	140.1	226.89	421.2	696.5
Non-financial Business	100	165.1	277.9	468.8	762.3
Financial Business	100	200.5	421.6	917.0	1920.2
Total	100	144.5	236.5	414.4	742.4

Notes : (a) Government includes—Federal, State, and local governments.

(b) This category is called households in source of these statistics. It includes also personal trusts, non-profit foundations, private schools, hospitals, labour Unions and churches.

Source : Federal Reserve Board, Flow of Funds Accounts.

Fig. 1

Billion Dollars Outstanding Debt and Gross National Production in U.S.

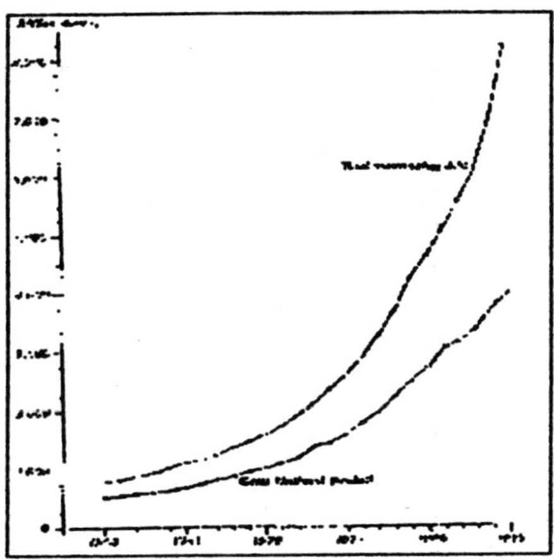

Source : Federal Reserve Board; Flow of funds and survey of current business, Feb. 1986. quoted for Harry Magdoff, "Stagnation is financial, Paul M. Sweezy Monthly Explanational Review Press, 2008.

Fig. 2

Speculation *vs.* Production in Real Economy in U.S.

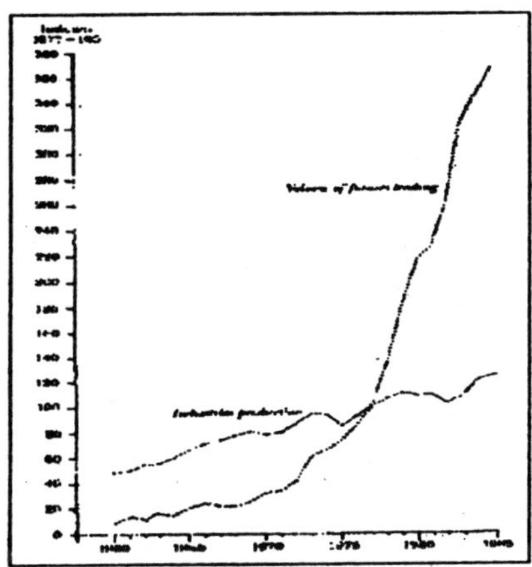

Source : Futures Trading Association and Federal Reserve Board of U.S.

These forces, no doubt acts a counter àcting forces against stagnation, as long as they last but it always creates the danger that if such policies carried forward they will erupt into an old fashioned panic of the kind, the U.S. economy has not seen since 1929-33 period. The present financial melt down is of the same mature as it appeared earlier. So, the present debate is left off where it was in 1930. Illustration below show the twenty-five years' behaviours of U.S. Economy which followed the Second World War during which we did not have a problem of stagnation.

TABLE 2

Growth of the Financial Sectors in U.S. Economy

Gross National Product

	Goods Production Billions dollars	*Financial Sectors*	*Financial sector as percentage goods production*
1950	153.3	32.2	21.0
1960	250.5	72.8	29.1
1970	440.5	145.8	33.1
1980	1144.6	400.6	35.0
1985	1566.7	626.1	40.0

Notes : (a) Agriculture, Construction, Manufacturing, Transportation and Public Utilities.

(b) Banks, other finance companies, real estate, and insurance.

Source : National Income and Product Accounts.

The above two figures depicting behaviour of U.S. world economies. The outstanding debt of U.S. economy has increased manifold compared to its Gross national product. Figure one compares total public-private debt with Gross National Production Debt has become a natural and necessary ingredient of business economy following its trends originated from U.S. and spread over to world over and it grows with business activity and declining during business down turn and expanding to fuel recoveries with installation of refineries and Petro-chemical units in far east and Arab world. The ratio of debt which was 1.5 to G.N.P. during 1950-60 went over to 1.57 to 1.7 between 1970-80. By 1985 the debt was twice as large as the years GNP. The worsening fact is that this debt is not composed of government debt. The total government expenditure has increased during past II war period from 13 per cent G.N.P. to 20 per cent in 1985, but in earlier years the surplus of good years balanced the deficits of recession years, but later on in 1960 and 1970 onwards deficits began to outweigh surpluses and thereafter reliance of deficit increased.

The spectacular rise in consumer debt in second line shows a strong desire to own homes and cars on the one hand and energetic promotion of lending by banks, finance companies on the others. Whenever effective demand for these big ticket items showed a tendency to decline lending terms were eased to widen the market. This practice was stimulated not by only manufactures and house builders but also by finance companies in order to seek a bigger share in the profitable business. As result of it, we have a proped up sales of homes and consumer durable goods, which helped piling up a mountain of consumer debt fast approaching to its unsustainable limit that is 68 per cent of after tax consumer income in 1970's and was close to 85 per cent in 1985.

The worsening fact of the U.S. economy is that as matter of fact government debt in its strict sense declined from 34 per cent in 1965 to 27 per cent in 1985, what is not worthy here is that debt dependency in last fifteen years of vast consumer class (Masses) has steedily increasing and in order compensate the weakening private economy via declining lending terms to widen market by the manufactures as well finance companies. Thus the government debt. increased not only by government expenditure influence effect, but by balancing the recession burden of manufacturing firms and finance companies, which ultimately out weight the surplus of both government, manufacturing units and finance companies, leading the system to explosive future trading which emergised this process, as depicted from Growth of financial sectors contribution to Gross National Product from 32.2 billion dollars in 1952 to 621.1 billion dollars in 1985 on wards. This contribution of finance sector to G.N.P. was 21 per cent greater than goods in 1950 which almost doubled to 40 per cent in 1985.

The point that comes in review is that U.S. Economy as mature monopoly capitalist economy indeed is dominated by the very growth of its productive potential which puts obstacles in the way of making full use of available human and material resources for the satisfaction of the needs of the greater mass of population. This means in the absence of powerful counteracting forces, normal state is stagnation. Capitalist system real history is composed of or determined by interaction tendency to stagnation and the forces countering this tendency. Thus monopolistic hegemony of U.S. and European economies with its gigantic productive potential, acts as obstacles in the way of making full use of resources and manpower of the third world countries in the interest of their common people, thus faits to producing a counteracting force against accumulation and as a result we have see weakening of investment demand.

INDIAN ECONOMY SITUATION AND THE CRISIS

How the government of India will face the economic fallout of the present economic impasse is question. It requires further analysis. We can draw certain analytical mechanism from analysis of US Monopoly capitalist behaviour. The Stimules packages provided by the UPA Government on Dec. 2008 and Jan. 2009 to counter the negative fallout of global slowdown. The government has provided huge fiscal stimulus during the fiscal year 2008-09 amounting to over Rs. 1,93,000 crores or 4.5 per cent of GDP over and above what was envisaged in last year's budget which already provided for a deficit of over Rs. 1,33,000 crores.

The true fiscal stimulus must include not only what was announced under two packages—Dec. 2008 and Jan. 2009 but also exspenditure under two supplementary demands for grants approved by Parliament in last Sept. and Dec. It is another matter that these supplementary demands were made for the creative under provisioning of some known items of expenditure in the last year's budget to remain within fiscal parameter of FRBM (Fiscal Regulation of Budgetary Management Act). The total consolidated deficit of 2008-09 including the actual deficit of central government (6 per cent) the state government 3.9 per cent and some of budget items such as the additional contingent liability for oil, and fertilizer bonds (1.8 per cent) amounts to (11.5 per cent) of GDP or nearly 6,26,000 crores.

It is this massive fiscal stimulus combined with sustained monetary stimulus measures from RBI in terms of reducing RR rate, adverse RRs have kept Indian economy chugging along at 6-7 per cent growth rate on an average between 2001-02 to 2006-07) even as most developed countries gone into recession.

The stimulus also helped to arrest the free fall of stock market and depreciation of rupees. It is out of the conventional wisdom which suggest that to be successful such stimulus packages have to be timely and targeted and but of temporary nature. The government of India adopted these measures within a few weeks of collapse of the Lehman Brothers in Sept. 2008 and with much of the stimulus directed at the worst affected sectors like—Exports, infrastructure, real estate, transport. The government, the central bank clearly passed the first two tests.

So far from interim Budget-projections it becomes clear that the Central government deficit would be 5.5 per cent in 2009-10 with a hint to rise upto 1 per cent by interim Finance Minister Pranab Mukherjee. Adding to this 3.5 per cent deficit of the state governments, and the possibilities of certain off-budget provisions in the year 2009-10, which could end up with a massive deficit of 10 per cent at end of the year 2010.

All these stimulus interms of fiscal deficit and monetary steps of rate reduction go a long way in pumping demand, compensating the loss on export demand from developed world due to slow down effect. That is why most of the additional spending is targeted towards infrastructure building, employment programmes, education and health.

The financing of this massive deficit is done through large government borrowing, which has crowded out the private borrowing. That is why interest rates have not come down substantially and Indian banks are shy of lending to private borrowers despite all the policy measures taken by RBI. If next year's deficit is too financed by private borrowing, it could be a bad news for private sectors and severly put at risk the recovery of private investment.

The law of inflation minimizes the risk of inflationary pressures arising from consequent increase in money supply. It is therefore, important that a large part of the deficit be monetized that is it should be financial by government borrowing from the RBI by temporarily shelving the MOU between finance ministry and RBI which prevents the RBI financing the government deficits.

Thus, the shelving at FRBM, and putting on hold of the MOU with RBI would set aside the two key anchors of prudence that have guided fiscal policy in recent years. It is true that the present economic crises have given rise exceptional situation and exceptional circumstances require exceptional measures.

India should abandon fiscal prudence since it is fraught with risk and we have learned to our cost in past and the test of time has suggested that fiscal stimulus measures, the government of India adopted in financing fiscal deficit via borrowing from R.B.I. must be temporary. Thus, the fiscal and monetary stimulus are like major shocks being applied now to revive the Indian economy in the wake of new economic crisis that has ingulfed the world economy taking its origin from American economy.

There are researches which shows that Lag generated by such major shocks being applied now can last for years making the recovery itself fragile. It is therefore, imperative that fiscal and monetary breaks be applied as soon as the economy returns to high growth path. It makes it clear that Indian policy-makers are also running the Indian fiscal and mometary policy and taking wider economic policy division on the same western line followed by America. The only difference is that the commanding economy of America has fastened the path of extravagance and we as a starter on the same line decided to follow the path of prudence with temporary fiscal and monetary stimuli. That is why Pranab Mukherjee in his latest interim budget speech indicated strong fiscal monetary compression, the return to FRBM regime and the M.O.U. with RBI will remain high priorities in future. Hopefully, then recovery will occur in 2010. So fiscal consolidation can be initiated within first half of next government tenure before compulsions of the insuing electoral cycle take over.

CONCLUSION

How to come out of this stagnation cycle or why this stagnation. In all market economies this question comes to fore in times of crisis and then relegated to the ground when because of certain externalities, pushed up demand comes into being setting motion of the multiplier effect of investment demand and the consequent boom. This issue was raised in 1930 and was dropped with advent of keynes, but without any satisfactory answer. Reality is now posing it again in wake of new crisis getting expressed in Meltdown analysis, we should as an academician accept this challenge and resume the search for an answer. The beginning point for the wayout is where Hanson in 1930 began. The structure of the economy both in its corporate and individual dimension is the same as it was half a century ago. Its saving potential is still enormous and what changes has taken place during capitalists' development decade have tended to make it greater rather than smaller in the intervening period. We have seen how corporate concentration has increased because of enormous saving potential of the system. This makes the distribution of individual income highly unequal. Morever, changes in tax structure have been more and more favourable to the corporations and the rich. Always under such conditions, a strong and sustained investment performance is needed to prevent to the economy from following into the recession trap and prolonged recession period. Thus it turns into stagnation. This is what has been missing for long time now and specially in the last few years. So the immediate cause of stagnation is the same now as it was in 1930—a strong propensity to save and a weak propensity to invest.

This can be changed only by providing alternative to this system and not by taking remedial measure which will use the resources at the disposal to provide livelihood bases and improving their livelihood condition by increasing their capacity building via generating creative psychology in their mind which in turn will enhance their confidence level in any endeavour of their own to ameliorate their poor living condition. This require drive against concentration, positive steps in terms of policies to establish an egalitarian order where every body will have access to natural resources at their disposal to use it in a proper way to make the development goals sustainable cycle. Only then stagnation will never show its ugly face.

References

Anger Maddison (2001), The World Economy: A Millennium Perspective, OECD, Paris.

Arun Maria, "A matter of Trust; Accountability Inspires Confidence in Free Markets", *Times of India*, Feb. 2, 2009.

Central Bank Cuts Key Rates, *Times of India*, Patna, Jan. 3, 2009.

Hanson, Alvin H., "Pull Recovery or Stagnation", 1938, Harward University Press.

Heonard Silk, Editor, *New York Times*, What is happening is not Depression, It is a Chronic State of Unemployment and Industrial Slack, also Business Section of the Sunday, March 14, 1965. The Roots of the Problem Go a Long way.

Lester Thurow, (Harward trained Professor of Economics), "The Great Stagnation", *New York Times*, Oct. 17, 1982.

Kaleki Michal (1968), "Determinants of Investment Decision", "Social Science Information, Dec. 1968), this Polish Economist is Credited with Inventing Keynesian Revolution before Keynes. He Says at the time of his death in 1968, that Long Run Growth of National Income involves Satisfactory Utilization of Equipment is far from obvious.

Keynes, J.M., General Theory on Employment Interest and Money, 1936.

Kiran Majumdar, Its in the DNA, *Times of India*, Jan 14, 2009.

Magdaff Harry and Sweezy, M. Paul, Stagnation and the Financial Explosion, pp. 7-79. Monthly Review Press, New York, 2009.

Magdoff Harry, The World Debt: Past and Present, Article presented at Allied Social Science Association Meetings, New York city, Dec. 1985, Feb. 1986, issue monthly review.

Marx Karl, Das Capital, Vol. I, "Marx referred to the quarrel between industrial capital and aristocratic landed property", which elicited the participation of England's outstanding economic thinkers in the decade of 1820's.

Mundule Sudipto, "No goodies here", *Times of India, Patna-Ranchi National*, Tuesday, Feb. 17, 2009.

N. Mohan Chandra, "Who will Light the Fire? *Hindustan Times*, Tuesday, Feb. 7, 2009.

Perelman Michael, "How to Think about the Crisis", Tuesday, 7 Oct. 2008, *Home Archive*, Left clicks search http://Radicalnotes/com/content view 73/79.

Sanjeev Sanyal, Go Beyond Statistics, GDP as Measure of Human Progress is out dated, *Times of India*, Jan. 10, 2009.

Schumpeter, A. Joseph, "The Business Cycles", 1938.

Stanley Aronowitz, "Facing the Economic Crisis, Socialist Project, *E. Bulletin*, No. 170, Dec. 26, 2008.

Steindl Josef, "Maturity and Stagnation in American Capitalism, Oxford Institute of Statistic, Oxford University Press, 1952.

Sudipto Mundle, "No Goodies here: The Interim Budget has Struck the Right Balance." *Times of India*, Feb. 17, 2009.

Sweezy, M. Paul, "Why Stagnation, Talk given by the author to Harward Economics Club on March 22, 1982, appeared in June 1982 issue of *Monthly Review.*

The dynamics of US Capitalism: Corporate structure, Inflation, Credit, Gold, and the Dollar (1972).

The End of American Prosperity in 1970 (1977).

Tseodore Shauin (ed.), Late Marx and the Russian Road: Marx and the "Peripheries of Capital", *Monthly Review*, Press, 1984.

Inflation in India
A Result to the Excess Supply of Money

C.B. SHARMA

INTRODUCTION

The term inflation has been defined differently by different economists. According to Chamber's Twentieth Century Dictionary inflation is defined as an "due increase in quantity of money in proportion to buying power, as on an excessive use of fiduciary money." Crowther was of the opinion that inflation is a state in which the value of money is falling, i.e. prices are rising. According to Pigou, "Inflation exists when money income is expanding more than in proportion to income earning activity". In brief the common concept of inflation is the evidence of a state of disequilibrium between the demand for and supply of goods which causes rise in the level of prices in the economy.

How evei J.L. Hanson was of the opinion that inflation is considered as a monetary condition where the volume of purchasing power is persistently running a head of the output of goods and services available to consumers and producers, with the result that there is a persistent tendency for prices and wages to rise, that is, for the value of money to fall. This type of inflationary situation can arise in wartime mainly.

FULL AND PARTIAL INFLATION

While inflation always indicates instability and rising prices in the economy it would be improper to describe every rise in the price level in a country as full inflation, notwithstanding the fact that such a rise in the level of prices may be inflationary in character indicating partial inflation. Every rise in the level of prices can not be called full inflation, rather only increase in the prices above full employment can be called full inflation. But the situation of full employment is not found to be happened in our real economic world.

INFLATION IN INDIA SINCE-1947

As we have already discussed that inflation is completely a monetary phenomena and is the resultant of price rise. We find in India that price level since 1947 has gone up 52 times and destroyed over 98% of the value of the rupees left by the British government and that was mainly due to excess supply of money. As we know prices of individual goods can keep rising or falling due to several factors affecting their demand and supply. But price level as a whole is determined primarily by the quantum of good and services available in the country and the total amount of money chasing them. Increase in the prices of some goods is bound to lead to fall in the prices of some other goods, unless the quantity of money is increased. Price level as a whole goes up only when more money is injected into the system or its velocity of circulation goes up due to changes in habits and practices.

As the monetary theory tells us that the price level does not fall when the total output of goods and services is increasing in an economy, money supply has to be increased. But if increase in money supply is greater than the increase in the quantum of goods and services, then the entire price level is bound to go up. Therefore, we find that better managed countries, therefore ensure that a reasonable relationship is maintained between the two such countries do not allow money supply to expand much faster than the amount required to take care of rising GDP.

Our above discussion is related with the simple quantity theory of money which many economists do not accept, but its basic proposition is simply a matter of common sense. Excess supply of money:

> Since a few decades our government continues to expand money supply several times more than increase in GDP, as the data tabulated in this article will prove. Considering the entire post-independence period, for every rupee of increase in GDP, currency in circulation has been increased by more than 30 rupees. This has led to the disastrous result of pushing up the price level by 52 times during the period of 61 years, i.e. from 1947 to 2008.

M3, which includes not only currency in circulation but also deposits of various types and other large liquid assets, represents a more comprehensive measure of money supply both have to remain under strict control to ensure a reasonably stable price level.

In the under given Table 1 we find the currency in circulation and total money supply as (M3) in a few selected years along with the whole sale price index.

As we have seen in the Table 1 between 47-48 to 60-61 currency supply did not even double. But with the passage of item it's supply has been found to be increasing in a very rapid way. Between 1947-48 to 2008, it has been found to be multiplied 463 times and that very excess supply of money from mere Rs. 12,382 crores to Rs. 6,04,185 crores took place after 79-80.

In more than 100 years ending in 1980, the total amount of currency in circulation increased gradually to only 12,382 crores. Now that much amount is being added every 45 days. In last one year alone a further amount of Rs. 97,606 crore was pushed into circulation which is currently playing havoc with the price level.

TABLE I

Year	*Currency in Circulation (Rs. Cr.)*	*Total Money supply (M3) (Rs. Cr.)*	*Wholesale Price Index Base year (1993-94=100)*
1919-20	154	NA	
1929-30	159	NA	
1938-39	189	NA	
1947-48	1304	NA	4.5
1951-52	1292	2196	7
1960-61	2154	3902	8
1970-71	4547	10326	14
1979-80	12382	43792	37
1990-91	55,282	249493	74
1998-99	175846	901294	142
2003-04	327028	1861604	176
May 2008	604185	4099957	235

Source : File-H—New Folder Indian Inflation uncontrollable-htm D-6.23.2008.

M3 was merely Rs. 43,792 crore in 1979-80 it has now touched the astronomical figure of Rs. 40,99,957 crores since 1951-52 and it has gone up 1867 times.

Massive expansion of currency and M3 is very much reflected in the rapid increase in the price level. Since 1947-48 price level has gone up from 4.5 to 253 percent (93-94 = 100).

After 1947 while GDP has increase only 15 times currency in circulation has been multiplied 463 times. This constituted an open invitation to large scale inflation.

Government officials and even some economists art of irrelevant factors for inflation in the country.

The historical data of growth in money supply (M3) and inflation for India since April 2002 gives amazing finding.

There as a negative correlation between these two variables between April 2002 and March 2005, which is really surprising for monetary economists. But the trend changed in 2005-06 which indicates a weaker positive correlation among growth in M3 and inflation.

But as apparent in Table 1 the real reason is the excess supply of money with a view to please the business community and finance the budget deficit of the government.

The currency was managed during the years prior to the second world war is apparent from the fact there in 19 years, i.e. from 19-20 to 38-39 currency in circulation went up from Rs. 154 crores to merely 189 crores. A comparative study of Money supply :

For comparative study the data was not available about money supply in a few selected countries of the world, but selected what could be gathered is given below in Table 2.

TABLE 2
M3

Country	*Increase in No. of times*
USA	35
Sweden	29
Singapore	38
Australia	95
India	677

Source : File-H—New Folder Indian inflation uncontrollable htm-6.23.2008.

In the above Table 2 we find that the number of times to the supply of total money (M3) increased during the period of 46 years, i.e. between 1990-2006. We are seeing in the above given Table 2 that there is a wide gap in the number of times of total money supply (M3) made by India and other selected countries of the world. It proves that India is acting beyond the norms of financial discipline in terms of money supply (M3) in respect to other important countries of the world a few among those are given in the above Table 2.

The undergiven Table 3 shows the number of times the price level increased in different countries during the period of 50 years, i.e. between 1956-2006.

TABLE 3

Country	*Increase in price level (Number of Times)*
Singapore	3
Germany	4
Switzerland	4
Japan	6
France	7
USA	7
Canada	8
India	

Source : *Ibid.*, Table 2.

In the above Table 3 we find that the better a country is managed the smaller is the increase in money supply and consequently the level of price. When we compare the countries listed in the Table 3 we find that by pushing up the price level so fast India is playing havoc with the finances of the lower strata of society and shifting huge amount of wealth in the most undesirable direction.

However, India can be proud of its record when it looks to countries like Turkey where price level went up 600 times (i.e. from 100 to 60,000) in only 15 years, i.e. (between 1991 to 2006). In Zimbabwe the position is much worse. It has recently introduced 500 million dollar currency notes which can buy only two loaves of bread.

INDIA AND SINGAPORE COMPARED

Singapore has the highest regard for the welfare and basic rights of its common people since its independence in 1961. Its price level has gone up 3 times only while its real GDP has jumped up 35 times. A comparison between India and Singapore covering period of 34 years (Singapore stated having its own currency in 1974) will show the vast difference in the way the two countries deal with such a vital matter affecting the life of their citizens.

In the under given Table 4 we find the actual position of India and Singapore in respect to their GDP, currency, M3, and Price level.

TABLE 4
Indian and Singapore Compared Increase between 1974 to 2008

	India *Increase in No of times*	*Singapore* *Increase in No of times*
GDP	6	10
Currency	87	15
M3	249	47
Price level	16	2

File-H—New Folder Indian inflation- uncontrollable htm 6.23.2008.

In the above Table 4 we find that during the period of last 34 years Singapore GDP increase 10 times and currency in circulation went up 15 times, i.e. 1.5 times only. In India's case GDP went up 6 times, but currency jumped up 87 times. A country which multiplies its currency by 14.5 times (8716) in respect to its increase in GDP is bound to suffer from high rate of inflation and inflict immense misery on its poor people.

INFLATION AND GOVERNMENT

Increase in currency in respect to the increase in GDP is certainly legitimate and necessary. But 14.5 times of its increase in respect to increase in GDP means encouraging the rate of inflation and that is due mainly to the policy of the government. Our government goes on blaming the cause like increase in price of imported oil. Government spokes men always talk about the policy of fighting inflation as if it is the creation of some external force. Increase in price of imported oil simply reduce India's GDP. By itself it cannot increase the price level as a whole. If people have to spend more on oil, they will spend less on other goods and that will lead to fall in the prices of other goods. As such in the long-run, the price level as a whole cannot rise merely because price of one commodity or some other commodities has already gone up.

BRITISH PERIOD

As we find the government of Britain never indulged in massive printing of money (except for a few fears of the Second World War). During the period even before the war, it ensured that the price level did not go up even 3 times more in the long span of 82 years, i.e. from 1857 to 1939 (with 48-49 as base year, price index stood at 10.2 in 1857 and 29.0 in 1939).

POLICY FOLLOWED IN INDIA

For a few years even after independence India increased its currency in tune with the increase in GDP and consequently the price level did not go up too high. During the period of 15 years immediately after independence, i.e. between 1947-48 to 1962-63, the Indian leaders continued to follow the policy of their British predecessors. During this period India increased its currency in circulation by only 87%, (from Rs. 1304 crores to Rs. 2439 crores) while GDP increased by 64%. Because of the sensible policy of not expanding the currency to much the price level went up only by 30% during this period of 15 years.

GDP AND MONEY SUPPLY

Government and big business groups are the main beneficiaries of inflation and the people belonging to these sections have succeeded in establishing the widespread myth that large expansion of money supply is necessary for rapid growth of GDP. They always talk about the trade off between inflation and growth implying that a country has to suffer inflation in order to have economic growth. Singapore has established the view that for rapid economic growth huge expansion of money is not necessary since its independence in 1961, real GDP has jumped up 35 times while price level has gone up only 3 times because money supply (as apparent from the data given in the Table 4) has been kept under strict control.

News paper, articles often contain remarks like "Reserve Bank will have to choose between control of inflation and economic growth".

Indeed Reserve Bank can control inflation without damaging growth. By printing money it does not increase the quantum of physical resources required for economic growth. It merely snatches away physical resources from the poor through the process of inflation and hand over them to the entrepreneurs. This is not the way for promoting growth rather to disturb the monetary stability of the country only. However we have seen that since 1947, India's real GDP has gone up 15 times but that is not due to massive expansion of money supply rather it has increase due to three-fold reasons that is increase in population (three-fold) the second entrance of skilled and educated workers are associated with work force and the last is availability of much improved technology.

HARMING THE POOR

In course of inflationary situation fall in the value of the rupee keep raising the value of physical assets and reducing the value of monetary assets. The rich and super rich normally borrow money and charged it into physical assets people of normal income group are normally lender of money through deposits with banks, post offices and others consequently the wealth of the rich and super rich has been going up and the lower sections of the society is going down. This is the fundamental reason behind the day-to-day rising in equalities between rich and poors since independence.

Fall in the value of the rupee through inflation does not destroy the real wealth of the country. It simply leads to the transfer of wealth from the poorer to the richer sections of the people. This is mainly because better managed countries like Singapore, Switzerland and Germany have not allowed the value of their currency to fall excessively.

In India, in the course of last 34 years, the price level has gone up 16 times with the result that value of money is reduced by 94%. Take the case of a widow who inherited Rs.

10 lakhs in 1976 and has been keeping it in a fixed deposit in a bank with the interest income left after paying income tax she has been meeting the household expenses. But in the course of 34 years, 94% of the real value of her deposit has been meeting the household expenses. But in the course of 34 years 94% of the real value of her deposit has been snatched away by the beneficiaries of inflation. Conclusively her deposit of Rs. 10 lakhs is now worth only Rs. 60,000 in terms of the money of 1974.

By printing money and promoting inflation government also causes immense damage to the poorest of the poor and the labour classes, because wages are sticky and do not keep pace with fall in the value of money, particularly in the short run.

Large scale printing of money provides the most subtle way of taxing the poor and the lower middle class people as well. They are forced to part with a major part of their hard earned income.

SOME DAMAGING CONSEQUENCES

Since the time of abandoning the Barter system, most of the human activity takes place in terms of costing and pricing, which is done in monetary amounts. If the value of money goes on changing rapidly all amounts of costs and prices need to be revised and a lot of time is wasted in renegotiating the transactions again and again, which reduces national output.

Fast rising prices and fall in the value of money adversely affect the household Budget of every body. Fixed income earners the worst sufferer. Employees of public and private sectors are all have to keep fighting continuously for increase in salary and wages rather than concentrate on production work.

SUGGESTIONS

After coming through discussions we come on the suggestions that for curbing the problem of inflation we are not supposed to adopt the traditional measures, i.e. monetary, non-monetary and fiscal only rather we should must be vigilant in supplying our currency in respect to the increase in the GDP. The example to the adoption of such tight monetary policy has already been quoted above by the example of a few developed countries of the world such as Singapore, Switzerland and Germany, etc. Hence the concerned ministry of finance should be very hard in giving permission to the concerned body for making excess supply of money in comparison to the increase in GDP.

This should be also suggested that in the interest of justice fairness and welfare of the common man, stability of the price level is very essential, the most ideal course would be to increase money supply to the extent of the increase in GDP so that the price level does not go up at all. But in order to energies rapid growth of the economy, some excess of money supply may be unavoidable. Moreover, it is not possible to match the two exactly. However, this excess supply of money should be so marginal that the price level should not be permitted to go up by more than one or two percent per year, as we find it to be happened in the countries like Singapore and even in India. During British rule—Hence, conclusively it is suggested that for economic prosperity and monetary stability an ideal relation between money supply and GDP should be maintained by the financial authority of the country concerned.

References

Chamber's Twentieth Century Dictionary.

Crowther, G., Outline of Money, 1958, Edition, p. 197.

Pigou, A.C., Theveil of Money, p. 34.

Hanson, J.L., Dictionary of Economics and Commerce, The English Language Book Society, Third Edition, p. 263.

Pallavi, Mulay, Monetary Tightening May not Curb Inflation. *The Economic Times*, Kolkata, 2.4.2007.

Bagi, S.S., Prices Rising Due to Reckless Supply of Money, June 2008 (6.23.2008).

File-H—New folder Indian Inflation Uncontrollable, htm 6.23.2008 (vii) *Ibid.*, p. 8 (viii) *Ibid.*, p. 11.

Ibid., p. 8.

Ibid., p. 11.

5

Inflationary Trends in India

ANIL KUMAR THAKUR AND APARNA BHARDWAJ

"Inflation may be defined as a state of disequilibrium in which an expansion of purchasing power tends to cause or is the effect of an increase of the price level."

—By Paul Einzig...

In a broad sense, inflation is that state in which the prices of goods and services rise on the one hand and value of money falls on the other. When money circulation exceeds the production of goods and services, the state of inflation takes place in the economy.

Inflation is a global phenomenon in present-day times. There is hardly any country in the capitalist world today which is not afflicted by the spectre of inflation. It is on account of this that the phenomenon of inflation has widely attracted the attention of the economists all the world over, but despite that there is no generally accepted definition of the term inflation. Inflation in the popular mind is generally associated with rapidly rising prices which cause a decline in the purchasing power of money.

Presently, inflationary trend exists in a very troublesome state. Inflation rate, soon after the price hike in petrol, diesel and cooking gas, has jumped to two digit figure table. The inflation based on the wholesale price index crossed double digits to touch 11.91 per cent for the week ended July 5, 2008, the highest since May 6, 1995. Earlier before petroleum price hike, inflation rate was also showing upward trend but components responsible for high inflation rate were different. On May 31, 2008, inflation rate rose to 8.75 per cent on account of higher prices of food items like edible oil, cereals, etc. But this time oil price hike fuels inflation rate to 11.42 per cent.

With two digit inflation rate India has joined the ranks of a few other Asian economies with double digit inflation like Vietnam (25 per cent), Indonesia (10.4 per cent).

EFFECTS OF INFLATION

The impact of inflation on different sectors of economy can be discussed under two sub-heads:

1. Effects on production, and
2. Effects on distribution.

As we know well that the effect of inflation is faced by each community of our society. Now we will discuss the various impact of inflation by above sub-heads.

I. Effects on Production

The phenomenon of inflation produces a very deep impact on the production of wealth in the economy. In fact, the impact of inflation can be studied under two situations. One is Mild Inflation which is not detrimental to productive activities in the economy. An expansion of money supply in an underemployed economy will result in a slow and gradual rise in the price. But such the situations exist until full employment is attained. Other is Hyperinflation which disrupts the smooth functioning of the economy.

Since hyperinflation results in a serious depreciation of the value of money, it discourages saving on the part of the

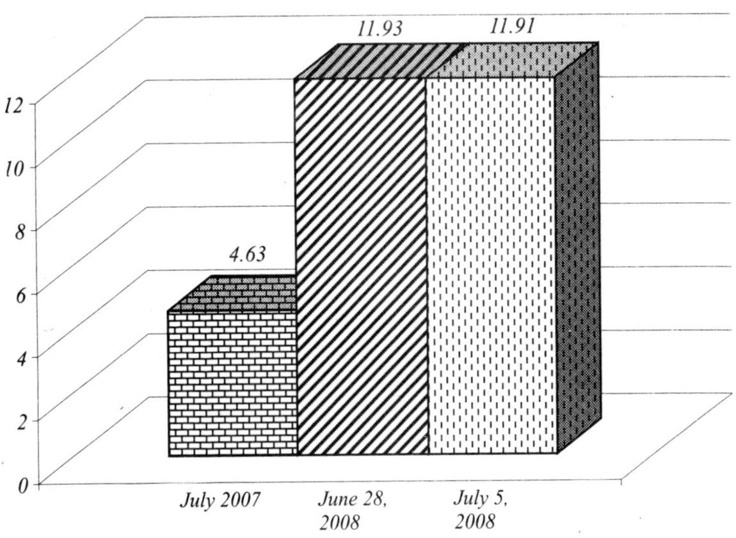

public. Consequently the process of capital formation suffers a serious setback. As inflation results in a seller's market, it may lead to a serious deterioration in the quality of goods produced in the economy.

The most serious effect of inflation is that it disrupts the smooth working of the price mechanism. It also loses the flexibility under the inflationary forces, which results in the reduction of mobilization of productive resources.

2. Effects on Distribution

Inflation produces a deep impact on the distribution of income and wealth in the society. Businessmen, traders, merchants and speculators reap rich harvests on account of windfall profits accruing to them as a result of the inflationary rise in price. The impact of inflation on various groups of society are as below:

(i) Debtors and Creditors

During inflation debtors are generally the gainers while the creditors are losers. The reason behind it is the purchasing power of money was high at the time creditor lent the money, while the purchasing power of money is low right now.

(ii) Wages and Salary Earners

Wages and salary earners mostly suffer during inflation because wages and salaries generally do not rise in the same proportion as the cost of living standard. When workers are well-organized into powerful trade unions, they may not suffer much during inflation, but if they are unorganized they may suffer much during inflation.

(iii) Fixed Income Groups

The fixed income groups are the hardest hit during inflation because their income being fixed, do not bear any relationship with the rising cost of living. The main targets of this hit are pensioners, interest and rent receivers, etc. as their income remain fixed while the prices soar highest.

(iv) Entrepreneurs

Inflation is a boon to the entrepreneurs. Whether they be manufacturers, traders, merchants, or businessmen, because it serves as a tonic for business enterprises. The costs of labour, raw materials and equipment etc. do not catch up with the rise in prices of products, which converts them into profiteers.

(v) Investors

Investors are generally of two kinds:

(a) Investors in Equities (Shares), and
(b) Investors in fixed interest yielding bonds and debentures.

Investors in equities earn profit during inflation as dividends on equities increases with the increase in price and corporate earnings.

On the other hand, investors in fixed interest yielding instruments are adversely affected during inflation as interest or returns on bonds and debentures remain fixed despite rise in the price level.

The middle class investors generally invest in fixed interest yielding instruments and thus suffer a loss while the rich class investors invest in equities and receive high returns.

(vi) Farmers

Farmers are generally gainers during inflation. The price of farm products go up while the costs incurred by them do not go up to the same extent. Moreover, the farmers are generally debtors and can repay their debts during inflation in terms of less purchasing power scenario of money.

Thus, inflation redistributes wealth and income in such a manner as to injure the interests of consumers, creditors, salary and wages earners, fixed income groups, small investors and to favour businessmen, merchants, traders and farmers. Socially, inflation is unjust and iniquitous. It transfers wealth to those sections who have too much.

MEASUREMENT OF INFLATION

The measurement of inflation is very much required in order to find a rational solution of inflation. There are broadly two measures of inflation:

1. Wholesale price index, and
2. Consumer price index.

I. Wholesale Price Index

It is also known as producer price index. It measures the mean of the changes of goods and services prices on the basis of wholesale price. It explains the market economy as well as the economy growth. Usually the change of prices of 26 selected groups of taken to determine the wholesale price index. In India, it is the most popular price index used in business industry and policy market.

The data are taken capital cities and other cities. The data taken from directly from the respondents by interview. The respondents are chosen from such companies who will be able to represent the commercial commodities.

Wholesale price index is divided into five commodities groups. These are:

(a) Agriculture
(b) Manufacturing
(c) Quarrying
(d) Import and Export
(e) Mining

Each of these divisions has again been grouped into many sub-commodity groups. Altogether there are 257 commodities.

In economics, Wholesale Price Index is taken as an indicator of the rate of inflation. It analyzes the market and monetary conditions. WPI focuses on the changing mature of the economy of different kinds of services like railway, road transportation, telecoms and banking sector etc.

Table 1 shows the trends of WPI from 2006-07 to 2008-09. Here base year for WPI Calculation is 1993-94. WPI for all commodities is estimated to 10.3 per cent for April-December quarter of 2008-09, which was 4.3 per cent one year back. Likewise, all India CPI-IW (industrial workers) is estimated to 9.1 per cent in April-December quarter of 2008-09, which was 6.1 per cent one year back.

2. Consumer Price Index

It is related to the increase or decrease in retail price. It has a direct bearing on the living standard of a consumer as there are different categories of consumers so we different types of consumer price indices, they are:

(i) *Consumer Price Index (CPI) for agricultural Labour (CPI):* It measures rural consumer prices. Since most of people are dependent on agriculture for their survival in the rural areas, so CPI best fit here
(ii) *Consumer Price Index (CPI) for Industrial Works (CPI):* It measures the price Index for urban consumer. It is very much useful in the urban areas. It is further sub-divided into CPIUNPM, i.e. CPI for urban non-manual employee.

TABLE I

Wholesale Consumer Price Movements in the Indian Economy and Comparative Inflation Rates (Financial Year)

Month	WPI Numbers* for Commodities (Base: 1993-94=100)			CPI for Industrial Workers (Base: 2000-01=100)			Percentage Change over Previous Year			
							All Commodities WPI		All India CPI-IW	
	2006-07	2007-08	2008-09	2006-07	2007-08	2008-09	2007-08	2008-09	2007-08	2008-09
(1)	(2)	(3)	(4)	(5)	(6)	(7)	(8)	(9)	(10)	(11)
April	199.0	211.5	228.5	120.0	127.0	138.0	6.3	6.3	5.8	8.6
May	201.3	212.0	231.1	121.0	129.0	139.0	5.3	9.0	6.6	7.7
June	203.1	212.3	237.4	123.0	130.0	140.0	4.5	11.8	5.6	7.6
July	204.0	213.6	240.0	124.0	132.0	143.0	4.7	12.4	6.4	8.3
August	204.8	213.8	241.2	124.0	133.0	145.0	4.4	12.8	7.2	9.0
September	207.8	214.7	241.5	125.0	133.0	146.0	3.3	12.5	6.4	9.7
October	208.7	215.2	238.8	127.0	134.0	148.0	3.1	11.0	5.5	10.4
November	209.1	215.9	234.2	127.0	134.0	148.0	3.3	8.5	5.5	10.4
December	208.4	216.4	230.5	127.0	134.0	147.0	3.8	6.5	5.5	5.5

(Contd.)

TABLE 1 (*Contd.*)

(1)	*(2)*	*(3)*	*(4)*	*(5)*	*(6)*	*(7)*		*(8)*	*(9)*	*(10)*
January	208.8	215.2		127.0	134.0		3.1		5.5	
February	208.9	219.9		128.0	135.0		5.3		5.4	
March	209.8	225.5		128.0	137.0		7.5		7.0	
				Monthly Average of Calendar Months						
Apr.-Mar.	206.1	215.5		125.0	132.6		4.5		6.0	
Apr.-Jun.	201.1	211.9	232.2	121.3	128.7	139.0	5.4	9.6	5.9	8.0
Apr.-Sep.	203.3	213.0	236.6	122.8	130.7	141.8	4.7	11.1	6.4	8.4
Apr.-Dec.	205.1	213.9	235.9	124.2	131.8	141.8	4.3	10.3	6.1	9.1

Notes : Provisional (and subject to revision).
* = WPI Numbers are averages of week-ended Saturday.
(CPI-IW Index figures up to January 2006 based on 1982=100 base year.

Sources : 1. Office of the Economic Adviser, Ministry of Industry, GoI for WPI Data/PTI Economic Service, Feb. 16-28, 2009.
2. Labour Bureau, Ministry of Labour, GoI, for CPI-IW Data/PTI Economic Service, Feb. 16-28, 2009.

The Consumer price Index (CPI)-Industrial Workers moderated to 147 in December from 148 in the preceding month. It clocked the annual growth of 9.7 per cent as compared to previous month's 10.4 per cent. The magnitude of moderation in CPI-based inflation, when compared to previous month, is only a third of that in WPI-based inflation. This is because the weight of fuel items, that had contributed the most in the sharp drop in WPI-based inflation, is very low in the CPI basket of commodities. The retail inflation stood at 5.5 per cent during December 2007.

Inflation in primary articles moderated further in December 2008 as all the main components of the group, that is food, non-food and minerals showed a deceleration in prices. Food articles, in particular, saw a decline in annual price variation for the first time during the current fiscal year. This was due to cheaper vegetables and tea. However, it continued to be the major driver in overall inflation of the primary articles group, as its contribution rose to as much as 59.2 per cent in December 2008. This is in sharp contrast with its contribution of a mere 37.5 per cent during the corresponding month of the previous year, exceptionally low prices of food articles marked this period, driving the overall inflation to record low levels.

Among non-food articles, fibres continued to experience a deceleration in price variation while oilseeds followed the reverse pattern. Inflation in minerals fell to the lowest level since February 2008. Overall, inflation in primary articles was recorded at 11.5 per cent as compared to 4.5 per cent during same month of the previous year. It can be seen in the Table 2.

Following the persistent fall in the crude price, the government reduced the prices of petrol and diesel by Rs. 5 and Rs. 2 respectively on December 6, 2008. This resulted in the decline in price indices of petrol and diesel to the tune of 10 and 5.7 per cent respectively over their previous month levels. This, together with the sharp drop in the prices of industrial fuels, dragged the inflation in mineral oils sub-group to –1.8 per cent in December. In yet another round of price cut, the government slashed the petrol and diesel price cut, the government slashed the petrol and diesel prices further by

TABLE 2

Inflation in Major Product Groups (y-o-y per cent)

April-December

Sectors	*Weight*	*Dec. 2007*	*Dec. 2008*	*2007-08*	*2008-09*
General	100	3.8	6.3	4.3	10.2
Primary	22	4.5	11.5	7.7	10.9
Fuel	14.2	2.9	-0.2	-0.4	11.2
Manufacturing	63.8	3.9	6.8	4.8	9.5
Contribution to inflation					
Primary		26.2	41.3	40	24.6
Fuel		16.7	-0.7	-2.2	23.7
Manufacturing		56.6	59.5	62.3	51.7

Source : Ministry of Industry/Crisil Eco view.

Rs. 5 and Rs. 2 respectively in addition to a reduction in LPG gas cylinder by Rs. 25, with effect from January 28, 2009. This is expected to bring down the fuel inflation by at least 400 basic points for the week ending January 30 and consequently the week's overall inflation by over 60 bps.

TABLE 3

Inflation in Primary Articles (y-o-y per cent)

April-December

Sectors	*Weight*	*Dec. 2007*	*Dec. 2008*	*2007-08*	*2008-09*
Gereals	4.4	3.4	9.3	6.6	7.7
Pulses	0.6	-12.3	12.9	-0.3	4.8
Fruits and Vegetables	2.9	-4.5	15.9	4.7	8
Eggs, Meat and Fish	2.2	3.1	6.8	6.6	4.4
Fibres	1.5	17	19.3	12.8	25.8
Oilseeds	2.7	16.6	15.8	26.2	17.6
Metallic Minerals	0.3	2.8	42.7	5.7	48.5
Other Minerals	0.2	6.9	21	2.3	21.8

Source : Ministry of Industry/Crisil Eco view.

Inflation in manufactured products moderated further to 6.8 per cent in December on the back of weak demand and low industrial activity. After touching its peak of 11.7 per cent in August 2008, inflation in this group kept declining as the indices witnessed deflation on a monthly basis. Tumbling energy prices too contributed to the deceleration in the price indices of energy intensive manufacturing product like chemicals, rubber and plastic products and metals.

TABLE 4

Inflation in Manufactured Products (y-o-y per cent)

April-December

Sectors	*Weight*	*Dec. 2007*	*Dec. 2008*	*2007-08*	*2008-09*
Chemicals	11.9	6.6	5.9	5.1	8.9
Food Products	11.5	3.2	4	3.2	10.5
Textiles	9.8	-3	10.2	-0.1	5
Machine Tools	8.4	5.7	5.5	8	5.6
Metal and Alloy	8.3	2.8	12.6	6.5	19.6
Transport Eqp.	4.3	4.6	3.6	2	6.2
NMMP	2.5	8.6	2.8	9.2	4.3
Rubber and Plastic	2.4	7	3.4	5	5.6

Source : Ministry of Industry/Crisil Eco view.

CONTROL OF INFLATION

There are various measures to control inflation, but monetary and fiscal are most effective and significant tools. Now we will discuss how these policies helps to control inflation.

I. Monetary Policy

Inflation is primarily a monetary phenomenon and it has been accepted by many classical and neo-classical economists. Hence, the most logical situation to check inflation is to check the flow of money supply by devising appropriate monetary policy and carefully implementing them.

In order to control inflation, it is necessary to control total outlays because under full employment, increase in total outlays will be reflected in a general rise in prices, i.e. Inflation. The central bank's monetary management method, the devices for decreasing or increasing the supply of money and credit for monetary stability is called monetary policy.

Reserve Bank of India, which works as central bank of India generally use three quantitative tools:

(a) Bank Rate policy,
(b) Open Market Operations, and
(c) Variable Reserve Ratio to control the volume of credit in an economy.

A dear money policy is used in order to curb inflationary pressures. In this context bank rate may be raised, open market sales operation may be taken and the reserve requirement ratio may be increased.

On June 11, 2008 RBI has raised the repo rate 25 basic points to 8 per cent and again hiked repo rate to 8.5 per cent on June 24, 2008 which is the highest in past 5 years. The repo rate has been raised for the second time within a fortnight in a bid to curb demand that is widely seen as stocking inflation. As a complementary support to control inflation rate, RBI also raised Cash Reserve Ratio (CRR) by 50 basic points to 8.75 per cent on June 24, 2004. Again on July 29, 2008, RBI raised repo rate to 9 per cent with immediate effect and also CRR to 9 per cent w.e.f. August 30, 2008.

2. Fiscal Policy

Fiscal policy is budgetary policy in relation to taxation, public borrowing, and public expenditure. Changes in the total expenditure can be effected by fiscal measures. To combat inflation, fiscal measures would involve increase in taxation and decrease in government spending.

Obviously, during a period of full employment inflation, the aggregate demand in relation to the limited supply of goods and services is reduced to the extent that government expenditures are curtailed.

A certain public expenditure may is not be sufficient. Government must simultaneously increase taxes to effect a cut in private expenditure also, in order to minimize inflationary pressures. As we know, when more taxes are imposed the size of the disposable income diminishes, as also the magnitude of the inflationary gap, given the available supply of goods and services. Inflationary pressure is significantly weakened by the simultaneous curtailment of government expenditure and an increase in taxation because, more resources are released for expanding the productive capacity in the private sector, the supply curve of aggregate goods and services shifts upwards with a contraction of monetary demand due to a decline in disposable income with people.

A tax policy can be directed towards restricting demand without restricting production. For instance, excise duties or sales tax on various commodities take away the buying power from the consumer goods market without discouraging the expansion of production capacity. However, some economists point out that this is not a correct way of combating inflation because of its regressive nature. On the other hand, this may lead to a further rise in prices of such commodities, and inflation can spread from one sector to another and from one commodity to another. But, during inflation, a progressive direct tax is considered best; it is also justified in the interest of social equity.

References

Civil Services Chronicle, March 2009, Vol. XIX, No. 9, Publisher Mrinal Ojha, pp. 104, 105, 106 and 107.

Crisil Eco View, Feb. 2009, pp. 10 and 11.

M.L. Seth, Money, Banking, International Trade and Public Finance, pp. 131, 132, 145 and 146.

PTI Economic Service (Feb. 16-28, 2009), Vol. XXXV, No. 4, Press Trust of India, p. 64.

Pratiyogita Darpan, Extra Issue—Indian Economy, 2009 Edition, Upkar Publication, pp. 162 and 163.

6

Role of Fiscal and Monetary Policies to Control Inflation

V.D. SHARMA AND BRIJESH SHARMA

Government policy regarding revenue and expenditure is known as Fiscal policy. It should stabilize the economic activity at high levels of output and employment. Monetary policy is the exercise of the central bank's (i.e. Reserve Bank of India in Indian Context) control over the money supply as an instrument for achieving the objectives of general economic policy. In policy measures the federal government generally makes efforts to increase the size of taxpayers and thus amount of revenue with an unchanged tax rate. Federal tax received is increased. But in the expenditure government does not like to grow the productive expenditure to generate more employment and resultant, it may raise the purchasing power and further may create the effective demand. In Monetary policy with the consultation of the Department of Economic Affairs and Ministry of Finance, Government of India, the Central Bank (i.e Reserve Bank of India in Indian Context) formulates the strategy regarding regulation of fund flow or money flow in the economy. The RBI should formulate the monetary policy in such a nice way that black money and fake money (which is known as parallel economy) can be stopped and the black money which 85% of total assets and kept unutilized in secret accounts of overseas can be brought here in the country to utilize for the well-being of our economy. Thus, we may become financially so sound and affluent and resultant we may develop our basic infrastructure to develop our rural economy. We may emerge as super power in the world economy

INTRODUCTION

Government policy in spending and taxing is known as Fiscal policy. In the years since the Great Desperation, it has become generally accepted that the fiscal policy of the federal government should contribute to the attainment of certain economic goals. If the economy is operating at a level of income and output below that at which there is reasonably full utilization of its resources, the appropriate fiscal policy is an expansionary one. If on the other hand the economy is at the level of income and output at which there is not only full utilization of resources but strong upward pressure on prices, the appropriate fiscal policy is a concretionary one. In other words, fiscal policy should operate in a countercyclical fashion, promotion of stabilization of economic activity at high levels of output and employment.

Monetary policy is concerned with government's attempts to provide a more stable economy by regulating the rate of growth of the money supply. Monetary policy is the exercise of the central bank's control over the money supply as an instrument for achieving the objectives of general economy policy. Monetary policy primarily contributes to the achievement of such objectives as full employment, stable prices and economic growth by influencing the level of aggregate demand and thereby the level of money income. Although the central bank's influence over the level of aggregate demand and money income stems from its ability to control the money supply, there are various measures of the money supply. In carrying out monetary policy, the federal reserves seeks to keep the growth rate of each of these monetary aggregates within the range that it believes will contribute most to the achievement of the ultimate objectives.

FISCAL DRAG AND THE FISCAL DIVIDEND

The level of output produced at full employment will naturally increase as the labour force and the productivity of labour increased. With an unchanged tax rate, federal tax received will increase, as will the FEBS so long as federal expenditure does not grow. If the economy is operating below full employment, the obvious will increase and become equal to the FEBES if and when the economy moves to the new full employment level of output, however the fact that the ABS increases in this way will itself restrain the growth of income and make it more difficult for the actual income level to reach the new full employment level.

FLEXIBILITY OF FISCAL POLICY

Economists generally on the FEBS to indicate whether the federal budget program is expansionary or concretionary from period to period. Increases in the FEBS (Full Employment Budget Surplus) from one quarter to the next suggests that the federal budget program is turning more concretionary or less expansionary, a decrease from one quarter to the next suggests that it is turning less concretionary or more expansionary. If at one time the intent of the policy-makers is to be fiscal policy to combat an ongoing recession, how much it is doing in the direction will be indicated by the extent to which the FEBS falls from one quarter to the next. Some measures like the FEBS is essential to give the policy-makers an indication of the expansionary or concretionary effect of the policy actions they have taken.

We here turn to another matter faced by policy-makers: Is it possible to secure the required degree of flexibility in government expenditures and/or tax rates to produce at one time the change in the EFBS in one direction and at another time the change in the opposite direction that may be required to meet the needs of the situation?

If we start off with a comparison of the relative flexibility of fiscal and monetary policy it is generally conceded that monetary policy has the advantage. Although this is due in part to the inherent flexibility of the tools of monetary management, it is also due in part to the fact that the decision-making authority lies in an essentially independent agency the political aims of which are limited to its own perpetuation and the preservation of its customary role and the power of which is concentrated in the hands of few people.

HOW DOES MONETARY POLICY WORK? KEYNESIANISM VERSUS MONETARISM

Firstly, we know that how monetary policy does affect the economy's income level? It is one thing to outline, as in the basic Keynesian model. A major development in monetary theory during the 1950s and early 1960s was the development of an explanation of that transmission process in terms of a systematic theory of portfolio adjustments. A change in the money supply produces a change in the income level by setting of a complex sequence of substitutions among the financial and real assets that make-up wealth-holders' portfolios.

THE PORTFOLIO ADJUSTMENT PROCESS

In a broad sense there is a rate of return on all assets in that all assets provide their owners with benefit. This is quite apparent in the case of plants and producers durable equipment for which a specific rate of return may be readily computed and for interested-bearing financial assets like bonds for which yields are reported each day in the page of financial newspapers. All thoughtless apparent, it is also true for money and goods held by consumers. The finally automobile and home appliances provide obvious flow of services to their owners. Less obvious but still present in the flow of services provided to its owners by money in the form of convenience and security that immediately available purchasing power offers. All thoughts the flow of services provided by such assets can not be expressed as a rate of return as we express the income from a capital good or a bond a rate of return nonetheless exits for these other assets.

CHANGES IN MONEY AND CHANGES IN WEALTH

Not even the staunchest anti-monetarist denies that there may indeed be a relation of the kind just described. However, he will hold that this relation is not a unique result of the fact that there has been a change in the money supply but is rather a result of the fact that the changing in the money supply involved a change in the public's total wealth. He will hold that, in the absence of a change wealth, a change in the money supply has the no direct effect on the demand for the goods. Accordingly, whether or not a change in the money supply causes a change in wealth becomes a very important issue. The answer is that some changes in the money supply do and others.

SUSTAINABILITY AMONG ASSETS

The Keynesians and the monetarists present very similar descriptions of the process of portfolio adjustment, but they disagree on a critical aspect of this process the closeness of substitution between money and other financial assets and between money and real assets. As the Keynesians see it, money and other financial assets are close substitutes. Accordingly, because arise in the price of any good will increase the demand for another good that is a close substitutes, the rise in the prices of another financial assets—here caused by an increases in the money supply—will produce and increase in the amount of money wealth-owners wish to hold.

RESEARCH FINDINGS/CONCLUSION

Government policy regarding revenue and expenditure is known as Fiscal policy. Fiscal policy should operate in a countercyclical fashion, promotion of stabilization of economic activity at high levels of output and employment. Monetary policy is the exercise of the central bank's (i.e Reserve Bank of India in Indian Context) control over the money supply as an instrument for achieving the objectives of general economic policy. On the FEBS time to time generally Economists indicate whether the federal budget program is expansionary or concretionary. In policy measures the federal government generally makes efforts to increase the size of taxpayers and thus amount of revenue with an unchanged tax rate. Federal tax received is increased. But in the expenditure government does not like to grow the productive expenditure which may generate the more and more employment and resultant it may raise the purchasing power and further may create the effective demand. In Monetary policy with the consultation of the Department of Economic Affairs and Ministry of Finance, Government of India, the Central Bank ((i.e Reserve Bank of India in Indian Context) formulates the strategy regarding regulation of fund flow or money flow in the economy. The RBI should formulate the monetary policy in such a nice way that black money and fake money (which is known as parallel economy) can be stopped and the black money which 85% of total assets and kept unutilized in secret accounts of overseas can be brought here in the country to utilize for the well-being of our economy. Thus, we may become financially so sound and affluent and resultant we may develop our basic infrastructure to develop our rural economy. We may emerge as super power in the world economy.

References

Anker, Richard (1983), Female Labour Force Participation in Developing Countries, *International Labour Review*, Dec.

Deogharia, Prakash (1993), Work Participation of Female Tribal's—A Case Study of South Chhotanagpur, *Social Change,* Vol. 23, No. 4.

Dholakia, Bakla and Dholakia, Ravindra (1978), Inter-State, Variation in Female Labour Force Participation Rates in India, *IJLE.*

Gulati, Leela (1975), Female Work Participation : A Study of Inter-State Difference, *EPW,* June 11.

Macro-economics Analysis, Edward Shapiro University of Toledo, 1999. Galgotia Publications (P) Ltd.

Inflation in India
An Analysis

SHRAWAN KUMAR SINGH

This article makes an attempt to analyse some of the complications that cloud the perception of the link in the short-run and tries to show that policy-makers cannot escape theory when dealing with the short-run. Money is generalised purchasing power, hence the monetary policy is very much concerned with the general price level. If the aggregate demand, as represented by purchasing power in the form of money, exceeds the value of the available goods and services there is a general price rise as a result of too much money chasing too few supplies.

Money Output and Prices

The interrelationship between money, output and prices is one area in macroeconomics subject to very intense and wide research. The relation between money and prices under stationary and dynamic, as well as steady state and growth, conditions is a central issue in theoretical and empirical monetary economics. In the latter, different perceptions emerge because other conditions are not always equal when the focus is on the relation between money and prices. There is a strong view that in the long-run, the various other conditions cancel out, and the direct relation *between money and prices* tends to be clearly established. But, *over the short-run, it is difficult to empirically establish the relationship*.

The central message of the *quantity theory of money* is that it is the price level that is the equilibrating factor between the supply of and demand for money. The concept of money is that of demand as the circulating medium, or the *medium of exchange*. Hence, it is customary to use M1 as the relevant empirical concept when dealing with price levels. When bringing in the *store of value function*, the *asset demand* for money becomes important, and here M3 becomes the critical magnitude along with other assets, which are like money as an asset.

What happens when interest rates change is that the asset demand for money becomes operative. Hence, when the price level has risen with an increase in the quantity of money and the interest rate also has been reduced, the asset demand portion of money gets weakened. Thus, of given M3, a larger proportion becomes M1, and this should generally cause the price level to go up. It follows that when the money supply is increased and the interest rate reduced, the price level effect would be much greater than otherwise. That is why when an increase in the supply of money occurs, it would be worth making the interest rate go up, to increase the proportion of time deposits in M3. We must note that a reduction in the rate of interest reduces the velocity of money and a rise in the rate increases the velocity. The effects of shifts in the composition of broad money should be taken along with the effects of a change in the rate of interest, if any, on velocity.

But there is no control over the course *of the output*, whose growth rate fluctuates. Consequently, many other variables are involved in the clear relation between money and prices, in the short-run. *Keynes said that the long run belongs to the classrooms. The short-run, then, should belong to the practitioners, especially policy-makers*. Policy-makers may have short tenures. But policies continue for long [*P.R. Brahmananda*, 1998].

Pattanaik and Samantaraya (2006) have emphasized that the major criticism against single equation method or causality tests is that they ignore simultaneity in the relationship between money, output and prices. Not only is output an important argument in the money demand function, monetary expansion also supports output growth through credit expansion. *The net impact of monetary expansion on prices will actually depend on output elasticity of credit (money) and elasticity of prices with respect to money and output*. Thus, a system of simultaneous equations incorporating all the related variables is better equipped to capture the determinants of prices as compared to a single equation.

Do investors bother about interest rates, if other conditions are propitious? What matters to the investor is what he gets after paying all costs, including interest. *Interest rates do matter to investors*. Policy-makers should appreciate the serious adverse impact of high interest rates on the profitability of investments. Such rates do give negative signals to fresh starts. Why should anyone go through the rigmarole of clearance of projects if the margin has to go to the lenders as interest? *High rates are a definite disincentive to new investment. The central bank has a conflict of roles. As a monetary arbiter, it has to decide what is good for the economy. As a guardian of bank viability, it has to weigh the impact*.

A look at the trend in real and nominal interest rates, and inflation, world over shows that while real interest rates are usually low, nominal rates rise or fall to compensate for the increase or decrease in inflation. In other words, *real interest rates remain fairly steady*, to be determined more by changes in productivity and public savings. This is in line with what the famous *Fisher hypothesis states. Accordingly, the proposition that a one per cent increase in inflation would be matched by a one per cent increase in nominal interest rates, thereby leaving the real interest rate constant, is a pretty useful rule of thumb*. Studies highlighted that while a substantial increase in government capital expenditure increases output, its impact on output and prices also depends on the extent of resource gap met by borrowing from the RBI. As the proportion of the resource gap financed by the RBI increases, the trade-off between output and prices worsens sharply. By early 1990s high fiscal dominance on monetary policy became a matter of serious concern [*Pattanaik and Samantaraya*, 2006].

According to Y.V. Reddy (1999), "it is necessary to recognize that the evolving transmission mechanism consequent upon financial sector reform would imply certain changes in the nature and magnitudes of the underlying relationship between the growth in money supply and inflation, matters on which further and intense research and analysis is required". "With complexities in statistical measurement of inflation, evolving relationships between money supply and prices, uncertain time lags in such relationship, conduct of monetary policy is a challenging task. On top of the normal growth cycles, our economy is undergoing a wide ranging and deep structural transformation, adjusting simultaneously to international price pressures". New Zealand's experience to developing countries particularly in the context of "fiscal dominance"; multiple objectives of monetary policy, especially growth and exchange rate; and lack of sophistication in inflation-forecasting, inflation-measurement and overall financial system. According to Mr. Donald Brash, Governor of the Reserve Bank of New Zealand, inflation targeting was in no sense a panacea but a very sensible policy option. (i) There is a need for working out a national consensus on the acceptable level of inflation. The Tarapore Committee on Capital Account Convertibility recommended a mandated rate of inflation for the three-year period 1997-98 to 1999-2000 in the average of 3 to 5 per cent. In brief, there is a growing consensus on acceptable level of the inflation-rate, but this needs to be better articulated, formalized and perhaps converted in due course into a mandate from Government to RBI and, in the process to all economic agents. This approach should have, among other things, a significant impact on inflationary expectations in India. (ii) Weights in regard to Wholesale Price Index and Consumer Price Index. The issues relating to base year, coverage and weights have to be resolved. (iii) analytical work on defining appropriate "Core Inflation" for India may be worth exploring. (iv) In analyzing inflation, we need also to look at the asset price inflation, particularly in the context of financial market liberalization. In India, the asset prices are not covered in both the indices of inflation indicators despite their increasing importance in terms of one of the important channels for the transmission mechanism of monetary policy. However, there are significant difficulties in constructing an appropriate index for this purpose. (v) analytical work on inflation-targeting needs to be continued. (vi) Well informed debate on the issue of inflationary expectations is necessary to take a view on the computation of real interest rates. (vii) there are a variety of policy-perspectives that have a bearing on inflation, and these too need to be analysed on an on-going basis. These relate to the evolving role of quantity variables and rate variables in monetary policy, the changing lags, and the improvements in transmission-mechanisms. The transmission-mechanisms are being enhanced but serious rigidities such as the interest-rates for Provident Funds, administered small savings, etc. persist. Liberalisation of various markets, including agricultural markets cut into rent-margin in commodities. Fiscal policy would be relevant not only in terms of aggregate demand effects through direct and indirect monetization, but also because of changing composition of tax and expenditure-structure. Perhaps we should also have an analytical-construct to differentiate between the extent of externally-induced inflation, or for that matter deflation and domestically induced inflation. (viii) The public distribution system has its costs but also has its benefits –particularly in terms of moderating the variability in inflation rate. To conclude, our track record on inflation has been satisfactory; and there are good chances that we would improve on it if we continue to keep our analytical tools rather sharp and ensure the timeliness and coordination especially between fiscal-monetary operations as well as effectiveness of policy-responses [*Pattanaik and Samantaraya*, 2006].

THE CONCEPTS OF INFLATION

An issue closely related to definitional aspect of inflation is concerned with use of "*headline*" versus "*core*" inflation. While "*headline inflation*" covers the entire set of goods and services included in the general index, *"core inflation"* otherwise known as *"underlying inflation"* ignores the volatile items in the general index. *Headline inflation* reflects not only the effect of demand pressures but also supply shocks which impart *transitory noise and bias to the index*. Thus, a supply shock arising from crop failures or the international oil price hike will have the effect of raising the headline inflation. On the other hand, a *positive supply shock such as a good harvest may reduce the headline inflation for some time even if underlying inflationary pressures are building up*. In the event of such supply disturbances, policy actions to counter the impact on the aggregate price level will tend to accentuate the output effects of the disturbances, generating a short-run conflict between the central bank's inflation and output objectives. Thus, the volatility of *"headline"* inflation without any discernible change in the associated fundamentals but due to supply shocks constrains its usefulness.

The concept of *'core'* inflation has gained importance in the monetary policy framework of several countries in recent years. *Core inflation* provides a measure of long-term inflation movements in the economy when various types of supply shocks or administered price changes produce fluctuations in the price index. Thus, the core inflation essentially captures the underlying cost and demand conditions which affect inflation when output is at its normal level.

According to *Raghbendra Jha* (2001), Central bankers use the notion of *'core inflation'* especially when inflation remains stubbornly high or when enunciating a medium-term perspective. *Otto Eckstein* popularized this notion and conceived of core inflation as consisting of changes in CPI or, alternatively, the GDP deflator bereft of changes in prices of fuel, food (and sometimes tradables). It is argued that these prices are rather volatile or, more pertinently, *'outside' the purview of the central bank*. Thus, considering changes in the prices of such goods could give a misleading picture of how well the central bank was handling inflation.

Central banks, particularly in developing countries, are attracted to core inflation because this notion appears to have a dual advantage for them. On the one hand, the central bank can claim that it is responsible for core inflation only and, on the other, it can blame headline inflation on raises in administered prices or fuel and energy price shocks. This subtly adds to the populist case for keeping administered prices low or changing them only infrequently. Core inflation is certainly the wrong target for any policy of inflation targeting. The pursuit of inflation targeting by a central bank has often been viewed as a contract of trust between the central bank and the public. The central bank sets realistic targets for an indicator of inflation that the public can relate to, especially in the important matter of forming inflationary expectations. Surely core inflation or for that matter the WPI does not suit this purpose. A representative CPI does [*Raghbendra Jha*, 2001].

Tolerance levels vary for inflation. Some countries can tolerate higher levels of it without growth slowing down. For others, the threshold is lower. Developed countries have lower inflation thresholds and developing countries have higher thresholds. But for those charged with the conduct of economic policies, knowing just this much is not enough. They also need to know *where the threshold actually lies so that corrective action can be taken in time*. This is not as easy as it sounds because it involves what is basically *a political choice of balancing inflation with unemployment. Often the central bank comes into conflict with the government*.

This is not to argue for zero inflation. Received wisdom has it that some inflation does help all the wheels of the economy. The question then boils down to what is the acceptable level of inflation. This varies from country to country and is broadly a function of past experience. In India the acceptable level is somewhere around 4-5 per cent. Anything beyond this could jeopardize the very foundations of growth.

MEASUREMENT OF INFLATION

To calculate inflation, the inflation-computing agency has to collect prices of identified commodities. The agency can take into account wholesale prices, retail prices or factory prices. As the wholesale markets are few, it is easier to collect prices of goods traded there. WPI takes into account wholesale prices of over 400 commodities. *The base year for the present WPI index, which is computed by the ministry of commerce and industry, is 1993-94*. The 100-point index is sub-divided into three groups. *Primary articles*, including food and non-food agriculture products, has a weight of 22.02 per cent. *Manufactured goods* have the highest weight of 63.75 per cent. Fuel and power has a weight of 14.23 per cent. The government is working out a revised index with a new base year. *The WPI must reflect the consumption pattern of the society to truly reflect the cost of living*. To be relevant, the basket of commodities whose prices are tracked must be relevant. The working group on WPI, headed by Planning Commission member *Abhijit Sen* has worked out a new index. The base year of the new index will be 2000-01. The basket of commodities will be expanded to around 1,200 to be truly reflective of the post-liberalisation consumption pattern.

None of the existing measures provided a reliable gauge of inflation at any point of time. "*An index can be constructed for different baskets of goods and services, with varying weights, to cover different sets of consumers or locations. There is thus no all-purpose, all-inclusive, universally valid index*". Operationally, there could be problems that distort an index. For example, the basket of goods and weights may be held constant for too long, and, over a period, some goods may go out of production. Also, change in quality of goods cannot be captured, though the quality of many industrial goods has been improving. "Further, the Government machinery that collects the data, even with best efforts, would not be able to capture the offers of discounts at the retail level".

Experts differ both about its extent and causes. How dependable is our inflation data? M3 has maintained a steady rate of growth. So too, fiscal deficit, which is at a high level. We should really look at the average rate of inflation—the average of the weekly rate of increase of prices over the year not the point-to-point or year-on-year rate. To this, one can only respond that *the truer measure of a fever at any point is the level at which it stands at that point, although averages also matter*.

The second argument is that one should look at *retail prices*. While *CPI* numbers are, indeed, important, the method of their collection and updating leaves much to be desired. The Government must, of course, revamp its methodology, both from the point of view of its basket of goods and the sample size. The urgency is all the greater, considering how CPI numbers figure in the calculation of dearness allowance for most labour settlements, particularly in government. A credible and accurate set of inflation data is a prerequisite to efficient management of the government's establishment costs.

Any amount of explanation that inflation measures the change in the rate of increase in wholesale prices, and not the actual increase in retail prices, fails to convince the common man. None other than the RBI Governor, Dr. Y.V. Reddy, has said that none of the existing indices (of measuring inflation, including the wholesale price index—WPI—used by the government and the RBI) *"provides a truly reliable gauge of inflation at any point of time"*.

In many parts of the world, the retail price index is used for measuring inflation. *Dr. Reddy, however, justified the use of the WPI*, principally, because it is available at shorter frequency (weekly) with a shorter time lag (two months) than the other measures—the consumer price indices for industrial labour (CPI-IW), agricultural labour (CPI-AL) and urban non-manual employees (CPI-UNME), and the implicit deflator in National Income (NID). Other grounds for the preference are: (i) the WPI is computed on an all-India basis as against the CPI-IW, which is computed for specific centres and combined to obtain an all-India index; (ii) the coverage of tradeable goods, especially manufactured items, is higher in the WPI than in the CPI; (iii) the correlation between the annual average variation of broad money (M3) and the WPI, in the long-term, is stronger than that between the former and the CPI-IW; and (iv) the three principal indices—the WPI, the CPI-IW and the NID—display broadly similar trends over a long-term, despite the divergences in their annual or short-term movements.

The grounds on which the case for the WPI stands are not particularly strong. The WPI is primarily an index covering transactions at the initial stages and far removed from final consumption, which is the objective of all economic activities. It does not cover the services sector, which now contributes more than half of the national income. The prices of services impact the cost of living, both directly and through wholesale prices via the cost-push route.

The issue of realistically measuring inflation has gained urgency and increased academic attention. In today's real world interest rates which are now free of direct control by the RBI, have become much more sensitive to inflation. Market participants, including the generality of savers, investors and financial intermediaries, track inflation data to anticipate monetary policy changes to do better than the market.

With the opening up of the economy, especially the current account transactions, the integral link between inter-country interest rate differentials, inflation rate differentials and forward foreign exchange premia has become more effectively operational. Besides, whichever party comes to power, further opening up of the economy and a radical reform of the financial sector cannot be postponed without paying a high price in terms of delaying growth. *With a market-determined exchange rate regime, inflation-tracking assumes critical importance in maintaining the competitiveness of the domestic industry*. We need a measure of inflation that will truly reflect, in the short and the long-run, the relationship between variations in broad money and the forces of effective demand and supply. This may require revamping the entire price-monitoring platforms that are in place.

INFLATION AND GROWTH

There is a pervasive belief that inflation can be reduced only at the cost of giving up growth, despite evidence to the contrary. A major determinant of results as seen in other countries is the policy mix and instruments used to reduce inflation and promote growth. The key to effective solutions appears to be identifying causes and formulating effective solutions with minimal negative consequences, not rote responses. This applies to managing capital inflows, too. India needs to devise ways to handle large capital inflows that are causing undue currency appreciation and inflation. One aspect is the long-term response of structural reforms, to enable efficient conversion of funding to productive projects, i.e. increasing supply. A second is of appropriate responses to mitigate short-term pressures, i.e. not automatically raising interest rates or defending the exchange rate, but taking coordinated fiscal and monetary action to contain excess liquidity (which might include possible actions on interest and exchange rates). Nor does credit growth at 30 per cent necessarily deserve clamping down. *Pattanaik and Samantaraya* (2006) have stressed that the debate on the nature of relationship between inflation and growth is still quite open, but there is a convergence of views on the adverse impact of high inflation on economic growth. *Fischer* (1993) and *Barro* (1995) established the non-linearity in the association of inflation and growth which subsequently led to emergence of the concept of *"threshold inflation"*. In the Indian context, *Rangarajan* (1998), introduced the concept of *"threshold inflation"* to *identify the level of inflation from which the adverse consequences begin to set in*. Below and around this threshold level, there is greater manoeuvrability for the policy-makers to take into account other considerations including economic growth.

The Chakravarty Committee [RBI, 1985] first made a reference to 4 per cent level of inflation, which is regarded as the first influential fix on the threshold level of inflation in India. *Rangarajan* (1998) regarded 6 per cent of inflation to be the outer tolerance limit. The *threshold level of inflation for India is found to be in the range of 4 to 7 per cent*. The appropriate measure of threshold inflation gives greater flexibility to the central bank in pursuing the objectives of growth and price stability, simultaneously. If expected inflation is below the threshold level, the growth objective can take precedence over the price stability. On the other hand, if expected inflation is above the threshold, price stability should be given greater relative importance. It can be noted that in a developing country context, the adverse impact of inflation on social justice has to be incorporated in any analysis of inflation. However, with structural changes in the economy and credible anchoring of inflationary expectations at a lower level, the threshold inflation could also move downwards [*Pattanaik and Samantaraya*, 2006].

Dr. Y. Venugopal Reddy, has called for a *national consensus on an acceptable level of inflation*. Dr. Reddy called for an inflation consensus followed by an explicit inflation mandate. The RBI, in its *annual report for 1993-94*, had argued that "it is here that there is need for a national consensus before prescribing a mandate for the central bank. Rapid changes in the world situation, and rapid process of our integration with the rest of the world, could be pushing this optimum level down from 6 per cent. In the average of 3 per cent to 5 per cent, there was a growing consensus on acceptable level of the inflation rate. This approach should have, among other things, a significant impact on inflationary expectations in India. Dr. Reddy has stressed on the need for a systematic revamping of factors such as *base year, coverage and weights in regard to WPI and CPI*. The issues relating to base year, coverage and weights have to be resolved. A detailed survey of the behaviour of individual commodity prices in both the wholesale price segment and retail price segment would perhaps help analyse changes in their behaviour in the past.

The permanent component is often called the *'underlying'* rate of inflation or the *'core'* rate of inflation. It is not the current rate of inflation, comprising transient components, but the future underlying rate of inflation, which should be the concern of monetary policy. Measurement of the underlying or more rate of inflation, however, does involve some amount of judgement or discretion.

According to *Y.V. Reddy (1999)*, "The economic rationale for considering the core rate of inflation in the framework of monetary policy which is governed by the fact that it is this rate, being permanent in nature, which is fully anticipated by economic agents and hence, incorporated into their decision-making processes thereby making it output-neutral. Viewed from another angle, *it is the existence of the permanent component, which imparts downward rigidity to the measured rate of inflation in the event of a positive supply shock*. Therefore, it would be valuable for the economy to ensure that permanent or core rate of inflation is reduced. The objective of reducing the rate of inflation as the prime objective of monetary policy should be viewed against this perspective". "With complexities in statistical measurement of inflation, evolving relationships between money supply and prices, uncertain time lags in such relationship, conduct of monetary policy is a challenging task. On top of the normal growth cycles, our economy is undergoing a wide ranging and deep structural transformation, adjusting simultaneously to international price pressures. When the headline measure of inflation indicated pressures, judgements were called for *in fine tuning monetary policy*".

Sugata Marjit (2008) has studied the relationship between the rate of growth of GDP and inflation rates. One would like to know, how they move together. Table 1 gives a picture of roughly a decade before and after the reform period of 1991-92. The overall correlation between GDP growth and inflation is negative (-0.102). But in the post-reform period it is rather strongly negative (-0.337); whereas in the pre-reform period it is positive (0.352). It is difficult to interpret the data, and also decipher what causes such correlation. But over the past 15 years they are negatively related. This is a relationship exactly opposite to what is predicted by the Phillips curve, higher inflation implies lower growth and hence possibly a higher rate of unemployment. Again the "unemployment" story is hard to rely on. First, if we are getting accustomed to a phase of moderately jobless growth in the organized sector, then the rate of unemployment should not be affected much by a decline in the GDP growth rate. On the other hand, we do have information that the real informal manufacturing wage has increased substantially during the same period. A simple negative correlation will not capture many such things. But it will be really worthwhile if some serious work is initiated in tracking the relationship between inflation and GDP growth.

INFLATIONARY TRENDS IN INDIA

While it is true that inflation outside of energy prices remains tame, there is a limit to which the effect of energy prices on inflation can be ignored. Oil prices have moved to a structurally higher plane and world expenditure on oil is back to 4.5 per cent of GDP—levels last seen in 1979-80. With the global economy continuing to exhibit strength, central banks are turning their attention back on ensuring the other side of the equation—inflation—does not get out of shape again.

India recorded relatively satisfactory levels of inflation since, for the entire period of analysis, i.e. 1950-51 to 1997-98, the average rate of inflation working out to 6.7 per cent and

TABLE 1

Pre- and Post-Reform Rate of Growth of GDP and the Rate of WPI Inflation (in %)

Years	*Growth Rate of GDP*	*Inflation Rate Based on WPI*
Pre-liberalisation		
1980-81	7.2	18.24
1981-82	6.0	9.33
1982-83	3.1	4.90
1983-84	7.7	7.53
1984-85	4.3	6.47
1985-86	4.5	4.41
1986-87	4.3	5.82
1987-88	3.8	8.14
1988-89	10.5	7.46
1989-90	6.7	7.46
1990-91	5.6	10.26
Post-liberalisation		
1991-92	1.3	13.74
1992-93	5.1	10.06
1993-94	5.9	8.35
1994-95	7.3	12.60
1995-96	7.3	7.99
1996-97	7.8	4.61
1997-98	4.8	4.40
1998-99	6.5	5.95
1999-2000	6.1	3.27
2000-01	4.4	7.16
2001-02	5.8	3.60
2002-03	4.0	3.41
2003-04	8.5	5.46
2004-05	6.9	6.48
2005-06	8.8	4.38
2006-07	9.7	5.42
2007-08	9.6	2.86

Correlations
Growth Rate of GDP

	Pre-reform	*Post-reform*	*All Years (1980-2008)*
Inflation rate based on WPI	0.352	-0.347	-0.102

Source : Sugata Marjit (2008), *EPW*, September 6, p. 13.

the modal value of distribution of inflation rates lying between 5 to 10 per cent. The maximum inflation recorded in the year 1974-75 at 25.2 per cent was mainly attributed to the failure of kharif crops in 1972-73 as also to the hike in crude oil prices in 1973. The inflation rate has also been far less volatile than in most developing countries, with standard deviation at 6.6 and the rate having crossed the 15 per cent mark on only four occasions during the last half a century or so. Moreover, the high pressures of inflation were felt on almost all occasions, due to exogenous shocks like oil price hike, gulf crisis, wars, etc. and domestic supply shocks such as adverse monsoon conditions [*Y.V. Reddy*, 1999].

The inflation record of India reveals that inflation increased from the 1970s onwards before moderating in the mid-1990s. Supply shocks both due to a setback in agricultural production and international oil prices, and monetary expansion due to automatic monetization of the fiscal deficit were the major contributory factors to higher inflation. Reform initiatives since the early 1990s towards developing a broad-based financial market, particularly activation of the government securities and forex markets coupled with *improved monetary-fiscal interface* enabled better monetary management since the second half of the 1990s. The success of price stability in India since mid-1990s has led to a reduction in inflationary expectations and consequently, inflation tolerance has also come down.

As measured by the Wholesale Price Index (WPI), inflation rose to 6.7 per cent (year over year) in early 2007 and has fallen to 3.2 per cent as of end September 2007. In assessing India's inflation situation, the first fundamental fact to note is that intra-year swings in y-o-y inflation are huge. This is not due to seasonal fluctuations which affect the intra-year price level, but get automatically cancelled out in measuring inflation y-o-y, when the price level jumps unusually in a given period (for example, week or month), the inflation rate also rises for that period, but falls back the same period the next year. This is the well-known *base effect*.

If the inflation decline is no big deal, by the same token the earlier rise between late 2006 and February 2007 is also much ado about nothing. Why then all the brouhaha during

2007 about rising inflation? What prompted the finance ministry to impose economically damaging export bans and price controls on wheat, sugar, milk and other commodities? And RBI actions also? But neither the press nor policy-makers bothered too much. But when the WPI rose to only 6.7 per cent in February 2007, there was wide discontent leading to policy reaction. Why the disparate response? The answer is reasonably obvious. What matters for the welfare of the public is not the WPI which is two-thirds manufacturing but the Consumer Price Index (CPI) in which primary food articles carry a much higher weight. The WPI matters for business India, while the various CPI (industrial workers, urban non-manual, agricultural labour and rural labour) matter for the people of India. The 8 per cent WPI rise in July-September, 2004 was mainly due to manufacturing which was at 7.6 per cent. Primary food inflation—notably in pulses—was very low. Conversely in January-February 2007, primary food inflation in the WPI was exorbitantly high, following similar highs, 25.1 per cent and 10.4 per cent in the previous fiscal years. The discontent due to this hardship transmitting itself through Parliament via the finance ministry seems to have led to the various price control and tightening measures. The 6.3 per cent WPI manufacturing inflation in January-March 2007 was not a sign of overheating because it has fallen back to 5.4 per cent in April-June 2007. Indeed, the three-year average for manufacturing WPI shows a decrease of late, despite unexpectedly robust GDP growth for four years. A productivity miracle is under way globally, leading to low inflation in items of sectors such as finished steel, despite rising iron ore costs.

Owing to the difference in commodity composition as well as the weights assigned to commodities and services in the CPI, inflation measured in terms of the CPI differs significantly from that measured in terms of the WPI. When the wholesale price index (WPI) had eased to below 6 per cent in January 2009 (from a year ago), the consumer price indices (CPI) continued to rise by more than 10 per cent for urban non-manual employees and industrial workers by about 10.4 per cent and for agricultural as well as rural labourers by more than 11 per cent on a year-on-year basis. To a casual observer of the index movement, such variation would seem strange. There are several reasons for this. For one, the basket of items that make up these indices as well as the weight assigned to each of these items have a bearing on the composite numbers. The WPI is made up of large number of primary, intermediate and manufactured items, most of which is not directly consumed by an average person. For that matter, much of items that form a household consumption basket have relatively low weight on WPI. The various consumer price indices, in contrast, assign higher weight for items that are commonly consumed by households. For instance, food, beverage, etc., account for nearly 49 per cent of the CPI for industrial workers (CPI-IW) but just a little more than 28 per cent on the WPI. Likewise, fuel accounts for a little over 6 per cent in EPI-IW but over 14 per cent on the WPI. As a consequence, fall in, say fuel prices would have greater impact on the WPI than the EPI headline numbers.

Secondly, the stage at which data is captured makes a lot of difference—the WPI reflects the ex-factory price of products of their administered price. This would mean most taxes other than excise are not reflected in that index. In comparison, the CPI captures the retail level prices and that includes all taxes, rebates, marketing costs and trade margins. When there is cost-push inflation, the WPI captures the price movement much before its effect is felt by the consumers. So while WPI reflects inflationary pressures in general and aids monetary and fiscal policy interventions, the CPI serves as a better barometer of the cost of living. Rather than be led by the headline WPI number, inflation analysis should be based on various components of the index [*The Economic Times*, March 30, 2009].

However, does this mean that the RBI should not tighten? No, because food inflation is unacceptably high. The pervasive focus on the WPI is obscuring information critical for the economic welfare of the people. The CPIs pertain to consumers with widely different expenditure patterns and incomes, but that does not justify ignoring them. A composite CPI weighted by population shares, or even a simple average, should be targeted. The booming world economy, especially China and India, is pushing up demand for food and energy. *Peter Brabeck*, CEO of Nestle, the world's largest food company, said in early July that "food prices are set for a period of significant and long-lasting inflation". It is misleading now to treat food inflation as due to transitory supply shocks and focus on core inflation.

Our Prime Minister, Dr. Manmohan Singh had himself stated, in his economist days, that low inflation was the best anti-poverty policy. Low primary food inflation, to be more precise, since money incomes of the poor are not automatically or fully indexed to inflation. Even if food inflation subsidies, unless it turns adequately negative, the price level at which food is bought remains higher. The *aam aurat* faces a difficulty that the ostensibly knowledge economics 'commentariat' trends to be ignorant about. The major task, in our opinion, for economic policy in emerging economies now is how best to tackle rising food prices, even when general inflation remains low. Food prices involve agriculture, trade, exchange rate, commodity futures markets and monetary policy. Even when overall inflation is low or on target, but food inflation is too high, to avoid knee jerk price controls, banning futures and similar tinkering, should a central bank squeeze GDP growth and reduce inflation (and also allow some real currency appreciation) to lower the burden of food prices?

WHAT DRIVES INFLATION LOWER?

Long-term trends in key monetary ratios such as the *broad money multiplier and the velocity measure of the money stock* support the view that the RBI may have effected such a policy shift. As the Table shows, the money multiplier (M3/RM) has displayed a secular upward trend whereas the GDP/M3 ratio (the velocity of money) has shown a secular downward trend. That long-term trend decline in the velocity of broad money is cause for concern as it means that a unit of broad money (created by the banking system acting on the monetary base provided by the RBI) results in lower and lower final output of goods and services. To that extent, the pressure on aggregate supply is higher and prices tend to move higher in that scenario. The GDP/M3 ratio does get affected by the increase in the demand for money (where people wish to hold more money in their portfolios) so that the velocity measure is reduced. But a long-term declining trend cannot be explained only by an increasing demand for money. Overall, the RBI strategy on liquidity, inflation and exchange rate management may have undergone a significant change in the recent past. Intervention in the forex market could become more selective and more phased out as we go forward.

TABLE 2
Movements in Key Monetary Ratios

	Multiplier M3/RM	*Income Velocity GDP/M3*
1990-91	3.11	2.28
1991-92	3.11	2.23
1992-93	3.20	2.17
1993-94	3.19	2.15
1994-95	3.12	2.12
1995-96	3.10	2.15
1996-97	3.39	2.13
1997-98	3.60	2.02
1998-99	3.84	1.93
1999-2000	4.03	1.85
2000-01	4.33	1.72
2001-02	4.52	1.61
2002-03	4.80	1.49
2003-04	4.76	1.48
2004-05	4.79	1.47
2005-06	4.79	1.43
2006-07	4.82	1.05

Source : RBI (reproduced from Kapali, 2007).

However, the government may have to do some tightrope walking as the wholesale prices of food articles, fuel, power and manufactured goods continued to rule firm. On its part, the government has decided to continue with its policy to rein in the rising prices through *fiscal measures and import of food articles to ease the supply side crunch.*

The concept behind the minimum support price (MSP), was essentially a mechanism to prevent prices from crashing when there was excessive supply in the market. The shortage of pulses would continue unless farmers shifted to sowing pulses in irrigated land instead of in rain-fed areas. To bring down inflation, the government has attempted to supplement the supply-demand gap by importing pulses and wheat.

Since in the largely liberalized environment the banks themselves fix most interest rates, there is very little that the regulator or the government can do beyond moral suasion. *The issue of rising interest rates has many dimensions.* At a basic level, it is the banking system's direct and immediate response to the monetary policy signals. During 2006-08 *RBI has raised the short-term repo rates and the cash reserve ratio* as part of a strategy to combat inflation. Faced with fewer resources and higher cost of funds, banks have been marking up their rates on both loans and deposits. This entirely logical response has, however, caught many a borrower unawares. In short, the reform era requires a greater level of diligence on the part of banks and their customers even as it opens up more choices. There is another important lesson to be learnt from the current high interest rate scenario. *Over the medium term at least, there is a divergence between macroeconomic goals and industrial policy.* Monetary tightening is necessary for price stability. But the high lending rates, apart from impacting adversely on the competitiveness of Indian industry, also draw attention to a major lacuna in financial sector reform. Banks, including the public sector banks, have profit targets. The "spread" income—the difference between the lending and borrowing rates continues to be the main source of profits. Various studies, including some by the RBI, suggest that banks, specially the dominant public sector ones, maintain an unacceptably high spread. Since competition for deposits has ensured that they can no longer maintain a tight lid on deposit rates, they are charging their borrowers more. It is only through further reform aimed at improving efficiency that the apparent conflict between bank profitability and larger macroeconomic goals can be resolved.

A great deal of popular attention is being paid to issues relating to inflation and its measurement in India, than ever before, reflecting some new realities (*Y.V. Reddy* (1999): They are: (i) dismantling of most administered interest-rates; (ii) with the progressive opening up of the economy, the integral link between inter-country interest rate differentials, inflation rate differentials and the forward exchange premia are closely observed when viewing exchange rate movement; (iii) in a liberalized trading regime and market determined exchange rate regime, and also if the country has to allow the economy to be "globalised" or more often, inflation-tracking is critical in terms of maintaining competitiveness of domestic industry; and (iv) the market participants carefully track inflation data to anticipate and assess monetary policy changes, in view of the recent trends in the manner of articulation of such policy changes.

CONTROLLING INFLATION : POLICY STANCE

Fiscal dominance on monetary policy in India through deficit financing is widely documented in terms of the impact of RBI credit to the government on reserve money and money supply. This monetary expansion, *ceteris paribus*, exerts upward pressure on prices. In turn, with an increase in prices government expenditure increases more rapidly than the revenues and hence widening government deficit. This *deficit-money-inflation-deficit*, spiral became popular in developing countries' perspective.

Monetary policy reforms during the 1990s hinged on easing the fiscal constraint. The first important step was introduction of an auction system for the central government's market borrowings in June 1992 and *switching to financing of the fiscal deficit by market borrowings*. This enabled RBI to scale down the statutory liquidity ratio *(SLR) to the statutory minimum of 25.0 per cent* by October 1997. The second major step was the historic *accord between the government and RBI in September 1994* for phasing out the issue of *ad hoc treasury bills having implications for eliminating automatic monetization*. A system of ways and means advances (WMA) to the central government was put in place to meet temporary mismatches providing greater flexibility to RBI in monetary management.

Increasing *monetary-fiscal coordination* in recent years facilitated better monetary management as well as smooth progression of market borrowings. It is important to note that the stipulation of the RBI's withdrawal from the primary government securities market from April 2006 under FRBM Act, reinforces greater fiscal monetary coordination. It is important to note that inflationary expectations are also dependent upon fiscal prudence. The enactment of the *Fiscal Responsibility and Budget Management Act* in 2003 by the central government and similar legislations by a majority of the state governments envisaged a reduction in key deficit indicators and this is expected to enhance the autonomy of the monetary authority. However, adherence to the fiscal rules as per the legislation will be important for stabilizing inflationary expectations in the country [*Pattanaik and Samantaraya*, 2006]. According to *Y.V. Reddy* (1999), following areas need attention:

(i) There is a need for working out a national consensus on the acceptable level of inflation. There is a growing consensus on acceptable level of the inflation-rate, but this needs to be better articulated, formalized and perhaps converted in due course into a mandate from Government to RBI and, in the process to all economic agents. This approach should have, among other things, a significant impact on inflationary expectations in India.

(ii) Weights in regard to Wholesale Price Index and Consumer Price Index, and the issues relating to base year, coverage and weights have to be resolved.

(iii) Analytical work on defining appropriate *'core inflation'* for India may be worth exploring.

(iv) In analysing inflation, we need also to look at the *asset price inflation*, particularly in the context of financial market liberalization. In India, the asset prices are not covered in both the indices of inflation indicators despite their increasing importance in terms of one of the important channels for the transmission mechanism of monetary policy. However, there are significant difficulties in constructing an appropriate index for this purpose.

(v) Analytical work on inflation-targeting needs to be continued.

(vi) Well informed debate on the issue of inflationary expectations is necessary to take a view on the computation of real interest rates.

(vii) There are a variety of policy-perspectives that have a bearing on inflation, and these too need to be analysed on an on-going basis. These relate to the evolving role of quantity variables and rate variables in monetary policy, the changing lags, and the improvements in transmission-mechanisms. The transmission-mechanisms are being enhanced but *serious rigidities* such as the *interest-rates for Provident Funds, administered small savings etc. persist.* Liberalisation of various markets, including agricultural markets cut into rent-margin in commodities. Fiscal policy would be relevant not only in terms of aggregate demand effects through direct and indirect monetization, but also because of changing composition of tax and expenditure-structure. Perhaps, we should also have an analytical-construct to differentiate between the extent of *externally-induced inflation, or for that matter deflation and domestically induced inflation,* and

(viii) The public-distribution system has its costs but also has its benefits—particularly in terms of moderating the variability in inflation rate.

Thus, *Y.V. Reddy* (1999) comes to the conclusion that "our track record on inflation has been satisfactory; and there are good chances that we would improve on it if we continue to keep our analytical tools rather sharp and *ensure the timeliness and coordination especially between fiscal-monetary operations as well as effectiveness of policy-responses.*"

CONCLUSION

The RBI is badly handicapped in its fight against inflation; not only for all the reasons we have heard so far, lack of independence, multiplicity of goals, dodgy statistics and so on. But also because of its poor transmission mechanism. *The monetary transmission mechanism determines how well signals from the central banks are transmitted to financial markets and the real economy.* As the RBI's *Report on Currency and Finance, 2004-05* points out, "successful implementation of (monetary) policy requires a reasonably accurate assessment of how rapidly the effects of policy action are transmitted through the financial system to the real economy, affecting aggregate spending decisions of households and firms and from there to aggregate demand and inflation".

Monetary policy is a very imprecise tool. It operates with a time lag that is both long and hard to quantify: Wise central banks, knowing the pitfalls of using monetary tools to tackle inflation take care to take pre-emptive action well before inflation takes root and inflationary expectations build up. It knows that despite its apparent success in containing inflation, it does not have an effective and credible mechanism to transmit its monetary policy impulses. The success of a monetary policy transmission framework that relies on indirect instruments of monetary management such as interest rates is, however, contingent upon the extent and speed with which changes in the central bank's policy rate are transmitted to interest rates and exchange rates and onward to the real sector. *So the bank is in a rather weak position in its fight against inflation.* The greater the influence of the central bank over interest rate levels the easier it is for it to manage demand in the economy and attain its objective of low inflation and sustained growth. *The first prerequisite to manage inflation, therefore, is that the central bank must be able to influence rates.*

People's income has changed, and so has their consumption pattern. This recognition is essential as we move towards an improved CPI. Additionally, these weights can be changed each year by gathering information on the present final consumption expenditure. Actual CPI inflation may be high and might warrant a tight policy stance, despite the weak industrial sector. But when WPI is close to touching zero, 10 per cent CPI inflation is most likely too high. The current very low rate of WPI is not therefore a cause for celebration, but much more a source of concern. What is required in this context is much more active intervention by the government, in terms of increased productive spending, to lift the economy out of recession. A small increase in the price level as a result of this could even be welcome if it is associated with more growth and employment generation in the system. The range of price variability has increased as inflation has receded.

References

Batura, Neha (2008), Understanding Recent Trends in Inflation, *Economic & Political Weekly*, June 14.

Brahmananda, P.R. (1998), The Complex Money-price Relationship, *The Hindu Business Line*, September 25.

Dutta, Bhaskar (2007), Heat is on, *The Times of India*, April 4.

Jalan, Bimal (2002), 'Is a Single Target Relevant?' in Bimal Jalan, *India's Economy in the New Millennium: Selected Essays*, UBSPD, New Delhi.

Jha, Raghbendra (2001), Core inflation, *The Economic Times*, September 24.

Kapali, T.B. (2007), Shift in RBI Strategy to fight inflation? *The Hindu Business Line*, July 4.

Marjit, Sugata (2008), Inflation and Public Policy: Contemporary Dilemmas, *Economic & Political Weekly*, September 6.

Moorthy, Vivek and Shrikant Kohlar (2007), Overheating and Undereating, *Business Standard*, August 11.

Moorthy, Vivek (2009), Will CPI stand up please? *Mint*, April 1.

Pattanaik, R.K. and Amaresh Samantaraya (2006), Indian-experience of Inflation: A Review of the evolving process, *The Economic and Political Weekly*, January 28.

Rangarajan, C. (1998), 'Development, Inflation and Monetary Policy' in I.J. Ahluwalia and I.M.D. Little (eds.) (1998), *India's Economic Reforms and Development: Essays for Manmohan Singh*, OUP, New Delhi, pp. 48-72.

Reddy, Y.V. (1999), Inflation in India: Status and Issues, address at Centre for Economic and Social Studies, Hyderabad, August 17.

Reserve Bank of India (1985), *Report of the Committee to Review the Working of the Monetary System* (Chairman, S. Chakravarty), RBI, Mumbai.

—— (2006 and 2007), *Report on Currency and Finance, 2004-05, 2005-06*, RBI, Mumbai.

Inflationary Trends in India
An Analysis

DALIP KUMAR, REKHA RANI AND BHARTI KUMARI

INTRODUCTION

This paper attempts to investigate the inflation trend in the period from January 2008 to February 2009. For this paper, methodology applied is based on secondary data. Weekly WPI collected from office of the Economic Advisor, Ministry of Commerce and Industry, Government of India. This paper basically covered only five groups of items. WPI-based Monthly inflation rate calculated by weekly (point to point) basis. As per weekly inflation rate calculated monthly average rate of inflation.

Inflation is defined as a sustained increase in the general level of prices for goods and services in an economy over a period of time. It is measured as an annual percentage increase. As inflation rises, the value of currency goes down. Inflation can also be described as a decline in the real value of money—a loss of purchasing power. Thus the purchasing power of the currency, i.e. the goods and services that can be bought in a unit of currency, too goes down. When the general price level rises, each unit of currency buys fewer goods and services. Inflation may widen an income gap between those with fixed incomes and those with variable incomes. High inflation may lead to shortages of goods as consumers begin hoarding them out of concern that their prices will increase in the future.

Standard measures of inflation are calculated based on an average consumption basket. However, there is a significant variation in the consumption basket across the population, including by income level (Arrow, 1958). A chief measure of price inflation is the inflation rate, which is the percentage change in a price index over time. In India two types of index: Consumer Price Index (CPI) and Wholesale Price Index (WPI) are used to monitor inflation. Of the two, WPI is the most widely used price index in India. WPI is the price of a representative basket of wholesale goods. India and use WPI changes as a central measure of inflation. It is used to measure the change in the average price level of goods traded in wholesale market and is available on a weekly basis with the shortest possible time lag of only two weeks. The WPI is an indicator designed to measure the changes in the price levels of commodities that flow into the wholesale trade intermediaries. The index is a vital guide in economic analysis and policy formulation, and as basis for price adjustments in business contracts and projects. It is also intended to serve as an additional source of information for comparison in the international front.

TRENDS OF WHOLESALE PRICES SINCE INDEPENDENCE

The inflation rate over the past five decades averaged 6.6 per cent per annum. However, decade-wise, the inflation rate accelerated steadily from an annual average of 1.7% during the 1950s to 6.4 per cent during the 1960s and further to 9.0 per cent in the 1970s before easing marginally to 8.0 per cent in the 1980s. On the other hand, the volatility in the inflation rate, as measured by the coefficient of variation, which was fairly high in the 1950s (4.4 per cent), moved in a narrow range of 0.4-1.0 per cent in the subsequent decades.

The pickup in inflation from 1970s onwards coincided with a sharp rise in growth, partly reflecting fiscal dominance. At that time, the inflationary dynamics also reflected supply shocks, such as the two wars (1962 and 1965), hike in crude oil prices (1973-74 and 1979-80) and crop failures. Demand pressures, emanating partly from the widening fiscal imbalances, sustained the inflation in the 1980s.

In the year 1990 saw a sharp increase in inflation. The decade began with double digit inflation. This was intensified by hikes in procurement prices as well as supply-demand imbalance in essential commodities like pluses, oilseeds and edible oils. The inflationary pressure continued during 1993-94 and 1994-95 in the wake of unprecedented capital inflows as the consequent higher monetary expansion. The inflation rate declined from an average of two digits (11.00%) during 1990-95 to single digit (5.3%) during the second half of the decade. Average annual WPI inflation declined from 10.6 per cent in the first half of 1990s to 4.1 per cent during 2001-02 to 2003-04.

The WPI registered a decade high growth rate at 12.85 per cent in August 2008 on surging global commodity and oil prices and partly due to domestic surge in food and non-food prices. The downward trend in global commodity prices resulted in the downtrend in prices of non-food article index to 3.09 per cent in February 2009 from 17 per cent in August 2008. On the other hand, in the food article index increased to 10 per cent in February 2009 compared with 6 per cent in August 2008. The rising food article index compelled the consumer price index to move up due to its higher weight age in consumer price index (CPI). The surge in CPI creates a barrier for the ultimate consumer to take benefit of underneath one percent WPI. The hike in minimum support price by government restricts the food articles index from coming down. (IER, 2009)

INFLATION RATE BASED ON CPI (IW)/CONSUMER INFLATION

It is generally argued that WPI inflation is not an appropriate index to determine the impact of price rise on the cost of living of the common man. Rather, the Consumer Price Index for Industrial Workers (CPI-IW), which also includes selected services and is measured on the basis of retail prices, and is used to determine the dearness allowance of employees in both the public and private sectors, is the appropriate indicator of general inflation. In sharp contrast to the WPI, CPI-IW inflation has been stable and moderate. This is because food items have higher weights in CPI-IW than in WPI, and in general the price increases of these items have been moderate in the current year.

Consumer Price Index (CPI) reflects changes in the retail prices of selected goods and services on which a homogeneous group of consumers spend a major part of their income. There are three distinct series of CPI—for industrial workers (IW), for agricultural labourers (AL) and for urban non-manual employees (UNME). Of these, the CPI (IW) is the most popular as the Central Government employees' wage compensation (dearness allowance) is calculated on the basis of movement in this index. CPI (IW) is constructed on a monthly basis, with a lag of one month. The base year for CPI (IW) is 1982.

The all-India consumer price index for agricultural labourers stood at 462 in February 2009 against 417 in February 2008. The index grew 10.79 per cent in February 2009 compared with a 6.38 per cent increase in February 2008. The index was up 10.31 per cent in April-February 2008-09 compared with 7.41 growth in April-February 2007-08. The index for industrial workers expanded 9.63 per cent in February 2009 compared with a 5.47 per cent increased in February 2008-09 compared with 6.05 per cent in April-February 2007-08. The index of rural laborers grew 10.79 per cent in February 2009 compared with 6.11 per cent increase in February 2008. It jumped 10.24 per cent (IER, 2009).

The world economy is passing through the most trying phase of recessions. The global economic downturn and simultaneous recession in major developed economies have forced Indian policy-makers to shift attention from fighting inflation to accelerating the economic growth which is slowing down. The government of India as well as the RBI has taken several steps to support the economic growth and financial stability. The interest rates have been lowered; there are reductions in taxes to boost the spending and economic growth. RBI took steps to boost economy by increasing liquidity. The bright side of the economy is the falling inflation rate due to decline in fuel prices and manufactured products. But the inflation rate in the primary articles group still continues to remain high at around 12 per cent in the month of February 2009.

Items-wise variation (inflation) can be seen as under:

All Commodities

The Chart indicates the annual variations in the wholesale price index in the period from 1995-96 to 2008-09 of all commodities. In the year 1995-96 annual variation of all commodities was 4.36 per cent but in 2001-02 came down to 1.63 per cent and lastly in the year 2008-09 it was less than 1 per cent (0.26%).

CHART I

Trends of Annual Variations of All Commodities

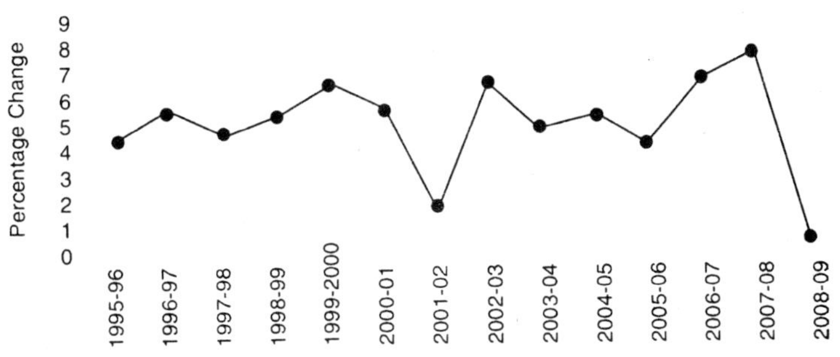

The paper attempts to reinvestigate the inflation trend in the period from Jan. 2008 to Feb. 2009.

As per Chart 2, average monthly inflation in India for all commodities was 4.47 per cent in January 2008 and continued to rise up to 12.74 per cent in August 2008. Thereafter, the rate continued to decline to just 3.67 per cent in February 2009.

CHART 2
Average Monthly Inflationary Trends of All Commodities (January-February 2009)

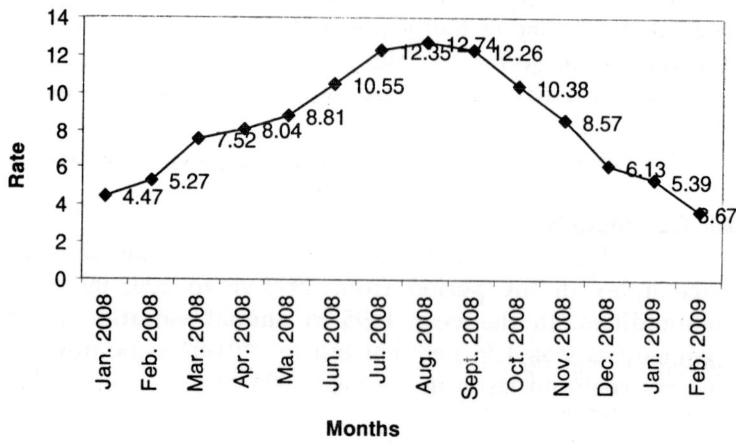

Food Articles

The effect of rising food prices will differ across household (ADB, 2008). In the one side some higher income class households may be benefited from higher price, but on the other side, the poor and low income class are adversely affected. (Son, 2008). The inflation rate of food articles remained high in the month of November, December and January 2009. It shows that price of food articles depend more on other factors like season, rainfall or socio-political factors like transport strike, festivals, etc. It does not depend more on global factors like global fuel price.

Chart 3 indicates the annual variations of food articles. The figure in 1995-96 was 7.75 per cent and reached 11.55 per cent in year 1996-97. In year 2000-01 it was negative (-0.18 per cent). Again gradually increased and reached 6.31 per cent in year 2008-09.

CHART 3

Trends of Annual Variations in Food Articles

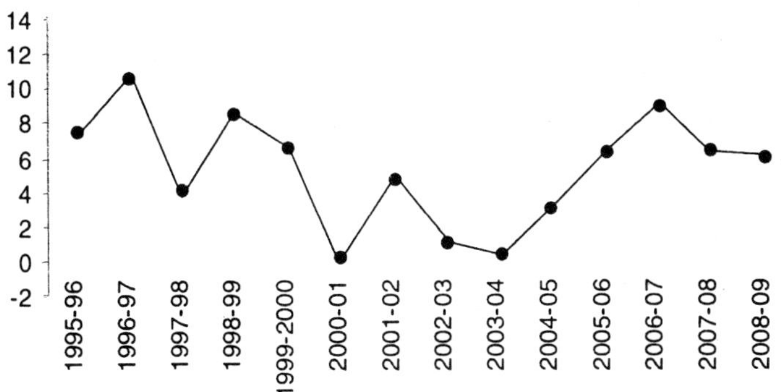

As per Chart 4, Inflation rate for food articles witnessed rising trend from 2.08 per cent in January 2008 to 10.87 per cent in January 2009. There has been fall in inflation in

CHART 4

Average Monthly Inflationary Trends of Food Articles (January 2008-February 2009)

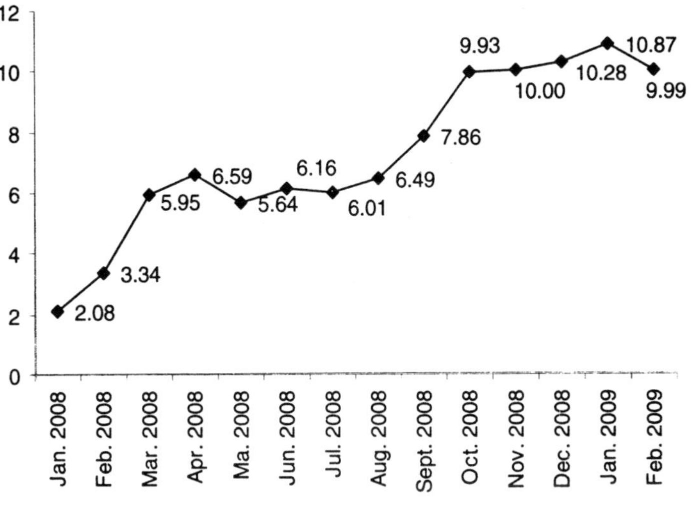

February 2009 to 9.99 per cent. The decline of inflation in the food articles is very slow. It is still 9.99 per cent which is much higher than that of other group of items.

Non-Food Articles

Non-food articles in the primary products group, including fibers, raw cotton oilseeds and sugarcane, etc. recorded a high price rise during the year 2003-04, consequence to the production shortfalls resulting from the draught of year 2002.

As per Chart 5, in year 1995-96, annual variation of non-food articles was negative (-6.06 per cent). In year 2001-02 it was less than one per cent (0.6%), because the shortfall of production with due to draught, but in year 2002-03 reached all year high of 22.07 per cent. Again in year 2008-09 its variation showing negative (-0.09%).

CHART 5
Trends of Annual Variations of All Commodities

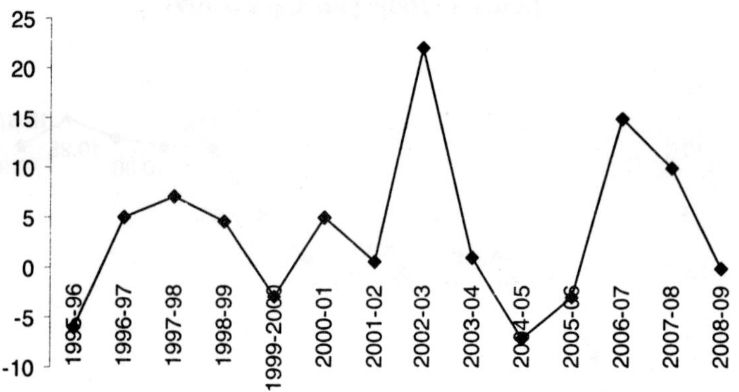

As per Chart 6, inflation of non-food articles reached from 11.08 per cent in January 2008 to the highest at 17.04 per cent in August 2008, thereafter there has been decline due to fall in prices of oil and power world-wide. It dipped down to the record lowest at 3.41 per cent in February 2009.

CHART 6
Average Monthly Inflation Trends of Non-Food Article (January 2008 to February 2009)

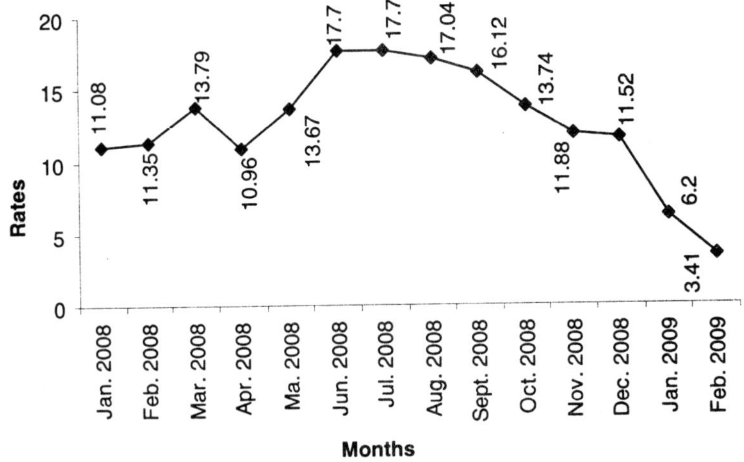

MANUFACTURING PRODUCTS

The manufacturing sector is the major contributor to inflation accounting for nearly 80 per cent of the inflation in 2003-04. The manufacturing group (with total weight of 63.75 per cent in WPI) an annual inflation of 5.1 per cent in January 2005. Within the manufacturing sector, food products, edible oils, textiles, leather and leather products, basic metal and alloys and iron and steel were the prime mover.

As per Chart 7, shows the annual trends of variation among manufacturing products. In year 1995-96 this variation was 3.8 per cent. But in year 1996-97 it was 10.55 per cent. Manufacturing products had negative trends, with -0.27 in year 1999-2000 and -3.07 in year 2000-01. In year 2001-02 it was showing 0 (Zero) level

As per Chart 8, manufacturing products inflation rate was 4.54 per cent in January 2008. It continued to rise till it reached a record high at 11.64 per cent in August 2008. Thereafter, the inflationary trend witnessed sharp decline till it came down to 4.91 per cent in February 2009.

CHART 7

Trends of Annual Variations in Manufacturing Products

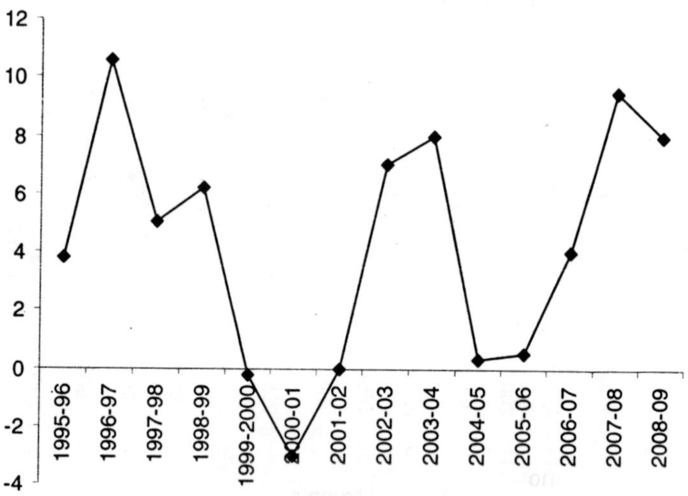

CHART 8

Average Monthly Inflation Trends of Manufacturing Products (January 2008 to February 2009)

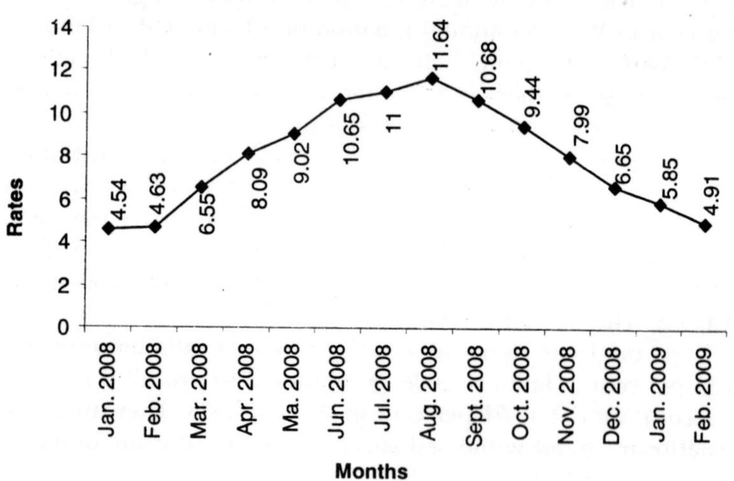

FUEL, POWER, LIGHT AND LUBRICANTS

The group with a weight of 14.2 per cent recorded an inflation rate of 10.1 per cent in January 2005. The fuel and lubricant group is broadly divided in three categories: coal mining, mineral oils and electricity. Major contribution to inflation was made by coal and petroleum products. Inflation in the oil sector has direct bearing on that in other sectors of products. The wholesale index price for light diesel oil showed an increase of 21 per cent in June 2008, liquefied petroleum gas 20 percent, naphtha 17 per cent, furnace oil 15 per cent, aviation turbine fuel 14 per cent, petrol 11 per cent, high speed diesel 10 per cent and bitumen seven per cent.

As per Chart 9, annual variation trends of fuel, power, light and lubricant recorded 5.13 per cent in year 1995-96. In year 1999-2000 it was highest 26.74 per cent. But in year 2008-09 this is showing negative trends (-6.11 per cent). This is with due to reduced the petroleum prices in international market.

CHART 9
Trends of Annual Variations in Fuel, Power, Light and Lubriants

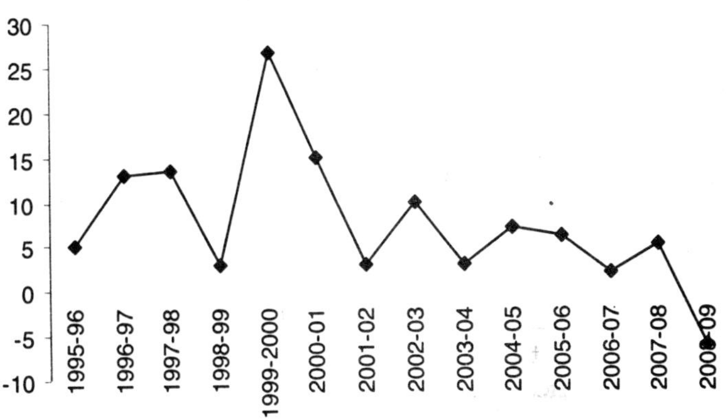

As per Chart 10, the WPI index of fuel, power, light and lubricant recorded the lowest level at 323.50 in month of February 2009 in the current financial year. It decreased -3.63

CHART 10

Average Monthly Inflation Trends of Fuel, Power, Light, etc. (January 2008 to February 2009)

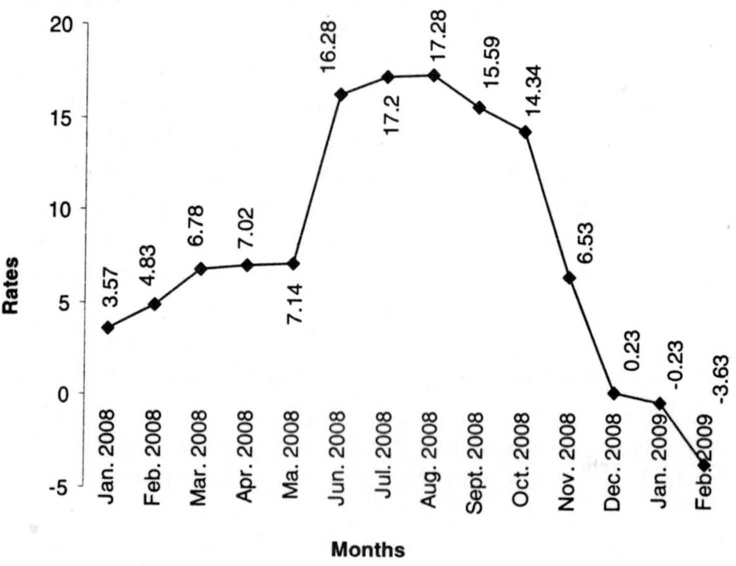

per cent in February 2009 compared with a 4.83 per cent rise in February 2008. Decreasing trend (negative growth) has noticed since December 2008. The WPI index showing lowest level in current financial year.

Chart 11 indicates the annual variation in the WPI in the period from 1995-96 to 2008-09. In the year 1995-96 WPI for all commodities stood at 4.36 per cent with food articles at 7.75 per cent, non-food articles at -6.11, manufacturing at 3.8 per cent and fuel, power, light and lubricants at 5.13 per cent. The figures in 1996-97 show that WPI for food articles reached 11.55, manufacturing products at 10.55 and fuel, power, light and lubricants at 13.34 per cent. In year 2001-02 this variation for food articles came down to -0.18 and manufacturing products at -3.07. This is showing the negative variations. Annual variation for fuel, power, light and lubricants reached at all time high of 26.74 per cent in year 1999-2000, but it dipped down now as low as -6.11 per cent in year 2008-09. For

CHART 11

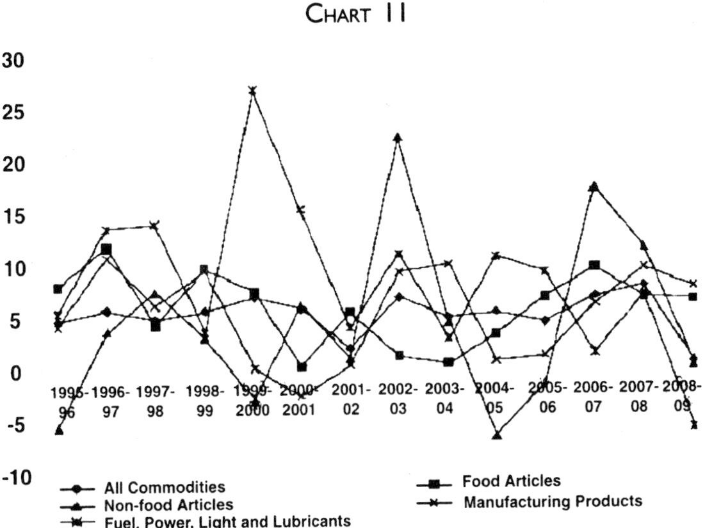

non-food articles WPI variation reached to 22.07 in 2002-03 but it come down to negative figure of -6.93 in year 2004-05, -1.92 in 2005-06 and -0.09 in year 2008-09. but the variation was at

CHART 12

Monthly Average Inflationary Trends in India (January 2008 to February 2009)

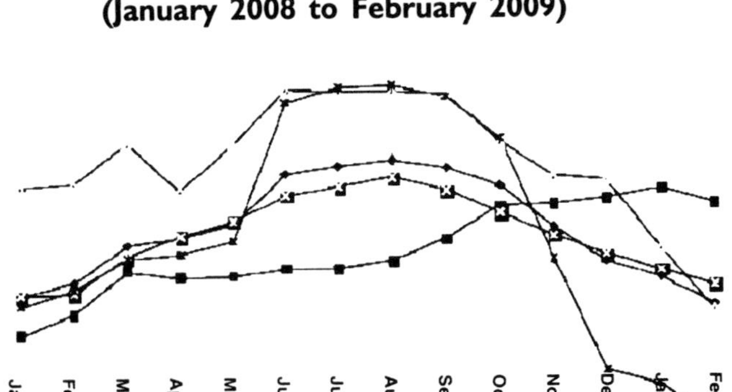

its peak at 22.07 in 2002-03. So far as WPI variation for manufacturing products in concerned it had negative trends with -0.27 in 1999-2000 and -3.07 where as it was the 0 (zero) level in year 2001-02.

All through the period of these 14 months, the direct correlation between inflationary trend in Fuel Power and light as well as the trend in all commodities Food Articles, non food articles and manufacturing products can be seen in Chart 12.

INFLATION TRENDS IN THE MONTH OF MARCH 2009

Inflation fell to an all-time low to 0.44 per cent with analysts expecting it to turn negative in the next couple of weeks. But this does not mean that prices of goods have begun to fall sharply.

Official data showed inflation measured by wholesale prices fell sharply for the week ended March 7 to 0.44 per cent from the previous week's 2.43 per cent. The previous low of 1.13 per cent was recorded on February 2, 2002.

Prices, however, continue to remain high, based on the consumer price index data that is released monthly, CPI inflation remains firm at 10.4 per cent in January.

Prices of food products continue to remain high, although there has been a slight moderation. 'Food articles' inflation ruled at 7.4 per cent, down from the previous week's 8.3 per cent.

The fall in inflation has been largely due to a sharp drop in the index of 'fuel and power' that has contracted by 6% compared with a contraction of 5.1 per cent in the previous week.

If at all, the low inflation will give more elbow room to the Reserve Bank of India (RBI) to cut interest rates.

"It is a good development", Planning Commission Deputy Chairperson Montek Singh Ahluwalia said. "It gives us reassurance that we can take measures to stimulate the economy".

The government said India was not headed for a deflationary situation where falling income lowers demand and prices of goods.

"It (low inflation) is more indicative of a base effect rather than any price effect," Cabinet Secretary, K.M. Chandrasekhar said, adding there were no signs of deflation.

Economists expect inflation to remain in the negative zone for the next few months.

"We expect negative readings to start in the late March or early April, lasting for around two quarters (six months)", said Sonal Varma of Nomura Financial.

Analysts expected a further cut in interest rates.

"This has provided more headroom to the RBI for further strong monetary measure to revive demand and support the economy," said Yashika Singh, economic analysts head. Dun & Bradstreet India.

The RBI has cut its key lending rate repo rate by 4 percentage points to 5 per cent since October 2008; the last one early this month to boost growth amid an unprecedented world economic slowdown. (Choudhary, 2009)

April 2009

India's wholesale price index rose 0.57 per cent in the 12 months to April 18 2009, above the previous week's annual rise of 0.26 per cent, government data showed. Prime Minister Manmohan Singh said, India's economy grew an estimated 6.5 per cent in the just-ended 2008-09 financial year and consumer price inflation is expected to moderate in five to six months. A global economic slump and slowdown economic slump and slowdown in domestic demand have weakened economic growth in Asia's third largest economy, but falls in commodity prices have helped moderate prices.

"The wholesale price inflation is already down to around 1 per cent and there is a time lag for the consumer price inflation to also fall", "Singh said. "But I am sure CPI inflation will moderate in five to six months", he said at the last lap of a month-long election campaign in the northern state of Punjab, India's wholesale price index rose 0.7 per cent in the 12 months to April 25, above the previous week's annual rise of 0.5 per cent. But annual CPI inflation stood at 9.6 per cent in February, as prices of food products remained firm.

References

ADB (2008), "Food Prices and Inflation in Developing Asia: Is Poverty Reduction Coming to an End"? A Special Report by the Economic and Research Department, Asian Development Bank, Manila

Arrow, K.J. (1958), "The Measurement of Price Change". In Joint Economic Committee, US Congress, *The Relationship of Prices to Economic Stability and Growth*. Washington, DC.

Choudhary, Gaurav (2009), Inflation at 0.44% but don't Celebrate, *The Hindustan Times,* 19th March, 2009, Delhi.

Kapila Uma (2006-07), (Eds). Indian Economy Since Independence, Academic Foundation, New Delhi.

IER (2009), Indian Economy Review, Capital Market Publishers India Private Limited, Mumbai, April 2009.

Son Hyun, H. (2008), Has Inflation Hurt the Poor? Regional Analysis in the Philippines, ERD Working Paper Series No. 112, Asian Development Bank, *Economic and Research Department*, Manila, May 2008.

Thaindian News (2008), 13-year High Inflation at 11. 05 per cent adds to Government Woes, June 20, 2008.

TOI (2009), Inflation May Moderate: PM, *The Times of India* (Delhi), 12 May, 2009.

9

Inflation Pendulum Strikes After 20 Years—2008

ABHA MITTAL

Rising inflation is a major issue worrying all the countries. Before analyzing inflation trend in India in 2008, lets analyze how is annual inflation rate measured in India. The barometer of macroeconomy in India is Wholesale Price Index (WPI) while in most countries inflation is measured by the Consumer Price Index (CPI). WPI is available at the end of every week (generally Saturday) for a period of one week ending that day. It has a time lag of 2 weeks (WPI for the year ending 2 weeks back will be available this week). WPI despite all its limitations is the conventional indicator for inflation. Every week, WPI of a set of 435 goods is calculated by the Indian Government (with base year: 1993-94). Since these are calculated at WPI, actual price paid by the consumer are far higher. In terms of rising inflation it means cost of living increase are much higher.

India witnessed the worst inflation in 2008 with double-digit inflation coming out month-after-month (June-September) with slight easing in mid-September. With the hike in administered fuel prices with most of India's vast population living close to below poverty line, inflation acts as a 'Poor Man's Tax'. This effect was amplified with rise in food prices, since food represents more than half of the expenditure of this group (poor). Quarter-wise analysis of inflation trend in 2008 reveals that the inflation rate raged continuously from first to the third quarter and reached double digit at the end of the second quarter (12%) 20-years—high. At the end of the third quarter (September) inflation rate moderated slightly to (11.8%) but decreased drastically to a single digit in the fourth quarter to approximately (8.6%). It reached a very low level to 5.9 per cent for which the entire credit goes to the efficient management by the Indian Government.

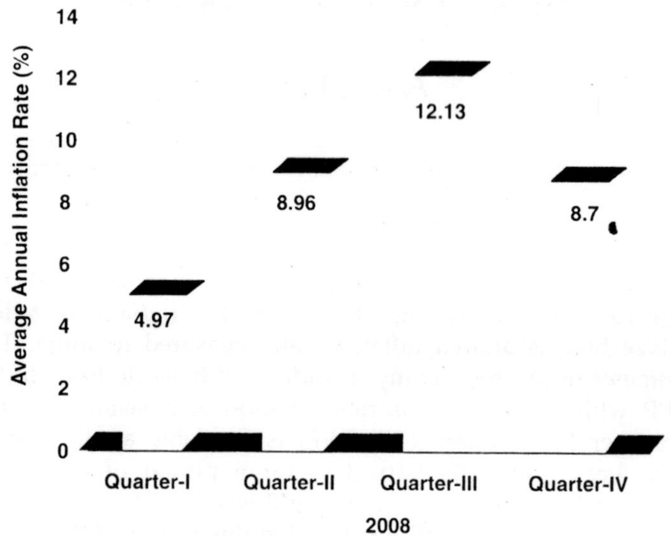

Quarter I (January-March)
Average Annual Rate—app. 4.97 per cent

Annual inflation rate which was at modest level in the first week of January (3.79%) zoomed to a 13 months high, doubling in few months to 7 per cent. This is the highest level since 6.69 per cent, Jan. 27, 2007. It was marked to beat its highest annual increase, a four-and-a-half-year high since mid-Nov. 2004. Rise was mainly due to sharp increase in

International oil prices which forced the Government to increase the retail prices of gasoline by 4.5 per cent for the first time in more than one and a half year so as to cut losses at oil company and lower burden of record crude oil costs. The domestic factors responsible for steep price rise were decrease in domestic demand, increase in price of fruits, vegetables, oil seeds, metals and decrease in industrial production to a four-and-a-half-year low of 5.3 per cent. Although the government tried to suppress inflation through measures like duty cuts, export bans, harsh measures against person detected hoarding up commodity to ease price pressure but was not successful.

According to RBI Governor Yaga Venugopal Reddy, pressure of inflation was increasing much swiftly than expected. In such a situation, monetary tightening was not ideal solution because domestic demand had decreased sharply.

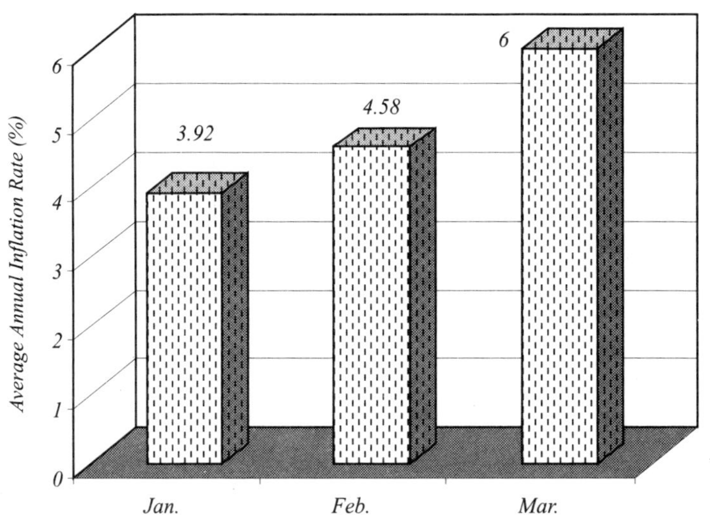

Quarter-1 (January-March) 2008

Quarter 2—(April-June)
Average Annual Inflation Rate Doubled—8.96 per cent

Inflation rate accelerated with fastest pace in more than 3 years at beginning of April, it jumped to a 7-year high in May (fastest increase witnessed since Feb. 2001) and further to double digit 11 per cent (20-year-high inflation) in June. With the world heading towards recession and oil prices booming inflation was bound to come. Annual inflation rate increased due to surging food and commodity prices. Wheat trading was at $ 13.495 a bushel which was almost double the price witnessed in 2007. Fuel prices increased by an average 10 per cent due to hike in International crude oil price. Oil Prices increased to $ 112.21 a barrel. This forced the Government to increase petroleum prices with effect from June 5. Prices of fuel, power and lubricants increased to 7.8 per cent, prices of ATF increased to 14 per cent, price of petrol increased by Rs. 5 per lt, of diesel by Rs. 3 per lt and of cooking gas by Rs. 50 per cylinder. The increase in price of gasoline led to increase in price of transport charges which led to drastic increase in prices of all consumer products which had to be transported. Need of the hour was to decrease inflation rate so that business operations could perform better. Inspite of RBI's measure to control inflation through increase in CRR to a 7-

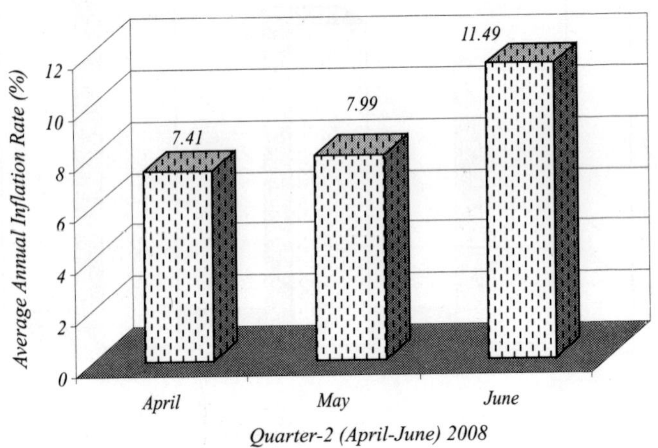

year-high of 8 per cent from 7.5 per cent and further to 8.75 per cent, increase in Repo rate to 8.5 per cent so as to decrease the money supply, i.e. suck of liquidity, was not successful.

Government efforts like decrease in food duties, scrapping import tax on oils and maize, ban on export of lentils and other staples were also not successful. One way to keep check on inflation was to maintain surplus foodgrains but that was not possible because foodgrains production increased at a small rate. However, nobody should expect miracles. Hopes remained with the monsoons.

Quarter-3 (July-September)

Average annual inflation rate in the third quarter compared to first quarter trebled—app.12.13 per cent. It was above 5.5 per cent the central bank target (for the end of fiscal year on March 2009). Inflation rate climbed to 11.91 per cent for the first time in more than 13 years in early July and further to 12.63 per cent in August, sending shivers through consumers this was more than 6 per cent higher than a year earlier and almost 2 times the RBI's target. Due to supply side measures like marginal easing of prices of essentials especially fruits, vegetables, drop in global oil prices, increase in industrial production by 4.8 per cent (below 7% in Sept. 2007 but above 1.4% in Aug. 2007) inflation rate showed some signs of moderation but the pressure still remained. The inflation rate in September still remained stubbornly at an unacceptable level of above 12 per cent for which the blame should not go to the Indian Government. It was the increase in oil price to $ 147 a barrel from $ 101.15 a barrel which proved to be the single most influential factor that led to high inflation. The Global meltdown triggered by the collapse of American investment banker Lehman Brothers was also responsible for high double digit inflation. This forced RBI to increase the repo rate to a 7-year high of 9 per cent (from 8.5% in June). However, compared to other countries e.g. Zimbabwe, India was in a comfortable position. Inflation during this period in Zimbabwe stood at 165,000 per cent. Bread prices doubled every week. In Zimbabwe it was due to bad run economy but in India sole and biggest reason was FUEL PRICES. Not much the government can do about it. If fuel prices rise, every part of your life is affected. Commodity prices have to go up.

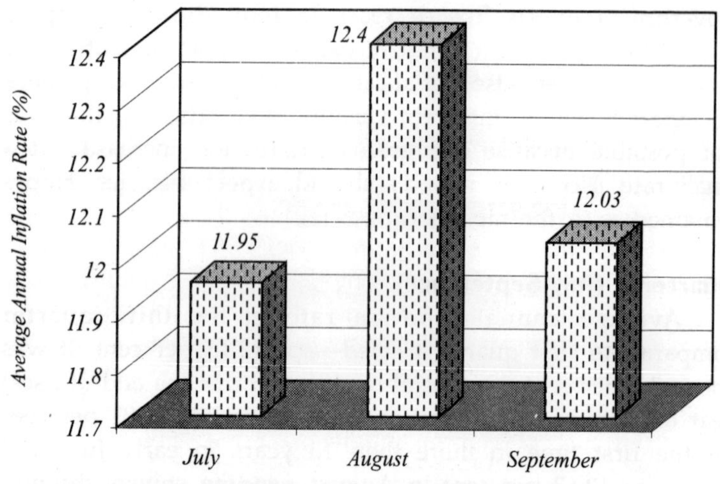

Quarter-3 (July-September) 2008

Quarter-4 (October-December)
Average Annual Inflation Rate—app. 8.7 per cent

It decreased below 11 per cent for the first time in over 4 months in October. Although inflation rose slightly for the week ended Oct. 25 it decreased drastically (in Nov.) to a single digit after 21 week (from 10.72 per cent per cent at the end of Oct. to 8 per cent at the end of Nov.) and further to 5.91 per cent (at the end of Dec.) for the 8th week in succession. It was good news for everyone. This was possible due to sharp fall in global crude oil prices from $ 165 a barrel in July to $ 55 a barrel in November. Government cut fuel prices by 0.9 per cent, Light and diesel price decreased by 11 per cent, Aviation Fuel price decreased by 5 per cent. WPI for commodities decreased by 0.2 per cent. In primary article group out of 98 articles, 20 articles (wheat, maize, urad, ragi, papaya, brinjal, okara, peas, sweet potatoes, sapota, ground nut, dry chillies, coriander, tea, cardamom, iron ore and raw rubber showed decrease in price, while 61 articles showed no increase in price. Index of manufactured product decreased by 0.3 per cent from 201.4 to 201. Imported edible oil, salt, cement, iron and steel became cheaper.

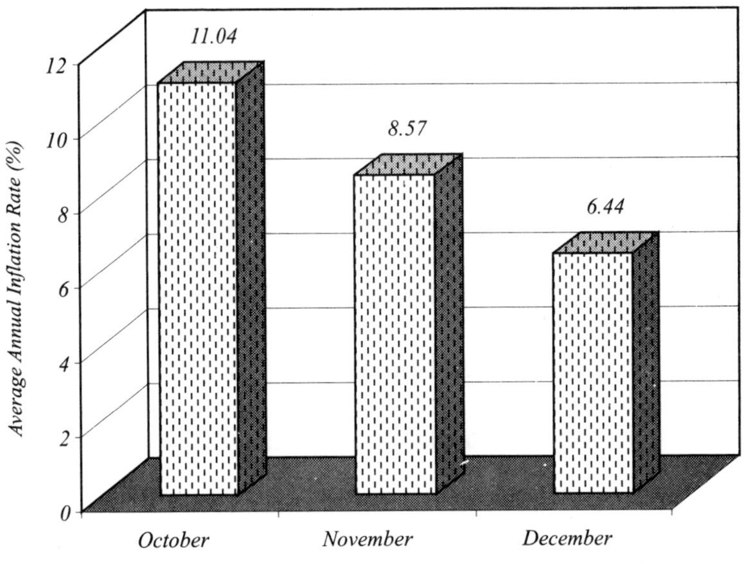

Quarter-4 (October-December) 2008

January 2009

Inflation rate maintained the downward trend. It decreased further from 5.91 per cent in the previous week (27 December) to 5.24 per cent. However, strike by truck drivers due to cut in fuel subsidies led to marginal increase in price of edible things like fruits and vegetables. Inflation rate in the second week of January increased marginally to 5.64 per cent (an increase in price seen after a gap of more than 2 months) but the increase was a temporary phase. Inflation rate decreased to 4.4 per cent on 31st January. Due to decrease in fuel rates globally and domestically the Index of fuel declined by 0.2 per cent due to low price of Aviation Turbine Fuel (ATF)—8 per cent and light diesel oil—(3%). There was further cut in fuel prices by 11 per cent, cooking gas price by 8 per cent, high speed diesel by 7 per cent. Index of food articles fell by 0.6 per cent as price of food articles (fruits and vegetables) fell by 3 per cent and (gram, barely and spices) by 1 per cent. Index of primary articles declined from 200.8 to 200.7. Index of manufacturing items fell by 0.1 per cent.

This meant that the country was able to control the inflation rate considerably.

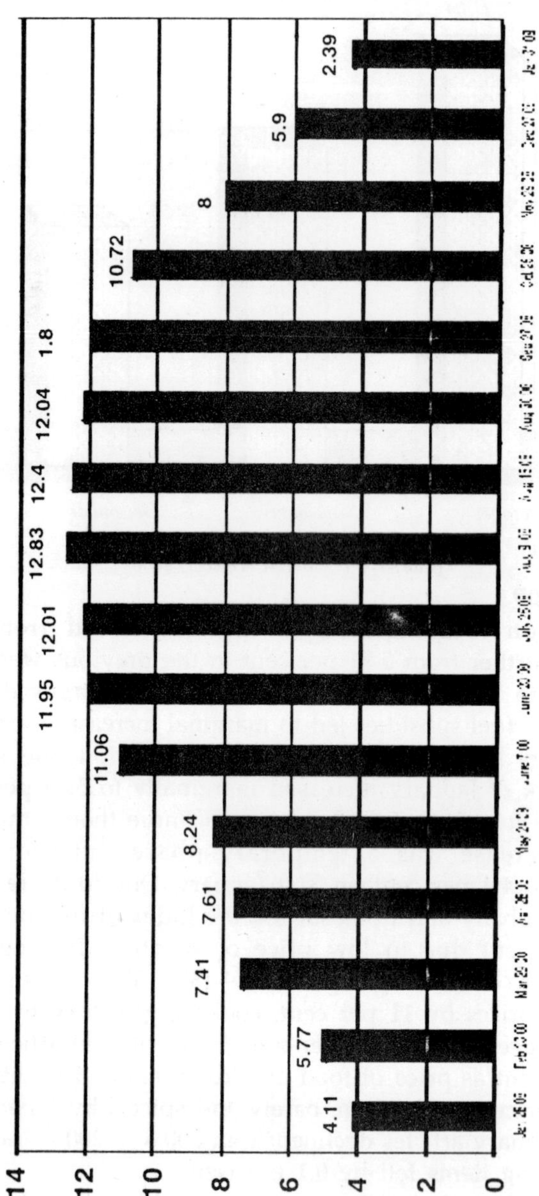
Inflation Trends in 2008
14
12
10
8
6
4
2
0
4.11
5.77
7.41
7.61
8.24
11.06
11.95
12.01
12.83
12.4
12.04
1.8
10.72
8
5.9
2.39

CONCLUSION

A deep study of the inflation trends in the year 2008 revealed that the basic reason of uphill in inflation was largely due to increase in price of food articles and fuel. In other words, it was due to supply-side factors which was controlled largely by using measures from the supply-side. The efficient handling of supply management by the Indian Government helped inflation to ease at the end of the year (December 2008). Thus, the single most important lesson from the events of 2008 is *"BE PREPARED FOR THE UNEXPECTED"*.

10

Issues and Policy Options for Inflationary Trends in India

B.M. JANI

INTRODUCTION

Inflation in India is the recent past experienced with recession and rising trends in prices of essential goods and services in India. For the last two years in Indian economy, the level of inflation remained as high as about kissing distance of 12 per cent as on 1/8/2008. The economy experienced 11.9 per cent rate of growth in wholesale price index looking as non-anticipated nature adversely affected growth rate of GNP, falling rate of unemployment with stagnant rate of growth of output. In calendar year 2008, the economy faced global recession, which again brought structural imbalances in the economy. Macroeconomic variables along with segmented markets affected adversely. Money markets, Capital markets and labour markets were adversely affected. Sluggish rate of industrial growth could not allowed the economy to achieve 9 per cent rate of growth as expected during the XIth Five Year Plan. During 2007 oil prices and in 2009 Gold prices escalated its highest pick

This paper aims to know causes and periodical changes of inflationary pressures as well as policy options to regulate inflation at tolerable level in era of recession with high rate of inflation in India. For this, the present paper is divided in to three parts: the first tries to know basic issues on the basis of work carried out on the subject by the economists in the past, the second one explores analysis of nature of inflation in the recent past, whereas the third one offer policy options to manage inflation at tolerable rate in Indian economy.

RETROSPECT AND BASIC ISSUES

There are several studies carried out by the economists in India and abroad so as to know theoretical base as well applied aspects of inflation related with behaviour at individual country level. These include Phillip Cagon, Thirwal, A.W. Phillips, Vakil, Shenoy, Brahmanand, C. Rangarajan, I.G. Patel, Rakesh Mohan, Alan Greenspan, Joseph Stiglitz, V.B. Angedi, Robert Samuelson and others those who gave tools and techniques to measure inflation, and related other issues for national and global policy. A common voice about inflation of these economists is centered on excessive expenditure over income of the state as well as budget deficit and balance of payments deficit are responsible for creation of new money and continuous rise in prices. However, non-economic happening of events are also responsible for continuous trend of inflation in any country

A cursory glance to the literature inspires the present researcher to pose following issues of debate: *whether current inflation in India is an outcome of:*

1. Transmission of global inflation into Indian economy,
2. Rising oil prices the recent past,
3. Rising balance of payment deficits in global trade,
4. Food inflation largely due to speculation in Agriculture Commodity Exchange Market price movement,

5. Exports drive of essential commodities so as to increase share of India's trade in global trade under the WTO regime,
6. Whether commodity inflation largely due to cost-push and demand-pull nature,
7. Pumping of liquidity in financial system by the RBI to manage efficient payment Mechanism in money markets,
8. Major difference between wholesale prices and retail prices paid by the consumers in retail markets,
9. Financial engineering in financial system failed to manage balance between capital markets and money markets,
10. Rising budget deficits due to excessive Plan and non-plan expenditure and Government of India failed to raise additional resources through tax and non-tax sources of income,
11. Whether financial packages declared by the government of India for committed Suicide by the farmers and survival packages to survive industries and corporate houses from global recession,
12. Inflation rate has eaten away growth rate of economy in general, excluded common poor man with exclusive growth and growth rate of real sector of our economy in particular.
13. Supply-side management of output has failed to reach demand of economy as a whole.
14. High cost of reforms, which are operated since 1991 in Indian economy,
15. High cost to keep idle foreign exchange reserves,
16. Global recession and appreciation of the US dollar. And several other reasons can be listed. By and large, economists have agreed that inflation is an outcome of happening of economic event resulting from excess expenditure over income with universal price rise.

An analysis of inflation is given by the different schools of economists as how it has affected the economy as whole or a sector or a life of people those whose level of living is seriously affected by constant rise in prices.

This paper tries to address and analyse a few of the said listed issues.

NATURE OF INFLATIONARY TRENDS IN INDIAN ECONOMY

It is a fact that inflation has not migrated from elsewhere, but it has generated in Indian economy. Still, however, it is necessary here to know main reasons and nature of inflationary pressures in India. Milton Friedman who categorized US families earning $21000 per year categorized as poor and he claimed that a given money supply, a rise in the price of any one item will be offset by a fall in the price of another cannot be true in all cases. Here, it should be noted that definition of poor is quiet different in India as person spending less than $2 per day is identified as poor. Movement of wholesale price behaviour and retail prices are quiet different in both the countries. There is extreme case of sub-Saharan countries facing more than 1000 per cent rate of inflation. Country-wise impact of inflation in different level of income is also different.

The RBI and Ministry of Finance have published periodically decadal changes in wholesale price index as well as price movement of essential commodities during the seventies, eighties, nineties, and the initial decade of the 21st Century. An attempt is made to show trend movement of the prices in the Table 1.

Trend analysis of the years of the nineties reveals that wholesale price index of all commodities have fallen from 10.30 per cent to 2.78 per cent considering percentage changes in the index. However, the index remained in control after 1995-96 largely due to FDI flows and FII investments in India as well as healthy forex reserves position in the economy. A gap between investment and savings is bridged by these two sources during the ninth five-year plan. Wholesale price index has been manufacturer group where price rise is found to be very low, this represents domestic drop in inflation. Still however, a group of economists believe that wholesale price

TABLE I
Inflation in Wholesale Price Index and Consumer Price Index (Percentage change over previous year)

Year	*Wholesale price index All commodities*	*Consumers Price Index of*		
		Ind. Workers	*Agri. Lab.*	*Urban non-manual*
1990-91	10.30	11.60	7.6	11.0
1991-92	13.70	13.50	19.3	13.7
1992-93	10.00	9.60	12.3	10.4
1993-94	8.40	7.50	3.5	6.9
1994-95	10.90	10.0	8.1	9.5
1995-96	7.70	10.0	10.8	9.5
1996-97	6.30	9.40	9.1	9.3
1997-98	4.80	6.80	4.3	7.2
1998-99	6.90	13.2	10.8	11.1
1999-2000 (Till Feb.)	2.78	3.3	4.9	4.5

Source : C.S.O.

index is not correct measure of inflation as people are paying retail price in the current market, which is fairly high. It is seen in the table that consumer price index of all three strata are fairly high as it is connected with human life consumption. As level of living depends up to real income and realized purchasing power of industrial workers, agriculture labourers and urban non-manual workers. This means the second half of the years of the nineties show favourable trend of inflation in Indian economy.

The RBI published data revealed in Table 2, expresses that there are convergence and divergence in the case of last eight year movement of GDP growth rate as well as average wholesale price index of inflation in India. However, monthly movement of the inflation rate has shown sharp ups and downs in general and during the year 2008-09. As far as growth and price stability twin objectives of the RBI has clear

TABLE 2
Trends of Growth Rate and Inflation in India

Year	*GDP growth Rate (%)*	*Average Wholesale Price Index Inflation (%)*
2003-04	8.5	5.4
2004-05	7.5	6.4
2005-06	9.4	4.4
2006-07	9.6	5.4
2007-08	9.0	4.7
2008-09	7.7*	7.0**

Note : *Projection, **Estimate for March 2009 by the RBI.
Source : *The Economic Times*, Ahmedabad, 1/9/2008, p. 8.

evidence as mentioned in the table. But robust foreign exchange reserves and healthy macroeconomic fundamentals are not doing the business of growth with stability. The expansion of the past few years was the part of global upswing, whereas, just slowdown now is a part of global downswing. RBI's effort to give housing loans and retail credit in 2004 prompted a lot of criticism. Moreover, bank's retaining securitized assets bitterly criticizes. As a result, many economists expressed that nuts and bolts of a sound banking system would be both incorrect as well as incorrect by the RBI. Similarly, there are 19 state co-operative banks and 732 urban co-operative banks were weak and sick in 2004, which increased to 563 in 2007 created financial tension for the RBI.

It is clarified from the large amount of doses of liquidity in banking system as well as other financial packages declared by the government are responsible to touch inflation rate at 11.9 in August 2008. Table 3 represents pumping of liquidity in banking sector by the RBI through different sources. Banking sector has eased monetary deal since mid-September 2008 as the crisis really hit emerging markets. The actual and potential increase in primary liquidity is order of Rs. 3,88,045 crore. Factor in the money multiplier, the addition to liquid funds on account of the 1 per cent reduction in statutory liquidity ratio (SLR) considered important. It is committed by the RBI

TABLE 3
Pumping of Liquidity in Banking System

Measure/Facility		*Amount in (Rs. Crore)*
1.	Cash-Reserve ratio	1,60,000
2.	MSS Unwinding	63,045
3.	Term Repo facility	60,000
4.	Increase in Export Credit Refinance	25,500
5.	Special Refinance facility for SCB (Non-NRRB)	38,500
6.	Refinance Facility for SIDBI/NHB/EXIM bank	16,000
7.	Liquidity Facility for NBFCs through SPV	25,000
	Total (1 to 7)	3,88,045

Source : *The Economic Times*, Ahmedabad, dt. 2/2/2009, p. 8.

governor up to 29 January 2009, the RBI has pumped Rs. 4 lakh crore of liquidity through various measures. However, Indian banking sector is not so responsible as US banking for credit crunch and down turn in credit markets for starting signals of recession. But it is a part and parcel to increase inflationary pressure in the economy. These huge cache of money in money market already impacted money market as well as government securities markets. It should be noted here that 10-year yields are now down to little over 5 per cent. Credit markets have been much less impacted, partly because of inefficiencies in the transmission mechanism, whereby RBI's signals are relayed to the market. All these happening of events fueled spirals in inflation in India economy.

It is visualized that the failure of *'Inflation Targeting'*, which means, whatever price growth exceeds the target level, interest rates need to increase. This phenomenon is based on little economic theory or empirical evidences. To day, inflation targeting is put to test and it will almost certainly fail. According to Cagon, anticipated inflation helps to manage inflationary accounting, whereas, non-anticipated inflation damages payment to all factors of production as they are not index-linked. Indexation of reward to all factors of production necessary so as to realized real income to them. Similarly, it is also debatable that for the central bank of a country should rule Vs. authority in money supply function to manage financial system both in the developed and the developing countries.

It is widely recognized that a central bank need to control the expectation of public to control expectation of inflation in order to measure actual inflation as price stability being prime function of the bank. If there is international transmission of inflation from one country to another or from the developed country like America to emerging market economy like India, one can realized that inflation has migrated and it is not local creation.

According to Joseph Stiglitz, recession in the US has brought the first phase of stagflation in India and other countries, which has caused low wages, high level of unemployment, and generated demand-pull factors. This has happened largely due to toxic mortgages and bad financial practices are exported from the US to the rest of the world those who parked international investments in the US private investment companies. It is also feared that there will be second wave of stagflation, which will also affect trade partners of the US. Central banks of the concerned country will have to manage global slowdown *vis-à-vis* local slowdown along with increasing pressures of inflation. During the last seven years, America's national debt rose from 5.6 billion to 9 trillion. This happened largely due to excess expenditure over the income. This means, a gift of stagflation in Indian economy is a result of global inflation with recession in the recent past, which has decreased purchasing power of people as well as loss of real value of investments in a country like India. Prosperity of capital market has been washed away due to dried global capital markets. It has caused crisis of payment in Indian capital and money markets and many share brokers in Mumbai and Gujarat committed suicide.

Treasury Inflation Protected Securities (TIPS) offer a win-win solution both for investors as well as for larger economies like India as they are useful tool for assessing inflationary expectations. Policy-makers can compare nominal yield with the yield of TIPS of comparable maturity so as to arrive at measurement of inflationary expectation and formulate monetary policy accordingly. It is argued that in the interest of lay investors only index-linked bonds can be issues. In money market, it is accepted that inflation would ease and rates soften. This makes a case for lender and investors to price their funds accordingly. Rates are likely to soften over a medium and lower term as and when growth rate or rise in supply side levels. From demand side, there has been dip in credit demand from key sectors such as real estate, personal loans, and capital markets. Overall credit has grown around 20 per cent during 2007-08 but money market operators feels closer to 15-16 per cent in the current financial year. This gives us a clue to know comfortable condition in the banking system, which give a way to lower interest rates in the long-run in India.

WHO IS PRICE-MAKER?

In financial market, which discovers the price of funds? Government raises funds at a price discovered by the market. It is a fact that price discovered for the funds raised by the central government is generally lowest reflecting better comfort for suppliers of funds. If government wishes to set the price, it will be price out of market largely due to our efficient and transparent financial market. Contrary to this, in labour market, labour is factor of production, it is not homogeneous. There is excess supply in labour market than demand though there are skill-specific shortages and hence price in labour market (wage determination) is not fully made by the market, which enables government to be a price maker. As a result, the price of labour market is not signaling device to get the right type of people as well as in solving agency problem.

MISCONCEPTION ABOUT WAGEFLATION

In order to have trust of monetary policy of the RBI, it has to fulfil expectation of people to maintain price stability to sustained purchasing power in the market. Looking to *non-anticipated inflation,* workers that prices are not going to increase rapidly but actually they are less likely to demand compensatory increase in wages. Thus, it is necessary to take of preventing an inflationary spiral. The organized sector has hardly 30 million employees in India out of the total workforce of the 430 million. Most of the government employees, whose wages are set by the sixth Pay Commission is not annual wage bargaining as they are less than index-linked. As employees are getting wage rate as on level of prices of 1-1-2006, whereas in retail market, they have to pay prevailing present abnormal high price, which means wages are always leg behind to the level of inflation in the case of developing countries. It means that there is no *wageflation* in Indian economy by higher wages but also due to other segment of excessive expenditure of the government. In Indian condition, inflation is not caused by spiraling food and fuel prices crisis, after droughts or oil crisis. Such inflation cannot be tamed by changes in the repo higher interest rates will hit industries without reducing inflation appreciably. Here monetary policy appears as relatively toothless.

POLICY OPTIONS TO ARREST CURRENT INFLATION

1. The Reserve Bank of India has acted as rule *vrs.* authority in money supply function, which has overruled basic objective of monetary policy to have price stability. Interest rate both for deposits and lending purpose is responsible for this. Fiscal policy for public expenditure programme or financial packages are decided by the government monetary policy has to manage subsequently. This means, Price targeting or inflation targeting along with steady interest rate policy is beyond the limit of the RBI.
2. The RBI is shouldered the responsibility of sustainable commodity markets. Here, interest rate mechanism and market mechanism have positive role in era of *stagflation*. It has to manage money market, commodity market and labour market
3. The RBI has to have a choice as revised Phillips curve to manage tolerable rate of unemployment and tolerable rate of price inflation. The US Federal Bank failed to manage liquidity in the economy on this ground as sub-prime crisis and financial crunch and

spread world-wide liquidity crisis for the rest of the world countries.

4. The RBI has paid price of keeping idle foreign exchange reserves. It could have utilized 25 per cent of them for infrastructure funding even after the years of mid-nineties.
5. Higher output growth rate may stop imports of foodgrains and save foreign exchange. Agro-based rural development programme may encourage alleviating poverty and unemployment.
6. For this, rural financial system needs to be economically viable and strong enough to manage and fund rural development programmes. It appears that growth-led credit and credit-led growth strategy to boost real sector in rural economy.
7. Pumping of liquidity in financial system by the RBI will not stop inflationary pressures. An industrialist or owner of a company goes in for financial fraud should be not awarded by financial package for its rehabilitation. Government funding to rehabilitate co-operatives and other public institutions need to be stopped by the RBI or a state. As India being capital-deficit country cannot afford leakage of revenue or financial scam in the economy.
8. According to Keynes, inflation would occur after full employment, which is experienced by Indian economy during the years of the seventies with under-employment and poor growth known as stagflation. For further funding by the RBI, it is necessary to bring down cost of funds and growth momentum and let economy to grow by market driven interest rates than that of administrative rates. It is equally necessary to have more transparency in the process of setting repo, reverse repo rate.
9. It is necessary to make use of easy liquidity in money and credit markets need to be utilized in fair ways not for hoarding purpose by the class of people enjoying bank credit. Political economy has allowed two NBFCs to fund for wastage of money and malpractices exercised by them.

CONCLUSION

It is clarified from the foregoing discussion that inflationary pressures are result of excess expenditure and excess credit in the economy. It is not wageflation. Very recently, Raghuram Rajan committee has suggested that the RBI should cut down its current multi-tasking, which covers exchange rates, growth and inflation and focus principally on inflation control. But in Indian condition, non-core inflation is often the dominant part of inflation. As such, monetary policy is a weak tool to curb the prices. Therefore, countries like China, Thailand, Indonesia, Vietnam, Egypt, Ethiopia and Cambodia made use of export-import policy than that of monetary policy. Current state of inflation is not due to deficit finance but largely due to public debt and borrowed fund utilized. Thus, Friedman's thesis related with trend analysis and consumption function has great relevance in western rich countries but not fit in Indian condition as growth less unemployed army is dominating. As such, income is main source for purchasing power. Neither interest rate policy nor other tools of the monetary policy proved successful to come out from global recession created by the US. Output-led growth and growth-led output policy in real sector of Indian economy appear to be more relevant in Indian condition to curb the inflationary pressures.

REFERENCES

Angedi, V.B. (2007), Glimpses of Emerging Trend in Trade and Development, Himalaya Publishing House, Mumbai.

Biotal Wang (2007), "The Nominal Income Targeting Rules of Monetary Policy and its Stability Properties in the Open Economy", *The Indian Economic Journal*, Vol. 65, No. 1.

Brahmanand, P.R. (1980), Growthless Inflation by the Means of Stockless Money, Himalaya Publishing House, Bombay.

Chaudhari, Sumitra (2008), "Inflation is the name of the game," *The Economic Times*, Ahmedabad, 25th April, p. 8.

M. Reinhart and Miguel Savastano (2003), "The Realities of Hyperinflation", *Finance and Development*, Washington, DC.

Patel, I.G. (2002), Glimpses of Indian Economy, Oxford Publishing House, New Delhi.

Peter Berunholz (2003), Monetary Regimes and Inflation, Edward Elgar, Surrey, U.K.

RBI (2008), Annual Report of the Reserve Bank of India, 2007-08, RBI, Mumbai.

Samuelson, R.J. (2008), The Great Inflation in its Aftermath, Random House, New York.

Thirwal, A.P. (1975), Inflation in Developing Countries, George Allen & Unwin.

11

Determinants of Inflation in India

An Empirical Analysis

ZAFAR AHMAD SULTAN AND SHARFUL HODA

INTRODUCTION

By the standard of many developing countries, India has been reasonably successful in maintaining an acceptable rate of inflation. Since the early eighties, inflation has not exceeded 17 per cent (measured by a year on year change in monthly wholesale price index (WPI) and has averaged about 8 per cent. While this is on par with other countries in Asian region, it compares well with an average inflation rate in all developing countries of around 35 per cent.

The reason might be that, one of the objectives of economic policy; particularly of monetary policy; in India is to maintain a reasonable degree of price stability together with ensuring adequate expansion of credit to assist economic growth. This would not only help in maintaining macroeconomic stability, but would also save the poor, who are the worst victim of inflation as they do not posses the effective inflation hedges. Therefore containing the inflation has always been considered as an important part of anti-poverty strategy in India.

The objective of the paper is to examine the factors causing change in prices in India during the reform period and comparing it with the determinants since 1970. Section gives a brief description of the theoretical foundation of inflation, examines the existing empirical literature of inflationary process in liberalized economy, the variables and the methodology, brief descriptions about the estimation procedure, empirical results and their interpretation, and conclusions of the paper.

THEORETICAL FOUNDATION OF INFLATION

The inflationary process has been a controversial topic in the literature, both theoretically as well as empirically. Number of factors acts on each other and in turn affects the price level in an economy. The precise nature of the relationship of price level with other macroeconomic variables has, despite years of research, remained an area of contention. The debate on the inflationary process in the closed economy context can be theoretically contained in these propositions:

The Monetarist School usually assumes a stable relationship between money-stock to nominal income. In their opinion 'fiscal deficit' is the root cause of the inflationary process in so far as it affects money supply. They argue that by reducing the rate of growth of base money (H or M_0), which in most cases requires cutting down the 'fiscal deficit' of the government, the rate of inflation could be brought down. Friedman argues, 'Inflation is always and everywhere a monetary phenomenon'. The role of money-financed fiscal deficits in the inflation process is theoretically well established and empirically documented

The Structuralist School, in contrast, argues that crucial sources of price rise are structural rigidities usually in the farm sector of a developing country. Excess demand drives up the price level triggering the inflationary process. Sectoral imbalances (caused by the rapid growth of the non-agricultural or industrial sector) could lead to an excess demand for wage goods and consequently it can result in rise in agricultural prices, as imports cannot come in. This is often complemented by the conflicting claims models which gives an account of the inflationary process, by which clashing claims of different social classes cannot be reconciled and inflation is argued to be a symptom of these conflicting claims (Sanyal, 1996; Bhaduri, 1986; Kalecki, 1972; Baer and Beckmann, 1974).

Cost-plus pricing is an important feature of the price formation process especially in the non-farm sector. This sector has been growing fairly rapidly in most of the developing countries. This argument is based on the cost-push factors in explaining the inflationary process. Interest rate and food prices are supposed to be the main cost transmission channels in this context.

However, in the context of the open economy, these relationships are likely to undergo significant changes and could weaken the influence of above described variables.

The openness of an economy can be defined in various ways, for example, in terms of trade to GDP ratio, lower average tariff barriers, pruned import quotas, export subsidies, no barriers to foreign investment, government procurement policies, etc. In the context of India, on the basis of all these indicators, one can safely say that India has opened up its economy to a large extent. Change in this direction in India started since 1980, but concrete steps were taken since 1991.

The mechanisms through which openness can affect the inflation outcome could be many, the important ones being the following:

1. According to 'new growth theory', openness is likely to affect inflation through its positive influence on the output, which is likely to ease the pressure on the prices (see for instance, Jin, 2000). This link could be operating mainly through—
   - Increased efficiency, which is likely to reduce costs through changes in the composition of inputs procured domestically and internationally;

- Better allocation of resources; and
- Improved capacity utilization.

2. Also increased openness could bring in foreign investment, which if channeled properly could stimulate output growth and correspondingly take further pressure off the price level.
3. As the economy opens up, the movement of goods across the border reduces the shocks to the price level due to the domestic farm sector output fluctuations. In the more open economies this is likely to diminish the price fluctuations (Sanyal, 1996; Okun, 1981; Kalecki, 1972).
4. The degree of integration of the domestic economy with the global economy could influence the level of domestic price level, as the domestic producers are likely to respond to international prices and not just to the domestic price level. This could result in upward pressure on the prices of those commodities, which usually are sold at lower than international prices in the domestic economy. The reverse is likely to happen for commodities, which are generally sold at higher than international prices. So, the net impact on domestic aggregate price level will depend on the interaction of overall effect on prices of various commodities in the domestic economy.
5. With the move towards opening up of the foreign exchange market, there has been a move away from a managed exchange rate regime towards floating exchange rate regime in many parts of the developing world. Exactly how this is going to affect the inflation outcome will depend on the degree to which the respective economies' import intensity changes in the more open trade regime, and the resultant influence on the cost structure of the various sectors of the economy.
6. With the World Trade Organization (WTO) committed to harmonization of tariff structure across countries, the import cost of a significant proportion of traded commodities is likely to go down. The

tariff barriers have been coming down in almost all countries in a synchronized manner in the last few years. This is likely to soften the impact on the price level for the member countries to the corresponding extent. However, this is going to have effect on domestic inflation rate only in the transition stage.

REVIEW OF EXISTING EMPIRICAL LITERATURE

The literature in economics on inflation and openness is relatively scant. The earliest papers by Triffin and Grudel (1962) had looked into economic performance of EEC and observed that more open economies tended to experience lower price inflation. Their explanation was that openness served as a safety valve and the domestic inflationary pressure spilled over into the BoPs in the open economy. Correspondingly this resulted in softening influence on domestic inflation.

Iyoha (1973) used a sample of 33 less developed countries and analysed the relationship for both yearly and 5-year averaged data from 1960/1 through 1964/5. The method used was OLS. The paper related inflation (proxied by rate of growth of WPI/CPI) and openness in simple bivariate framework. It was found that openness is negatively related to inflation. However, the results in the multivariate exercise were not unambiguous although openness variable always had negative sign but it was found to be significant only occasionally. Changes in income and money growth were the other explanatory variables found to be significant when used separately. Otherwise, change in income variable tended to dominate the money growth variable. This could possibly be due to the presence of high degree of multicollinearity between the two variables.

Kirkpatrick and Nixon (1977) in their comment on the paper by Iyoha (1973) argued that cut down of imports could worsen the inflationary situation. They argued that composition of imports needs to be examined to check the inflation and openness link and more reliable indicators of openness are needed for a thorough understanding of the issues involved.

IMF (1990) in a review of the literature of inflation brought in the openness variable and argued its potential influence on the inflationary process in the developing countries. The paper points out that Inflation in large part of the developing world had remained considerably higher than in the industrialized countries. In many of these countries inflation had still been a serious problem with some experiencing hyperinflationary situations. This paper besides the conventional variables, such as money growth and fiscal deficit, which influence inflation process, brought in the import price and degree of openness as other possible factors that might influence the inflationary dynamics. There was, however, no empirical or econometric estimation in the paper.

Romer (1993) argues that openness puts a check on the government's incentive to engage in unanticipated inflation, because of induced exchange rate depreciation. He demonstrated that average inflation rate to be lower for smaller and relatively more open economies. In addition, he finds this relationship to be significant, quantitatively large, and robust. This is supposed to be because the more open an economy the higher the possibility of her prices to come in alignment with the international prices. Romer's analysis started by regressing logarithm of inflation rate on openness for a cross-section of 114 countries. His results were found to hold for a wide range of countries, except for a small group of developed OECD countries. He also found that the empirical analysis finds the relationship between inflation and openness to be stronger in countries which are politically less stable and with less independent central banks. He divided the countries of his sample in 4 broad groups: first group excluded the hyperinflation countries, second group, excluded the countries whose monetary policy is tied up with that of other countries; thirdly, according to the quality of data, and excluding major oil producers; and fourthly, geographical region-wise. The results were on expected lines except for a small group of most highly developed countries (mainly OECD countries).

Lane (1997) using the same data set as Romer (1993) also found support for the above proposition of negative relationship between inflation and openness. An interesting finding was that the openness effect was stronger when country size was included as the control variable. This paper, like Romer (1993), also included the proxies for 'central bank independence' and 'political instability'. The grouping used by her was based on rich countries, OECD countries, and the overall sample.

Terra (1998) also observed similar evidence in her paper written in response to Romer (1993) but she found the negative relationship between inflation and openness to be significantly influenced by the extent of indebtedness of the country. The argument forwarded by the paper is that consider two countries with the same debt burden, therefore needing the same trade surplus to make the external transfer. Assuming identical price elasticity, the less open economy will need a larger exchange rate devaluation to generate the trade surplus. The devaluation, in turn, further tightens the internal constraint by raising the value of external liabilities in domestic currency; more resources will have to be transferred from private to the public sector. When inflation tax is the major mechanism for this transfer, a higher inflation rate will result. Hence, the less open a country is, the higher its inflation will be during a debt crisis.

Jin (2000) in his analysis of East Asian economies found openness to be an important variable for growth but fiscal policy and foreign price shocks were coming out to be even more important in his analysis, which was based on the time series data for these economies using vector auto-regression (VAR) framework.

Empirical studies of inflation in India have generally followed either a monetarist or structuralist approach. Moosa (1997), for instance, finds one to one correspondence between prices and money stock in case of Indian economy. Rao (1997) also finds similar evidence supporting monetarist approach.

In one of the papers following structuralist framework, Balakrishnan (1991) models prices of manufactures through an error-correction specification based on a mark-up pricing rule using annual data 1952-80. Labour and raw material costs are both found to be significant determinants of inflation in the industrial sector. Agricultural prices are modeled as a function of per capita output, per capita income of the non-agricultural sector, and government procurement of foodgrains through the public distribution system. Bhattacharya and Lodh (1990) too find the superiority of the structuralist over the monetarist model in explaining Indian inflation.

Mallick (1998) finds that cost-push factors are more important in causing price level than the excess demand, as the magnitude of its impact is very negligible. Price level, measured by the wholesale price index is positively and significantly affected by the domestic unit labour costs and the cost of imported inputs (measured in US dollars). This model combines both demand and supply factors and suggests a weak role of money in its influence on prices in India. However, the empirical literature in India does not report openness to be a significant factor in explaining the inflation outcome.

DATA AND METHODOLOGY

Inflation is a complex process and it is difficult to find a single empirical model that fits the circumstances of all the developing countries. It is, however, possible to identify key factors, which might influence the inflation process in different economies.

In a closed economy, price level is generally influenced by domestic factors. When an economy is opened to the world economy, change in price level takes place even when domestic variables show normal trend. This happens because in an open economy, the domestic price level and international price level are closely related and tend to equalize. The relation between the two prices could be expressed as:

$$P_i = (P_d)/(E)$$

Where P_i = International Price level

P_d = Domestic Price level

E = Exchange rate; i.e. Price of International currency in terms of Domestic Currency

Taking the rate of growth, we get

$$\Delta P_i/P_i = (\Delta P_d/P_d) - (\Delta E/E)$$

This shows that the domestic inflation minus the change in the exchange rate would be equated to international inflation. In other words, whenever there is change in any one of the three terms, for the equality to be restored adjustments would be required in at least one of the variables on the right hand side of the equation.

The trend in recent years has been towards greater opening up of the international trade in most of the developing countries. This exercise looks at the domestic price inflation and how it is influenced by the extent of openness. The openness variable is proxied by—

Trade-GDP ratio is computed from value of export of goods plus value of imports of goods as a proportion of gross domestic product (GDP), at nominal prices; and

Import-GDP ratio is computed by taking imports of goods as a proportion of gross domestic product, at nominal prices.

As discussed above, there are various other possible measures that could be used as a proxy for openness but for the sake of convenience and difficulty in obtaining long historical time series for most of these, we restricted ourselves to trade to income ratio, or import to income ratio. The former indicates the overall openness of the economy. The latter captures the impact of import on the inflationary process. Import to income ratio reveals the import penetration that represents the degree of openness: the more open an economy, the lesser the restrictions in world trade, higher will be the import penetration in the domestic economy. In addition to the openness variable/s, the other variables, which could influence the inflation outcome, were also considered. These included money stock defined as growth rate of stock of M3 (monetary variables), growth rate of agricultural output, growth rate of national income defined in terms of growth rate of GDP (output variables), and World inflation rate.

In order to examine the determinants of inflation in India, the following model has been used:

$$PI = f(GDP, Pw, M3, Agr, O)$$

Where

PI = Log of India's inflation rate (based on WPI).

GDP = Log of Growth rate of India's GDP.
Pw = Log of World Inflation rate.
M3 = Log of Growth rate of stock of money (M3).
Agr = Log of Growth rate of agricultural output.
O = Log of Openness index (measured in terms of trade GDP ratio, and Import GDP ratio separately).

Theoretically, we expect that GDP growth rate would have positive relationship with the rate of inflation as the rise in income would increase the level of aggregate demand in general and of food products in particular.

Similarly, the inflation rate in the world economy would have positive influence on the economy. A high rate of inflation in the world economy would, pull the price in the domestic market up by making the import costlier and export relatively attractive. Both these factors would lead to decrease in the availability of goods in the domestic economy, and hence rise in the general level of prices.

The influence of change in money supply, as is argued and established by many monetary economists, is also positive.

Increase in growth rate of agricultural output is generally expected to have dampening effect on the price rise by increase in supply of agricultural products (supply side effect). It may also have positive influence on prices through increase in aggregate demand in the economy because of rise in income of the countryside, who have greater propensity to spend (demand side effect).

Both the openness indices are expected to have negative influence on price level. Imports make the commodities available and reduce the shortage of goods and services in the economy, thus checks price from rising.

ESTIMATION PROCEDURE

The empirical analysis in this paper is based on time series data. But the problem with the time series data is that the data may not be stationary at level. Regressing the non-stationary variables on other non-stationary variables may sometimes give spurious results. In order to avoid that, first of all, a stationary test of these variables have been conducted.

For the purpose, Augmented Dicky-Fuller test (ADF-test) and Philips-Perron test (PP-test) were applied. Those variables, which were integrated of the same order, were included in regression equations. The stepwise regression analysis was used to find out the variables that were significantly related to the price behaviour in India. For the purpose, first inflation is regressed on each of the variables mentioned above individually. Then each time one variable is added in the equation on the basis of its AR^2. OLS method has been applied on log linear model to estimate the regression coefficients. Further, these regression equations were estimated for two time periods. One for the period extending from 1970 through 2006; and another for the period 1990 to 2006 in order to compare whether there is any difference in the determinants of inflation during the reform period and the overall period. Further, for both the time periods, the significance of openness factors has also been examined. The data has been taken from various issues of International Financial Statistics, International Monetary Fund.

RESULTS AND INTERPRETATION

The results of these equations are given in following tables from Table 1 to Table 5. Table 1 presents the result of unit root test. The results show that Inflation rate in India (P), Inflation rate in the world economy (Pw), growth rate of agriculture output (Agr), and growth rate of money supply (M3) are stationary, i.e. integrated of zero order I(0). The regression of inflation on these variables would give a long-run relationship. Further, the table shows that the growth rate of GDP (GDP), import-GDP ratio (Imp), and trade-GDP ratio (Tr) are not stationary at level. Since inflation in India; and GDP growth rate, import GDP ratio and trade GDP ratio are not integrated of the same order; we cannot have a long-run relationship between inflation and these variables.

The result of simple regression equations of inflation on world inflation, growth rate of agricultural output, and money supply for the period 1970 to 2006 and 1990 to 2006 are given in Tables 2 and 3 respectively. The Table 2 reveals that during the period 1970 to 2006, agricultural growth rate has been the

TABLE 1
Result of Unit Root Test at Level

Variables		*ADF-Test*		*PP-Test*	
		C	& TC	C	C & T
P		-5.862991	-5.893167	-4.170305	-4.478335
Agr.		-9.763782	-9.624258	-13.61555	-13.37490
Pw		-2.976638	-3.273706	-2.999677	-3.215535
M3		-4.810187	-4.731979	-6.126467	-6.278318
GDP		-0.546827	-0.571070	-0.546827	-0.571070
Tr.		0.466348	-0.990237	0.433871	-1.101723
Imp		-4.668488	-4.645581	-4.444556	-4.446522
Critical values	1%	-3.670170	-4.252879	-3.632900	-4.243644
	5%	-2.963972	-3.548491	-2.948404	-3.544284
	10%	-2.621007	-3.207094	-2.612874	-3.204627

TABLE 2
Results of Bi-variate Regression Equations (1970-2006)

Sl. No.	*Equations*	R^2	AR^2	*F*	*DW*
1.	P = 1.77 + 0.12 Agr. + 0.48AR(1)				
	(11.37) (1.98) (2.15)	0.61	0.52	6.94	2.11
2.	P = 0.60 + 0.59 Pw + 0.14 AR(1)				
	(1.61) (3.82) (0.7)	0.4	0.36	8.81	1.96
3.	P = -2.32 + 1.53 M3 + 0.39AR(1)				
	(-1.63) (3.01) (2.17)	0.34	0.29	6.70	1.88

TABLE 3
Results of Bi-variate Regression Equations (1990-2006)

Sl. No.	*Equations*	R^2	AR^2	*F*	*DW*
1.	P = 0.69 + 0.57 Pw				
	(2.62) (4.56)	0.63	0.60	20.75	1.82
2.	P = 1.61 + 0.20 Agr				
	(10.99) (2.17)	0.37	0.29	4.73	1.19
3.	P = -0.86 + 0.97 M3				
	(-0.45) (1.41)	0.13	0.07	1.99	0.66

most important factor contributing to inflation as revealed by the value of R^2. It has significant and positive relation with inflation with the coefficient value of 0.12. Normally, it is argued that inflation and agricultural growth has negative relationship, meaning thereby, that the decline in agricultural output leads to inflation by creating scarcity of agricultural products (supply side effect) and *vice-versa*. A positive relation between the two found in the case of India implies that increase in agricultural output gives more purchasing power in the hands of rural population, who have higher propensity to spend, thus causing increase in aggregate demand and hence general price level. This implies that in the case of India, demand side factor dominates the supply side. This is in line with the India's experience that despite the increase in agricultural production and achieving self-sufficiency in it, the price does show any sign of declining trend.

The result also shows that world inflation rate and money supply have positive and significant relation with inflation in India. On the other hand, the result for the post-reform period

TABLE 4

Results of Step-wise Regression Equations (1970-2006)

Variables	*Model 1*	*Model 2*	*Model 3*	*Model 4*
C	1.07 (3.31)	1.29 (0.61)	0.84 (2.75)	-1.71 (-1.35)
Pw	0.29 (2.24)	0.30 (1.88)	0.41 (3.13)	0.34 (2.71)
Agr.	0.13 (2.11)	0.13 (1.92)	0.14 (2.28)	0.16 (2.79)
M3		-0.08 (-0.10)		0.95 (2.07)
AR(1)	0.23 (0.88)	0.22 (0.82)		
R^2	0.74	0.74	0.51	0.61
AR^2	0.64	0.58	0.46	0.54
F	7.40	4.87	10.00	9.23
D.W.	2.18	2.17	0.82	1.16

TABLE 5
Results of Step-wise Regression Equations (1990-2006)

Variables	*Model 1*	*Model 2*
C	0.75 (3.30)	-1.33 (-1.01)
Pw	0.42 (4.08)	0.40 (4.19)
Agr.	0.19 (3.57)	0.20 (4.16)
M3		0.75 (1.59)
AR(1)		
R^2	0.81	0.87
AR^2	0.76	0.80
F	15.29	13.27
D.W.	2.22	2.59

shows that world price has been the most important factor influencing the price behaviour in India. This is followed by growth rate of agriculture output. Both these factors have significant and positive relation with inflation in India. The relationship between money supply and inflation has not been found significant, though the sign is positive. Several times India witnessed this kind of manifestations. For example, during the Janata Government rule despite the increase in money supply the price kept declining.

The result of multiple regression equations for both the time periods, i.e. for the period 1970 to 2006 and 1990 to 2006 (given in Tables 4 and 5) shows that inflation rate in India is significantly related to world inflation rate and growth in agricultural output, but it does not have significant relation with growth in money supply.

CONCLUSION

From the above analysis we find that inflation rate, growth rate of agricultural output and of money supply are stationary, whereas, growth rate of GDP and openness index are non-stationary. Therefore, regression equation of inflation on these two would be meaningless. Further, regression equations of inflation on inflation rate in the world economy, growth rate of agricultural output and of money supply shows that for both the periods, world inflation rate and growth rate of agricultural output have significant relations with price level in India. But money supply does not have significant relation with inflation, though the sign is in line with the earlier studies, which finds a positive and significant relationship between the two. Further, a positive relationship between growth rate of agricultural output and inflation is contrary to the findings of earlier studies.

References

Baer, Werner and Welch, John, H. (1987), "The Resurgence of Inflation in Latin America: Editor's Introduction", *World Development;* 15(8), August, pp. 989-90.

Balakrishnan, P. (1991), "Pricing and Inflation in India", *Oxford University Press,* New Delhi.

Barro, R. (1991), "Economic Growth in cross-section of Countries", *Quarterly Journal of Economics,* May, pp. 407-43.

Bhaduri, A. (1986), "Macroeconomics: the Dynamics of Commodity Production", Macmillan, London, (revised Indian edition, 1990).

Bhattacharya, B.B. (1985), "Public Expenditure, Inflation and Growth: A Macro-Economic Analysis for India", *Oxford University Press.* New Delhi.

Cukierman, *et. al.* (1992), "Measuring the Independence of Central Banks and its Effects on Policy Outcomes", *World Bank Economic Review,* September, pp. 353-98.

International Monetary Fund, "International Financial Statistics", *IMF,* various issues.

Iyoha, Milton A. (1977), "Inflation and "Openness" in Less Developed Economies: A Cross-Country Analysis: Reply", *Economic Development and Cultural Change;* 26(1), Oct., pp. 153-55.

Jin, Jang (2000), "Openness and Growth : An Interpretation of Empirical Evidence from East Asian Countries", *Journal of International Trade and Economic Development,* pp. 5-17.

Kalecki, M. (1972), "Selected Essays on the Economic Growth of the Socialist and the Mixed Economy", *Cambridge University Press,* London, pp. 1-37.

Kirkpatrick, C.H. and Nixon, F.I. (1977), "Inflation and Openness in Less Developed Economies: A Cross-Country Analysis: Comment", *Economic Development and Cultural Change*; 26(1), Oct. 1977, pp. 147-52.

Lane, Philip, R. (1997), "Inflation in Open Economies", *Journal of International Economics*, Vol. 42, pp. 327-47.

Mallick, S.K. (1998), "A Dynamic Macroeconometric Model For Short-Run Stabilisation In India", Warwick University Working Paper Series No. 523, available at warwick.ac.uk/fac/soc/Economics/research/papers/ecps.pdf

Moosa, I.A. (1997), "Testing the long-run neutrality of money in a developing economy: the case of India", *Journal of Development Economics*, Vol. 53, No. 1, pp. 139-156.

Okun, A.M. (1981), "Prices and Quantities: A Macroeconomic Analysis", *The Brookings Institution*, Washington D.C.

Rao, M.J.M. (1997), "Monetary Economics: An Econometric Investigation", in K.L. Krishna (ed.) *Econometric Applications in India*, Oxford University Press, Delhi.

Romer, David (1998), "A New Assessment of Openness and Inflation: Reply", *Quarterly Journal of Economics*, Vol. 113(2), pp. 649-52.

Sanyal, Amal (1996), "Access to credit and the inflation process in a developing economy", *Journal of Post-Keynesian Economics, Summer*, Vol. 18, No. 4, pp. 621-31.

Terra, Cristina T. (1998), "Openness and Inflation: A New Assessment", *Quarterly Journal of Economics*, May, pp. 641-52.

Triffin, R. and Grudel, H. (1962), "The Adjustment Mechanism to Differential Rates of Monetary Expansion among the Countries of the European Economic Community", *Review of Economics and Statistics*, Vol. 44, November, pp. 486-91.

12

Inflationary Trends and Measures Taken to Curb

S.P. SAHA AND BISHNU ROY

In 1995, 13 years ago, the Indian economy after having lived through the trauma of having to mortgage gold to fulfil debt obligations, the country had built up ample forex reserves of over $ 20 billion. The gross domestic product (GDP) growth rate, which was 1.4 per cent in 1991-92, had increased to 6.4 per cent in 1994-95. This had resulted in a spurt in demand for steel, cement and other consumer items. Companies had gone for huge investment outlays to expand their production capacity. But the euphoria did not last and economy faced suddenly with double digit inflation during first six to eight months of year 2008. By 1995, financial institutions like IDBI, ICICI and IFCI were raising funds at 16 per cent from the market and lending to corporate at 18 per cent.

The stock market which had touched an all time high of 4500 in June 1994, fell back to 3300 by June 1995. Facing a bearish stock market and soaring interest rates. Companies struggled to fund their ambitions plans even as the money supply tap went dry. By 1997-98 economic growth fell to the much derived 'Hindu Rate of Growth' of 4.3 per cent by 2006. Indian economy maintained a 9 per cent growth rate and forex reserves rose to over $300 billion. But there are troubling signs of raising inflation in spite of booming sensex which was on a triumphant charge till January, is now beating an equally dramatic retreat. There were initial public offers worth almost Rs. 1 lakh crore in the pipeline but companies were understandably apprehensive of tapping the capital markets at this stage.

The global slowdown and oil price crisis made the situation worsen and prices of food items and essential commodities like steel and cement were soaring and showed little sign of coming under control, "A slow down in economic growth is imminent, since the RBI is bound to pursue a tight money policy to combat inflation" (Sonal Verma, 2008). The high inflation rate will force RBI to take measures to increase the interest rate to capital demand. This in turn, will affect the profitability of companies and economic growth on a whole. In 2008-09, GDP growth might sustain itself at over 8 per cent, but in the following year, if inflationary pressure continues like this because of global developments, there will be no way to stop the growth rate from coming down (D.K. Joshi, 2008).

The saving grace is well and the saving rate in India is at high 35 per cent. And as interest rates rise, so will the temptation for investors to save money. At an investment capital-output ratio (capital inputs required to generate one percentage point of output growth) of around 4, that should help the economy to sustain a growth rate of 9 per cent for now, consumption demand too has defied dire predictions and remained strong.

GLOBAL CRISIS AND INFLATIONS

This is difficult to fully comprehend the depth of global crisis in a country like India that will record growth of around 7 per cent for fiscal year 2008 at a time when most developed countries are shrinking. Some sectors like exports, real estate, textiles, IT and transport equipment have been affected severely. But overall, the impact has been limited, thanks in no small measures to the prompt and sustained measures taken by the RBI and the government. The markets have stabilized and decline of the rupee has been arrested. The stock market has started recovering, the Satyam shock not withstanding, and the flow of credit is reviving.

The important question is what more should the government do now to contain the expected decline in growth in fiscal 2009. Critics point out that most of the steps so far have been monetary measures to ease the supply of credit, few fiscal measure to reduce inflation. Actually, a very substantial fiscal stimulus has been provided through the supplementary demand for grants in September 2008 and a second supplementary demand in December 2008.

INFLATION AND OIL BEARS

What actually is needed to battle inflation is a bunch of bad time bears. Oil or rather the rising price of oil at the end of year 2008 had been widely recognized as one of the main culprits responsible for inflation in India and elsewhere. The other, and possibly major part responsible for inflation, is speculation. The weak US dollar and market uncertainties across the globe have increasingly caused many investors to put their money into commodity futures, which include oil.

Market analyst Arjun Narain Murty has formulated a 'Super-spike' theory of oil prices by which it was predicted that the price crude oil would go $ 150-200 a barrel but Murthy again reveled that many parts of the world-including America, the planets biggest gas guzzler-individuals and organizations were figuring out ways including lifestyle change strategies would cut down on fuel consumption. What long-term lifestyle changes would that motivate in the most energy-prodigal country in the world? Government of India had imposed a hefty import duty and then energy conservation sector would need the oil bears: long-term speculators and the price of oil would decline to $ 75 a barrel and start short selling oil future. This has made a negative impact on oil futures and the price went down at the beginning of 2009.

By raising the repo and cash reserve ratio rates by 50 basic points each, the RBI had taken a firm step towards showing its willingness to fight inflation. The double stroke anti-inflationary measure by the central bank has tightened liquidity in the system and stock market had read out the RBI's move as a sign of the government determination to confront double-digit inflation. A tight monetary policy was imposed to avoid any further intensification of inflationary pressures and to firmly anchor inflationary expectations. Government took the priority to douse the fire of inflation as effectively as possible with all means of disposal. Since the current inflation was essentially a global phenomenon, driven largely by sky-high oil prices, controlling money supply alone could not have proved an effective measure to control inflation. If inflation is essentially driven by spike in oil prices, the RBI could have let the rupee rise a bit in time so that the cost of importing commodities, particularly oil, became cheaper.

MESURES TO BEAT INFLATION

In this context of inflation and oil bears, what had caused the inflation? And could it be tamed? Following measures are taken to beat inflation:

PHENOMENAL RISE OF WORLDWIDE OIL PRICE

Not because oil consumption has jumped all of a sudden but because speculators have become active in the oil futures market. We can not ban speculation or future trading but we can insulate ourselves from the oil shock. To achieve this, we should immediately allow the rupee to become stronger.

We should also curtail our energy consumption; Indian consumers consume three times more energy as percentage of GDP than the word average. Next is the transport sector where the railways consume only one-third the energy needed to move on one ton of material over a kilometer by road. The private sector should be encouraged to generate energy from renewable sources like solar, wind, waves, tides, geothermal hydro biomass and feed it into the grid.

FOREIGN INVESTMENT IN MANUFACTURING SECTOR

India has a foreign exchange reserve of $300 billion which is enough to meet out import needs for the next two years. China has an import cover of 11 months and Germany and US for few months. India's reserves have swollen due to capital inflows rather than exports exceeding important or profit earned in exports.

FOOD SITUATION

Higher food process can act as an incentive to farmers leading to increased production. Food prices then automatically come down. In every city or town some land should be earmarked for direct sales. In the mean time, food stamps should be issued to the poor to cushion the impact of high food prices.

SPECULATION IN COMMODITIES

Steel producers have formed a cartel and have started overcharging. The government owned SAIL need not become a part of cartel and supplied steel a reasonable prices and garnered a bigger market share. It was a matter of surprise that government was not asking SAIL to stabilize prices while making reasonable profit.

IMPROVING POOR INFRASTRUCTURE

If infrastructure improves, the cost of goods and services will come down. For this purpose, the government should allow infrastructure companies to float tax free infrastructure bonds. No question should be asked about the source of money being invested in these bonds. All those with black money would then be tempted to invest in these bonds. At the same time government should do away with Rs. 100, Rs. 500 and Rs. 1000 currency notes giving the holders of these notes an option to either deposit them in their bank account or pay income tax or invest it in tax free infrastructure bonds. The rich would be forced to transact all business through banking channel or credit cards. The poor would use coins or notes upto Rs. 50. Black money would instantly vanish immediately reducing inflation.

The current inflation was imported and fuelled by speculation. Developed nations were exporting inflation to Indian economy because these countries NR's no longer wished to invest in manufacturing sectors. Their idle funds were being used for speculation and for investing in commodities. Our economy was not able to fight such imported inflation by increasing domestic interest rates or reducing domestic money supply while giving free run to foreign money supply and that would result in stagnation of the economy.

STIMULUS PACKAGE AND INFLATION

Year 2009 could test India's economic pain threshold more than 2008 did. That's the challenge the governments second stimulus package that the RBI's fourth round of rate cuts have sought to address. The package has forward looking components where reality and infrastructure gain from eased rules on external commercial borrowings. Both sectors are key to stimulating investment and general economic activity with a raised cape on corporate bonds, FIIs can invest more in India and recent capital flight of over $ 13.5 billion mandates innovative ways to coax back overseas investors. Also, a deeper debt market is good for businesses seeking resources. These would make the ways to reduce inflation.

This package followed much awaited RBI rate cuts. The repo-RBIs lending rate to banks—and reverse repo—the rate it offers banks for depositing surplus funds—were cut to 5.5 per cent and 4.4 per cent respectively. These incentives banks to lend rather than tó park money. The cash-reserve ratio—money banks must keep in reserve—was also slashed to lubricate the system. Credit starved consumers and industry have reason to smile since banks have less ground for continued risk-wariness. India's interest rates are one of the highest in the world and can afford further trimming to lift demand, more so since inflation is at a nine month low of 6.38 per cent and expected to fall further.

Economists said that they had predicated the inflation rate to fall further because of a number of reasons, including the tight monetary policy adopted by the central banks in the beginning of New Year 2009, and supply factors. The reduction in inflation was expected as agriculture production has started reaching the markets now and reduction in fuel prices has also helped controlling inflation. It is also expected the inflation rate to come down further by 2 percentage points by next few months.

The government has also given liquidity support to infrastructure financing firms. State can access additional market borrowings for capital sending. Pushing infrastructure will generate economic activity in the short-term and is necessary for growth sustenance and investment friendliness in the long-term. Low and middle income housing a huge unmet demand—will get a fillip with states being asked to release land for projects. There are goodies for the export, auto, steel and cement sectors too, making for a please all package whose effectiveness will depend on quick, targeted government spending. Even if modest IMF-world bank or Goldman Sochs forecasts turn out right, India's growth would still be healthy at over 5.5 per cent compared to the world's recession hit countries. Fighting economic slowdown is as much a question of curbing inflation as of coming months.

CONCLUSION

Declining the prices of crude oil has helped India to manage the inflation rate. The trade deficit will be 10.4 per cent of GDP in the current year. The government has intended to tackle the temporarily inflation by demand compression and by raising interest rates. Even at the best times such a policy involves walking a tightrope. Having allowed the trade deficit to become as large as we have implementing such a policy will require all the skills that the policy-makers can muster. The choice is between an orderly retreat and market driven scuttle. Of course, going by past experience, nothing of the sort will happen.

References

Times of India, January 5, 2009.
Times of India, January 26, 2009.
Times of India, July 18, 2008.
Yojna, Budget Issue.

13

Inflation in India
Causes and Measures

SHAILESH KUMAR AND RATNESH KUMAR

INTRODUCTION

Inflation and global meltdown are the two things that are most rigorously discussed among politicians, academicians and public in general. Different people attribute different reasons for inflation. The Deputy Chairman, Planning Commission Prof. Montek Singh Ahluwalia is of the opinion that inflation is prevailing all over the world. Being integrated to the world economy in a globalize world is bound to bear the adversities being faced by the rest of the world. Even a country like china is facing the problem of inflation. George Bush, the President of USA owed it to rise in income of middle class who have higher propensity to spend on food items leading to rise in prices of food products and overall prices. Mr. Sharad Pawar, the Agricultural Minister of Union Government advised to control export of foodgrains from India to control inflation.

Rest of the paper is structured as follows. The theoretical foundation of inflation, the trend of inflation since 1980, the causes of inflation, policy measures, and conclusion.

THEORETICAL FOUNDATION OF INFLATION

The Classical Economists held the view that if demand is greater than supply this will lead to inflation. But this is not true. Since 1970 in India we are not only self-sufficient in food grains but also exporting. For example, the foodgrains, production in the year 2007-08 is estimated at 219.3 million tonnes. The production of cereals is expected at 205 million tonnes in 2007-08. The production of pulses is expected to remain almost at the 2006-07 level. The production of the oil seeds estimated to reach to 27.2 million tonnes. The production of cash crops particularly cotton is likely to remain buoyant. (Economic Survey, 2007-08, Government of India, Ministry of Finance, p. 15)

Our total exports have increased from US $ 18477 million in 1990-91 to US $ 128083 million in 2006-07. Thus both, our production and exports are on the rise. Exports as a percentage of GDP has increased from 5.8 per cent in 1990-91 to 14 per cent in 2006-07. These factors point to the fact that inflation in India is not because of supply shortage. (Economic Survey, Government of India, 2007-08, pp. 111-12)

Neo-Classical Economists such as Fisher contend that increase in money supply leads to increase in prices assuming 'V' (velocity of money circulation) and 'T' (total transactions) as constant. But this theory is developed only with reference to full employed countries. Moreover, there are several empirical studies, which showed that increase, or decrease in money supply does not lead to changes in the prices. There are instances in Indian Economy where prices have decreased even though money supply increased. (This was prevalent during the Janata Government rule in India).

Thus neither the increase in money supply nor the shortage of foodgrains supply is the only cause for present inflation in India. In fact for the last so many years we are maintaining the buffer stocks of foodgrains, part of which was eaten by rats. The procurement of rice in the year 2006-07 is of the order of 250.8 lakh tonnes whereas the procurement of wheat in the year 2007-08 has reached to 111.3 lakh tonnes. As on January 2008 we had 19.2 lakh tonnes of rice and wheat as buffer stocks. (Economic Survey, 2007-08, Governmentof India, Ministry of Finance, pp. 176-77). When this is the situation of production and existence of buffer stocks, there is no reason for the prevalence of inflation.

TRENDS OF PRICE IN INDIA

Price Movement during the Eighties

The Congress Party, which returned to power in January 1980, regarded inflation as its number one problem. Initially the price situation appeared to be hopeless. The poor agricultural crop of 1979-80 and the consequent adverse effect on industrial production and the hike in oil prices by 130 per cent in 1980 alone were responsible for boosting the price level still further (Table 3).

The wholesale price index (WPI) rose by 38 points in 1980-81—an increase of 17.4 per cent over the previous year. A vigorous anti-inflationary policy kept the rise in prices to moderate levels. The demand and supply management of the Government during the Sixth Plan (1980-85) was largely

TABLE 1

Price Movement during the Sixth Plan

(1970-71=100)

Year	*WPI of all commodities*	*% Variation over the previous year*
1980-81	256	17.4
1981-82	281	9.8
1982-83	289	2.9
1983-84	316	9.4
1984-85	338	7.0

Source : Compiled from Government of India, Economic Survey, 1988-89.

successful in containing the prices. The annual rate of increase in prices during this period ranged around 7 per cent.

Whenever inflationary pressures were high (as for instance during 1980-81 and since January 1983) the Government of India was prompt in taking anti-inflationary measures on both demand and supply side. On the demand side, Government made a series of adjustments in the cash-reserve ratio of the commercial banks to check the growth of liquidity in the banking system. The commercial banks were also asked to confine their lending operations within certain limits. In January 1984, the Government announced its decision to curtail public expenditure by 3 to 5 per cent, imposed a temporary ban on fresh Government recruitment, and so on. The objective of these monetary and fiscal measures was to check the increase in the volume of money supply in the country and to check effective demand.

On the supply side, the Government attempted to increase the supply of goods and services through both short-term and long-term measures. Short-term measures included larger releases of wheat, rice, sugar and edible oils through the public distribution system and imports of foodgrains and edible oils to augment domestic availability. Long-term measures included steps taken to increase production in critical areas.

During Seventh Plan period (1985-90), the wholesale prices moved upward rather steadily. The annual rate of inflation during this period ranged between 4.7 per cent (1985-86) to 9.4 per cent (1987-88) and averaged 7 per cent. The pressure on prices was due to the shortfall in production of essential agricultural commodities. In order to control inflationary rise of prices, during the Seventh Plan period, RBI tightened selective credit controls and took certain measures to mop up excess liquidity. The availability of large stocks of rice and wheat, built over many years was effectively used to combat drought and inflation. The food reserves were used to supply foodgrains to the lower income groups through public distribution system, to special employment programmes, relief programmes, etc. The Government took recourse to large imports of edible oils and pulses, rice and sugar to maintain adequate supplies. For some essential commodities, appropriate price bands were determined and suitable market intervention operations were undertaken to maintain stability of prices. By and large, inflationary situation was under control during the 1980's that is, during the Sixth and the Seventh Plans.

TABLE 2

Price Situation during the Seventh Plan (1985-90)

(1981-82=100)

Year	*Wholesale Price Index*	*Annual increase (%)*
1984-85	120	6.0
1985-86	125	4.9
1986-87	133	4.7
1987-88	144	10.7
1988-89	154	5.7
1989-90	166	8.1

Source : Economic Survey, (1992-93).

PRICE SITUATION IN RECENT YEARS

The price rise since the beginning of 1990 was almost engineered by the Government itself: through deliberately raising administered prices and indirect taxes. The increase in the prices of foodgrains on mere political considerations and the gulf-surcharge which raised the prices of petroleum products to an unprecedented level in one single jump were the other factors behind the rise in prices during the 1990's. Prices rose rapidly during 1990-91 and 1991-92 and the average annual rate of inflation were 10.3 per cent and 13.7 per cent respectively.

The inflation rate was controlled since then because of a better performance by the agricultural sector as also because of the macro-economic corrections adopted by the Narasimha Rao Congress Government, including reduction in the fiscal deficit and the resultant control in the expansion of money supply.

The price situation, however, took a severe turn from August 1993. The annual rate of inflation started rising again mainly because of heavy fiscal deficit resulting in expansion of money supply with the people. To this was added the rise in administered prices of sensitive goods. The double-digit inflation continued for the latter part of 1994-95. Since then, the inflationary situation came under control with a noticeable decline in the prices of primary food articles as well as manufactured food products. In fact, the average rate of inflation during the last year of the Eighth Plan (1992-97) had declined to 5 per cent. The improvement in the price situation was particularly welcome to the poorer sections of the society, as some items of mass consumption like cereals, pulses and edible oils actually registered a drop in their prices.

The price situation was stable and largely comfortable during the Ninth Plan (1997-2002) period and the first two years of the Tenth Plan period (see Table 3).

It would be clear from Table 3 that the annual rate of inflation (average of 52 weeks) was around 4 per cent except during 1998-99 and 2000-01. In fact, the annual average rate of inflation was 3.3 per cent (the lowest rate for many years) during 1999-2000 and 2001-02.

Although WPI increased by 7.1 per cent during 2000-01, but during 2001-02 and 2002-03, the increase in WPI was controlled and it averaged 3.5 per cent during 2003-04, WPI increased by 5.5 per cent. On the whole, it can be stated that during 1998-99 and 2003-04, the average increase in WPI was of the order of 4.6 per cent, which cannot be considered as inflationary. However since 2004-05, inflation rate once again started rising, but still can be said to under control, when we compare it with the arte in many of the developing countries.

During 2004-05, inflation rate has accelerated and as on 7th August 2004, it was 7.96 per cent compared to the corresponding period last year. This has unbalanced the economic equilibrium of the country. The main factors responsible for the situation are: scarcity of rains in some parts of the country and conditions of flood in some other parts; a sharp increase in the international price of oil to $ 50 per barrel which forced the government to increase oil prices-both petrol and diesel. Since 70 per cent of the total demand for oil is met

TABLE 3
Price Situation after 1990
(Average of 52 weeks)

Year	*Wholesale Price Indian*	*Annual Rate of Inflation*
	1981-82=100	
1990-91	182.7	10.3
1991-92	207.8	13.7
1992-93	228.7	10.1
1993-94	247.8	8.4
	1993-94=100	
1994-95	112.6	12.6
1995-96	121.6	8.0
1996-97	127.2	4.6
1997-98	132.8	4.4
1998-99	140.7	5.9
1999-2000	145.3	3.3
2000-01	155.7	7.1
2001-02	161.3	3.6
2002-03	166.8	3.4
2003-04	175.9	3.5
2004-05	187.3	6.5
2005-06	195.6	6.7
2006-07	206.2	5.4

Source : Government of India, Economic Survey, (2007-08).

by imports, it resulted in a considerable strain on the national economy.

CAUSES FOR THE RISE IN PRICES IN INDIA

Inflation in any country is the product of many factors acting upon each other. Recent rise in price level in India is not the result of any one set of factors like demand-pull, cost-push or structural factors. In fact a strong inflationary pressure has been built into the Indian economy for a long time partly through ever mounting demand on the one side and inadequate rise in supply, on the other. The planning process since 1951 has accentuated the inflationary situation in India. The expanding demand for goods and services is due to the rapid multiplication of our population, rising money incomes, expansion in money supply and liquidity in the country, rising volume of black money and continuous rise in demand for goods and services due to periodic wars, rapid economic development, etc.

Now, supply of goods and services too rose but the rise in supply has not been proportionate and matched the rise in demand; this is due to monsoon agriculture, use of backward technology, bottlenecks in transport and power and shortages of various inputs. At any given time there was demand supply imbalance; that was somehow managed by the government and brought the demand and supply in equilibrium to stabilize the price level.

A. Demand-Pull Factors

(i) *Mounting Government Expenditure*: Government expenditure has been steadily and continuously increasing over the years. The total expenditure of both Central and State Governments including Union Territories had risen from nearly Rs. 740 crores in 1950-51 to Rs. 37,000 crores in 1980-81 and nearly Rs. 12,15,329 crores in 2006-07. In a predominantly agricultural economy like India, big programmes of economic development involving huge public investments have been undertaken. The annual average rate of investment under the five year plans has risen from Rs. 1,000 crores in the 1950's to Rs. 2,000 crores during the 1960's to Rs. 7,000 crores in the 1970's, Rs. 30,000 crores in the 1980's and to over Rs. 80,000 crores during the 1990s and Rs. 3,00,000 crores during the Tenth Plan Period (2002-07), and the is expected to be more than Rs. 700,000 crores during Eleventh Plan. Not only development expenditure has been rising, but also non-development expenditure has been rising at much more rapid rate. Mounting Government expenditure implies a growing public demand for goods and services and thus, is an important factor for the rise in prices. Besides, continuous increase in Government expenditure has the effect of putting in large money incomes in the hands of the general public-expenditures of the Government becomes income for the people, thus stocking the fire of inflation.

(ii) *Deficit Financing and increase in money supply:* The Government of India is responsible for adopting deficit financing as a method of financing was quite modest in the first three plans (Rs. 330 crores to Rs. 1,130 crores), the magnitude of deficit financing rose rapidly from the Fourth Plan onwards.

Mounting Government expenditure financed through deficits directly pushes up the money supply in the country and consequently pushes up the public demand for goods and services. Money supply with the public (M) consisting of coins and currency notes and demand deposits of the public with commercial banks had gone up from Rs. 7,340 crores in 1970-71 to Rs. 5,73,140 crores during 2003-04.

More important than money supply with the people is the total volume of liquidity with the people, i.e. aggregate monetary resources (M3) of the public consisting of M1 plus time deposits with the banks had increased by 185 times. This enormous increase in money supply and monetary resources with the general public has a direct influence on the level of effective demand and therefore on the level of prices. The following equation manifests the relationship between price index (wholesale price Index) and supply of money (M3)

$$\text{Log}(P) = -5.73 + 0.76 \log(M3)$$
$$(-34.32)\quad(54.90)$$
$$R^2 = 0.99,\ AR^2 = 0.99,\ F = 3014.2$$

The t-value (given in parenthesis) and F-value shows

that price index and money supply is significantly related to each other in India during the period 1970-71 to 2006-07.

Thus money supply is an important factor for any spectacular rise in prices in all countries. Without monetary expansion, inflation cannot be sustained at all for any length of time. India is no exception to this. The Government of India has been responsible for the inflationary situation in the country through its policy of deficit financing and the State Governments contributed their share through persistent financial indiscipline, reckless expenditure and unauthorized over-drafts.

(iii) *Role of Black Money:* It is well known that there is large accumulation unaccounted money in the hands of income-tax evaders, smugglers, builders and corrupt politicians and government servants estimated at Rs. 6,00,000 crores in 1997-98. There is considerable slush money with politicians and Government servants, especially those dealing with licensing, registration, collection of taxes, etc. A large part of the unaccounted money is used in buying and selling of real estate in urban areas, extensive hoarding and black marketing in many essential and inflation-sensitive goods, such as sugar, edible oils, etc. It is difficult to estimate the amount of black money or the precise influence of this money in pushing up prices but there is no denying the fact that one the important factors responsible for inflationary pressures in recent years is the existence and the pernicious role of black money.

(iv) *Uncontrolled growth of population:* While discussing the role of demand-pull factors for inflation in India, we should emphasizes the pressure of growing population on aggregate demand and on the price level. The Planning Commission realized this fact quite early when it accepted that the major explanation for the continued up trend of wholesale prices during the Second Plan was undoubtedly the rising pressure of population and of money incomes.

"Increase in population by 18 to 19 million every year implies continued increase in demand for food stuffs and other materials. It is the continually rising population, which is responsible for the persistent gap between demand and supply, in almost all consumer goods and services, thus exerting continuous perssure on prices. It is indeed a pity that both the monetarists and the structuralists either ignore or under play the effect of the growth of population on prices. In fact, the problem of prices for that matter, every problem in India—cannot be solved satisfactorily, unless the growth of population is checked.

B. Cost-Push Factors

If supply of goods and services can be increased to correspondence with every increase in demand, price level will tend to stable. In the First Plan period, prices demand pull factors were exerting pressure on prices—increase in population, increase in investment, increase in Government expenditure and deficit financing. But the increase in production in agricultural goods was so much that there was no rise in prices; prices actually declaimed. Prices however rose whenever the production of foodgrains and other consumer goods declined or was stagnant.

(i) *Fluctuations in output and supply:* In this connection, after a record production of 108 million tonnes in 1970-71, foodgrains production declined to 97 millions tonnes in the next year—a fall of 11 million tonnes. After touching a record output of 132 declined to 110 tonnes in the next year—a decline of 22 million tonnes in just one year.

In 1983-84 foodgrains production touched a high level of 152.4 million tonnes but as a result of drought, it fell sharply to 138.4 million tonnes in 1987-88. In 1996-97 again, foodgrains production reached a high level of 199 million tonnes, but fell to 192 million tonnes in 1997-98. Again in 1999-2000, foodgrains production rose to a level of 209.8 million tonnes, but declined to 199.6 million tonnes in 2000-01. In 2001-02 foodgrains production touched the peak level of 212 million tonnes, but in 2002-03, it sharply declined to 174.2 million tonnes in 2003-04. Such fluctuations in the output of foodgrains in certain years thus were a major factor in the rise of foodgrains prices as well as of general prices. Likewise, we may also refer to the fact that the supply of manufactured goods, did not increase adequately in certain periods. Power breakdowns, strikes and lockouts and shortage of transport facilities are major factors for lower rate of production of manufactured goods with ever rising demand for manufactured products, the producers are often in a position to push up the prices of their products.

Apart from fluctuations in agricultural production, market arrivals have also tended to be erratic. In fact, the upward pressure on agricultural prices is also due to large hoarding by farmers, and boarding and speculation in foodgrains by traders and black marketers. At one time, only middlemen did hoarding but now farmers have also joined the traders in this vicious game. With increased credit facilities from the co-operative societies and commercial banks, even small farmers have now more holding capacity. They hold on to their stock in anticipation of higher prices.

(ii) *Taxation*, as a factor in rising costs. Cost-push factors consist mainly of rise in wages, profit margins and rise in other costs. In this connection the government and the public sector were also responsible, to a large extent, for pushing up the price level in the country. With every budget, the government imposed fresh commodity taxes and gave an opportunity to the trading classes to raise the prices, often more than the levy of the taxes.

(iii) *Administrated Price:* The public sector enterprises too were continuously raising the prices of their problems and services which generally consititute raw materials for other industries. A good example is the Railways which have been regularly raising fares and freight rates in the last few years. Likewise there has been regular upward revision of several administered prices such as those of petrol, diesel, steel cement, coal, etc. pushing up the price level further. Every rise in administered prices adds fuel to the inflationary potential in the country.

(iv) *Hike in oil prices and global inflation:* Serious inflationary pressure were also created because of the sharp like in the price of crude oil since September 1973 and the consequent upward revision of the prices of oil and oil-based goods. In 1980 alone, there was 130 per cent increase in all fuel prices by the OPEC. The gulf-surcharge which raised the prices of petroleum products to an unprecedented level in one single jump is major cause for rise in prices during 1990-91. Prices of petrol and diesal are changed frequently according to international prices of oil crude.

C. Other Factors

The failure of the Government policy on the price front at various times was serious factor in the inflationary rise in prices. We can cite specific cases. In 1973 the Government nationalised the wholesale trade in wheat along with a threat to introduce a similar measure for rice. This measure completely upset the normal trade and the price of open market wheat shot up. At the same time the Government failed to procure adequate amount of foodgrains for the public distribution system, nor was it able to import the necessary quantity from foreign countries.

The Government of India has generally followed a highly vacillating and anti-peasant policy in fixing procurement prices. This is equally true in fixing and controlling prices of such essential goods as sugar, properly enforced thus giving great scope for rampant black-marketing to exit, for the benefit of the traders.

There is now a strong agricultural lobby in India which azures for the dropping of all farm support prices on the one hand, and all sops to farmers in the form of subsidized fertilizers and free or highly subsidized, etc. trinity and irrigation water, on the other. This line of thinking is based on the following arguments:

- The Indian farmers have come of age and need no more artificial supports for their products and for their inputs.
- Support prices to major cereals and sugar have led to serious distortions in crop pattern in the country. This has resulted in excessive production of major cereals and water guzzling sugarcane at the expense of major cereals, pulse and oilseeds.
- Price support programmes and control of agricultural prices have generally worked in favour of the urban consumers at the expense of the rural folk.

REASONS FOR CURRENT PRICE RISE

The reasons for the current rise in price are building up of inflationary pressure and mismatch in demand and supply conditions.

On the demand side, large capital inflows exerted pressure on liquidity conditions. On the supply side, shortfall in the domestic availability of wheat, pulses and edible oils in 2006-07 aggravated mismatch. The production of wheat averaged 69 million tonnes during 2004-06. Lower production led to lower procurement and decline in the carryover stocks, which together resulted in a build up of inflationary expectations. This got compounded by a global decline in output and stocks, which was reflected in wheat prices of US SRW wheat averaging US $ 345 per tonne in December 2007 compared to an average of US $ 136 per tonne during Jan.-Dec. 2005, US $ 159 in Jan.-Dec. 2006 and US $ 239 in Jan.-Dec. 2007. So is the case with production of pulses and oilseeds.

Further, increase in international crude oil prices from an average of US $ 38/bbl in 2004 to US $ 54 in 2005 and to US

$ 70 in June 2006 necessitated an upward revision in prices of petrol and diesel in domestic market led to further rise in price level in the country.

CONTROL OF INFLATION IN INDIA

A wide range of measures have been are being adopted to ensure stable conditions as well as to prevent speculators from taking an undue advantage of the conditions of scarcity. Since the price situation is the outcome of shortages in basic goods and services and a rapid growth in money supply and bank credit, various types of measures relating to money supply, pricing and distribution of commodities have been pressed into service.

DEMAND MANAGEMENT

The price policy since 1973-74 has relied predominantly on fiscal and monetary measures with a view to check the demand of the general public for goods and services.

(i) *Fiscal measures:* The Government of India has generally insisted on controlling its own expenditure and keeping in check both its revenue deficit and fiscal deficit—this has been a major instrument of inflation-control.

It was only since 1990-91 that the Government of India has appreciated the importance of reducing fiscal deficit. The Budget of July 1991-92 took the first decisive action to limit the fiscal deficit by bringing it down from 8.4 per cent of GDP in 1990-91 to 6.2 per cent in 1991-92 and to 4.9 per cent in 1992-93. Since then the Government failed to reduce fiscal deficit until 2001-02 when it reached to above 6 per cent. After that fiscal deficit again started declining and reached to 3.2 per cent in 2006-07.

(ii) *Monetary measures:* The monetary policy of RBI consists of extensive use of general and selective credit control measures. The main thrust was to restrict bank-credit against inflation-sensitive goods and to influence the cost and availability of commercial bank credit. The RBI relied heavily on selective credit controls on bank loans against foodgrains, cotton, oil seeds and oils, sugar and textiles so as to discourage speculative hoarding.

During the Eighties and Nineties, monetary policy was directed essentially to prevent any excessive increased in liquidity and at the same time to ensure sector and the priority sectors were adequately met. The cash-reserve ratio (CRR) was raised from 6 to the statutory maximum of 15 per cent gradually. These steps resulted in a large measure, in mopping up excess liquidity in the economy, moderating monetary and credit expansion and consequently helped in bringing down the rate of inflation.

In general RBI uses its monetary policy to achieve a judicious balance between the growth of production and control of the general price level. Generally RBI uses Bank Rate, CRR, SLR and open market operations to increase bank credit and expansion of business activity (in times of business recession) or to contract bank credit and check business and speculative activity (in periods of inflation).

SUPPLY MANAGEMENT

Supply management is related to the volume of supply and its distribution system. On the commodity front the Government has generally focused its attention in securing greater control over the prices of rice, wheat, sugar, oils and other commodities of mass consumption. Through increase in domestic supplies, large release from official stocks of foodgrains and widening and streamlining of the network of public distribution, the Government attempts to prevent an undue increase in the prices of essential commodities. Let us touch on some of the important aspects of this policy.

(a) *Fixation of Maximum Prices:* For eliminating the incentive for hoarding and speculative activity in foodgrains, the State Governments were asked to fix the wholesale and retail prices of foodgrains. Further, the Government also fixes minimum procurement prices for major crops on the recommendation of the Agricultural Prices Commission (APC). Prices of other important goods like cloth, sugar, vanaspati, etc. were also controlled in the past.

(b) *The system of dual prices:* The government has adopted a system of dual prices in the case of goods like sugar, cement, paper, etc. Under this system the weaker sections of the community are supplied these goods through fair prices shops, at controlled prices and the rest re-allowed to purchase their requirements the higher prices from the open market. Dual pricing generally failed to serve the purpose; rather, it created confusion in the market and led to erratic price movements. Hence dual pricing of cement was given up and price of cement is allowed to be determined by market forces of demand and supply.

(c) *Increase in Supplies of Foodgrains:* The Government used to increase supplies of foodgrains and other essential goods in times of internal shortage through larger imports. This has become largely unnecessary except in the case of edible oils. During 1970's and 1980's the Central Government took advantage of the success of green revolution and gradually built up large reserves of foodgrains; at one time, reserve exceeded 30 million tonnes. During the last few years, the Food Corporation of India (FCI) used the open market sale of rice and wheat to check market prices of these essential foodgrains. For example, during 1995-96, one million tonnes of rice and 3.5 million tonnes of wheat were sold by the FCI in the open market to check market prices.

(d) *Problem of oilseeds and edible oils:* In recent years, steep rise in the prices of edible oils along with those of pulses, tea and sugar have been responsible for rise in the general price level. The Government has prepared medium and long-term plans to step up the production of oilseeds in the country. The

Government has announced higher support prices for groundnut, soybean and sunflower seed-the last two crops offer the maximum scope for augmenting the supply of edible oil in the country. In the short period, the Government has been relying on imports of edible oils; at reduced or confessional import duties even though it has found out that imports do not necessarily bring down prices for the domestic consumers.

In this connection, we should refer to the steps taken by the Government to increase the production of all other agricultural products.

(e) *Public Distribution System (PDS) and consumer protection.* An important asper of the Government policy was the strengthening of the PDS. The Government has set up a network of fair price shops numbering nearly 4,00,000 which cover a population of over 500 million and which distribute wheat rise, sugar, imported edible oils (palm oil), kerosene, soft coke and controlled cloth. The public distribution system serves two purpose, Firstly, it helps to hold down prices. Secondly. it provides essential commodities to low income groups at relatively low prices. But when ever the PDS is hard pressed due to inadequate supply. prices of essential goods tend to rise. PDS has been strengthened and extended to rural areas.

(f) *Control over Private Trade in Foodgrain*—To check prices and to eliminate hoarding and speculative activity in food grains trade, wholesale dealers in food grains were licensed in many States. Limits were also fixed beyond which traders and producers could not hold stock without declaration. At the end of September 1977, Pulses and Edible Oils (Storage Control) Order was issued under the Essential Commodities Act to fix the maximum limits of stocks that could be held by wholesalers and retailers in respect of pulses, edible oils and vanaspati. The Food Corporation of India has come in a big way to buy in surplus area and sell in deficit areas and thus moderate the difference in prices.

(g) *Other relevent measures:* Since 2000-01, the following important measures have been taken by the Government to control inflation.

(i) Adoption of OGL (Open General Licence) import policy for importing sugar pulse etc.

(ii) Adjustment in trade and tariff policies in recent Central Government budget to ensure that domestic prices of industrial products remain competitive.

(iii) Substantial reduction in excise duties on a number of items expected to accelarate the pace of industrial revival and raise industrial growth; and

Inflation has been by far the most pressing problem for the common man in India for the last many years. The Government has largely succeeded in controlling inflation. Containment of inflation in the present context largely depends upon containing fiscal deficit and checking monetary expansion. Besides these, it would be necessary to promote the recovery and expansion of industrial production, and manage the supply of food grains and other essential commodities like oils and sugar among the poorer sections of the people.

RECENT POLICY MEASURES

- To control inflation, the government has recently taken following policy measures.
- To augment the availability of wheat, public sector agencies such as STC, MMTC and PEC etc. have contracted of importing about 18 lakh tones of wheat upto January2008.
- To maximise the procurement of wheat and paddy, the procurement price has been increased to Rs. 745 and Rs.1000 per quintal respectively.
- Export of pulses and wheat.
- A minimum export price of US $ 500 has been fixed for export of non-basmati rice.

- Import of wheat and pulses is permitted to private sector at zero duty.
- Import duty on edible oil, crude palm oil and soybean oil is reduced.
- Hoarding of wheat, pulses has been controlled by invoking Stock Limits through Central Order dated August 29, 2006, under Essential Commodities Act.

CONCLUSION

Thus we find that inflation in India is structural as well as monetary phenomenon. In the short-term, localized demand supply imbalances in wage goods, often due to seasonal variations in production-coupled with market rigidities and failure of regulatory framework have supported the inflationary expectations. In the medium to long-term, increase in money supply fuelled the price rise in the economy. However, wide range of measures have been taken by the government to ensure stable conditions as well as to prevent speculators from taking an undue advantage of the conditions of scarcity.

References

Bhattacharya, B.B. (1985), "Public Expenditure, Inflation and Growth: A Macroeconomic Analysis for India", *Oxford University Press*. New Delhi.

Datt, R. and K.P.M. Sundharam (2005), *Indian Economy*, S. Chand and Company Ltd., New Delhi.

Ministry of Finance, Government of India, *Economic Survey*, various issues.

14

Inflationary Trends in India

JAGDISH PRASAD SHARMA, KANCHAN PRABHA
AND VIVEK KUMAR

INTRODUCTION

Inflation is an economic concept. What the cause of inflation is, is not important to us from the point of view of this article. What is important to us is the effect of inflation! The effect of inflation is the prices of everything going up over the years. Suppose a person's salary few years back was Rs. 4000 and over the years it has now become Rs. 75,000. This is what inflation is, the price of everything goes up. Because the price goes up, the salaries go up.

There are different commodities which specially face the problem of rise in prices. In the case of food, there are more than just demand forces at work, although it is certainly true that rising incomes in Asia and other parts of the developing world have led to increased demand for food. Five major aspects affecting supply conditions have been crucial in changing global market conditions for food crops.

First, there is the impact of high oil prices, which affect agricultural costs directly because of the significance of energy as an input in the cultivation process itself as well as in transporting food. Across the world, governments have reduced protection and subsidies on agriculture, which means that high costs of energy directly translate into higher costs of cultivation, and therefore higher prices of output.

Second, there is the impact of both oil prices and government policies in the US, Europe, Brazil and elsewhere that have promoted bio-fuels as an alternative to petroleum. This has led to significant shifts in acreage as well as use of certain grains. For example, in 2006 the US diverted more than 20 per cent of its maize production to the production of ethanol; Brazil used half of its sugarcane production to make bio-fuel, and the European Union used the greater part of its vegetable oil production as well as imported vegetable oils, to make bio-fuel. This has naturally reduced the available land for producing food.

Third, the impact of policy neglect of agriculture over the past two decades is finally being felt. The prolonged agrarian crisis in many parts of the developing world; the shifts in acreage from food crops to cash crops relying on purchased inputs; the excessive use of groundwater and inadequate attention to preserving or regenerating land and soil quality; the lack of attention to relevant agricultural research and extension; the overuse of chemical inputs that have long-run implications for both safety and productivity; the ecological implications of both pollution and climate change, including desertification and loss of cultivable land: all these are issues that have been highlighted by analysts but largely ignored by policy-makers in most countries.

Reversing these processes is possible but will take time and substantial public investment, so until then global supply conditions will remain problematic.

Fourth, there is the impact of changes in market structure, which allow for greater international speculation in commodities. It is often assumed that rising food prices automatically benefit farmers, but this is far from the case, especially as the global food trade has become more concentrated and vertically integrated.

A small number of agribusiness companies worldwide increasingly control all aspects of cultivation and distribution, from supplying inputs to farmers to buying crops and even in some cases to retail food distribution. This means that marketing margins are large and increasing, so that direct producers do not get the benefits of increases expect with a time lag and even then not to the full extent. This concentration also enables greater speculation in food, with more centralised storage.

Finally, primary commodity markets are also attracting financial speculators. As the global financial system remains fragile with the continuing implosion of the US housing finance market, commodity speculation is increasingly emerging as an important alternative investment market. Such speculation by large banks and financial companies is in both agricultural and non-agricultural commodities, and explains at least partly why the very recent period has seen such sharp hikes in price.

Commodity speculation has also affected the minerals and metals sector. For these commodities, it is evident that recent price increases have been largely the result of increased demand, especially from China and other rapidly growing developing countries, but also from the US and European Union.

A positive fallout of the recent growth in demand and diversification of sources of demand is that it has allowed primary metals producing countries, especially in Africa, to benefit from competition to extract better prices and conditions for their mined products. But there is also the unfortunate reality that higher mineral prices have rarely if ever translated into better incomes and living conditions of the local people, even if they may benefit the aggregate economy of the country concerned.

At any rate, metal prices are high and likely to remain so because of the growing imbalance between world supply and demand. A reduction in global output growth rates would definitely have some dampening effect on prices from their current highs, but the basic imbalance is likely to continue for some time. This is also because there has been a neglect of investment in this sector as well, so that building up new capacity will take time given the long gestation period involved in investments for metal production.

SURVEY

India's 2008 Economic Survey Report targeted a drop in India's Inflation Rate—but with food, oil and commodity price rises worldwide, the opposite is happening. According to the 2008 Economic Survey Report, India's inflation rate was targeted by the Reserve Bank of India (RBI) to be 4.1 per cent, down from a rate of 5.77 per cent in 2007. Inflation rates for many investment goods have decreased dramatically in recent years. The price of basic goods such as lentils, vegetables, fruits and poultry were expected to slow their rise. The price of various manufactured goods also fell in 2007, and this contributed to a reduced inflation rate. However, the beginning of 2008 has seen a dramatic rise in the price of rice and other basic food stuffs. There has also been a no-less alarming rise in the price of oil and gas. When coupled with rises in the price of the majority of commodities, higher inflation was the only likely outcome. Indeed, by July 2008, the key Indian Inflation Rate, the Wholesale Price Index, has risen above 11 per cent, its highest rate in 13 years. This is more than 6 per cent higher than a year earlier and almost three times the RBI's target of 4.1 per cent. Inflation has climbed steadily during the year, reaching 8.75 per cent at the end of May. There was an alarming increase in June, when the figure jumped to 11 per cent. This was driven in part by a reduction in government fuel subsidies, which have lifted gasoline prices by an average 10 per cent. The Indian method for calculating inflation, the Wholesale Price Index, is different to the rest of world. Each week, the wholesale price of a set of 435 goods is calculated by the Indian Government. Since these are wholesale prices, the actual prices paid by consumers are far higher. In times of rising inflation this also means that cost of living increases are much higher for the populace. Cooking gas prices, for example, have increased by around 20 per cent in 2008. With most of India's vast population living close to—or below—the poverty line, inflation acts as a 'Poor Man's Tax'. This effect is amplified when food prices rise, since food represents more than half of the expenditure of this group. The dramatic increase in inflation will have both economic and political implications for the government, with an election due within the year.

GOVERNMENT'S FRUITLESS STRATEGIES

The Government's response to the domestic price rise, which is already creating panic in official corridors in an election year, has been to reduce or eliminate import duties on several food items such as edible oils, so as to allow imports to bring the price down.

But that is a short-sighted and probably ineffective strategy. It provides direct competition to Indian farmers producing oilseeds, even as they suffer rapidly rising costs. It sends confused signals not only to farmers for the next sowing season, but also to consumers, and leaves the field open for domestic speculators as well because the imports are not under public supervision but left to private traders.

Most of all, given the tendency of international commodity prices noted here, it will not solve the basic problem of rising inflation in such commodities. Instead, it will make the Indian economy even more prone to the volatility and inflationary pressure of world markets. In fact, the increases in prices in India have not been as sharp for some commodities largely because of the vestiges of the intervention era.

Thus, prices of some commodities, like rice for example, have gone up less than world prices only because exports have been prohibited. This does suggest that the Indian economy cannot hope to remain insulated from these global trends without much more proactive policies that rely substantially on government intervention in several areas.

STICKINESS IN INFLATION TRENDS

Stickiness is a situation in economics to describe a situation in which a variable is resistant to change and continues to be around its previous levels. Another point to note is that stickiness normally applies in one direction e.g. a variable that is "sticky upward " will be reluctant to drop even if conditions dictate that it should.

This is actually expected, as prices don't change very often. The various items that form the inflation index like prices of various manufactured products, etc. don't change very often. Similarly, an indirect component like wages that leads to build up in costs and then in product prices, are also not revised very often. The companies also change prices looking at their competitors and usually make decisions after taking the others decisions into account. This implies two things—one, the actual inflation may be lower than it should actually be as prices have not risen, and two, it might take more time to bring the inflation to acceptable levels. Both the situations are very tricky for the policy-maker. In the first situation, the inflation expectations are building up and in the second, the policy-maker is never sure whether the policy actions taken so far have been enough.

HOW DOES INFLATION AFFECT OUR INVESTMENTS?

With inflation hovering around 6 per cent, our long-term investments, fetching less than or around 6 per cent, are in fact offering us no returns. So at this stage it is worthwhile to withdraw such investment, and reinvest at the current interest rate, which have moved up to, say for example 8.5 per cent. So in such inflationary situation investors should be alert enough to take such step.

When there is inflationary pressure, returns from the share investment also declines. Even the dividend payment from companies declines. Investors should only increase their exposure to "growth assets" such as shares, property if they can wait. Analysts believe that in the long-run shares can beat any other investment.

House buyers will also have to re-adjust their finances since in an inflationary situation both interest rates and prices are on the rise. So, house buyers have to face two situations, first, a rise in the property prices and second, a rise in interest rate on the loan. A higher monthly instalment may affect their financial planning in general.

Inflation can be Controlled by Adopting Following Measures:

(A) Monetary Measures

Monetary measures relate to the control in the supply and circulation of money in the country.

1. *Bank rate policy*: In case of inflation, the bank rate is increased; the supply of money is controlled.
2. *Open market operation*: During inflation, the central bank sells government securities and price bonds in the open market in order to contract the supply of money.
3. *Variable reserve ratio*: In order to control inflation, the central bank increases the reservation.
4. *Credit Rationing*: When there is inflationary pressure, the state bank adopts the policy of credit rationing.

(B) Fiscal Measures

Measures in connection with public borrowing, public expenditures and public revenues are called fiscal measures.

1. *Public Borrowing*: During inflation, increase the public borrowing, during deflation, decrease in public borrowing.
2. *Public Revenues*: In order to control inflation, the increase in public revenues by the Government.
3. *Public expenditures*: Inflation is also controlled by decreasing the public expenditures by the Government.

(C) Realistic Measures

1. *Increase the supply of goods and services*: When the supply of goods and services is increased, the prices will come down.
2. *Population planning*: Control on population by adopting different measures of family planning will reduce the demand and finally prices will be controlled.

3. *Price control policy*: The government should adopt strict price control policy against the profiteers and hoarders.
4. *Economic Planning*: Effective economic planning is necessary to control the inflation in the country.

CONCLUSION

This paper deals with the facts which bring out the impact of the Inflation on Indian economy. The inflation trends in India also follows some trends of globalised inflation. There are various measures led by the government to control the inflation and releave the stress created by the inflation in the market. The analysis have been made to bring out the importance of stickiness in the context of the inflation.

REFERENCES

The Purchasing Power of Money: Its Determination and Relation to Credit Interest and Crises.

Financial Crises; Kindleberger.

High Inflation: The Arne Ryde Memorial Lectures.

http://wikipedia.com

http://economywatch.com

15

An Analysis of Inflationary Trends in India

Pre and Post-Reform Period

SUNIL KUMAR AND SUNIL KUMAR

INTRODUCTION

Inflation, generally refers to the rising prices, is a common economic feature of the market economy. Moderate growth in the rate of inflation is considered a *sine-qua-non* for the growth of market economy as it encourages entrepreneurs to invest in new enterprises which leads to an increase in productive capacity and subsequently, in the volume of employment and production. However, the high growth in the rate of inflation is realized dangerous for an economy as it affects negatively the real factors like saving, investments, effective demand, employment, etc. on the one hand and on the other, gives rise of concentration of wealth, inequality of income, hoarding of stocks, speculative activities, deterioration in the quality of goods, etc. This is why, every economy based on market forces wants a mild and stable growth in the rate of inflation. This goal would be achieved through an efficient use of fiscal as well as monetary measures which requires a proper knowledge of the past trend in growth, causes and measures to control of the rate of inflation.

Inflation in India has been by far the most pressing problem for the common man for the last several years. There has been a steep rising trend in the wholesale price index right from the inception of the Five Years Plan in 1950-51. According to Economic Survey, 2007-08, the wholesale price index (base year = 1993-94) which stood at 6.8 per cent in 1950-51, reached 206.2 per cent in 2006-07, a total rise of about 30 times during nearly six decades. Several reasons like rapid growth of population, war, famine, political instability, external inflation, etc. have been responsible for this drastic situation. Government of India has been taking steps from time to time to control the steep rise in the rate of inflation and getting success too. However, the price situation during 70's and 80's was worse than ever. Due to the need to address this situation and also some others Govt. of India started structural Adjustment Programme (SAP) popularly known as Economic Reform in 1990-91. Nearly two decades have past since then. Now, it is pertinent to anlayse the growth and variability in the rate of inflation during the period before and after 1990-91. The present study aims at presenting the trends in the growth and variability in the annual rate of inflation in India during the pre and the post-reform periods and also tries to highlight the causes and the measures taken to control of the annual rate of inflation during the both periods.

DATA BASE AND METHODOLOGY

This study is based on secondary data and covers the period from 1971-72 to 2007-08. The period covered for the study has been divided into two parts—the pre-reform period or period I (from 1971-72 to 1990-91) and the post-reform period or period II (from 1991-91 to 2007-08). Each period has been further divided into two sub-periods, each of them having a time length of ten years approximately. As such the periods are:

(1) *Pre-reform period* or period I—From 1971-72 to 1990-91.
period IA—From 1971-72 to 1980-81.
period IB—From 1981-82 to 1990-91.

(2) *Post-reform period* or period II—From 1991-92 to 2007-08.
period IIA—From 1991-92 to 2000-01.
period IIB—From 2001-02 to 2007-08.

Time series data concerning to wholesale price index which is an expression of general inflation were collected from various issues of Economic Survey, published by Govt. of India. The collected data were of different series based on different base years. So, there arose the problem of discontinuity in data. This problem was removed by making adjustment through the method of splicing. Thereafter, annual rate of growth in inflation was calculated for the whole period which were further used to get average growth and variation in the annual rate of inflation for the every period mentioned above with the help of statistical tools like arithmetic mean, standard deviation and co-efficient of variation. The results thus found out provide a basis for comparison of the trends in growth and variation in the rate of inflation between the pre-reform and the post-reform periods.

RESULTS AND DISCUSSION

The average growth and co-efficient of variation in the annual rate of inflation during the various periods mentioned above have been shown in the following table. The average growth in the annual rate of inflation indicates the periodic trend of inflationary pressure and the co-efficient of variation in the annual rate of inflation shows the periodic instability in the price situation. The higher the co-efficient of variation in the annual rate of inflation, the higher the instability in the price situation.

Table 1 indicates the forth—written facts—First, the inflationary pressure as indicated from the average growth in the annual rate of inflation, during period I was higher than that during period II. Not only this but the variation in the annual rate of inflation during period I was also higher than that during period II. It indicates that the price situation

TABLE I

Trends in the Growth and Variation in Inflation in India during Pre- and Post-Reform Periods

Average Periods Growth	*Pre-reform period*			*Post-reform period*		
	Period I (1971-72 to 1990-91)	*Period IA (1971-72 to 1980-81)*	*Period IB (1980-81 to 1990-91)*	*Period II (1991-92 to 2007-08)*	*Period IIA (1991-92 to 2000-01)*	*Period IIB (2001-02 to 2007-08)*
(1)	(2)	(3)	(4)	(5)	(6)	(7)
1. Average Growth in Annual Rate of inflation	8.73	10.21	7.25	6.56	7.80	4.80
2. Standard Deviation in the Annual Rate of Inflation	6.59	8.80	2.22	2.77	2.93	1.01
3. Co-efficient of Variation in the Annual Rate of Inflation	75.49	86.19	30.62	42.23	37.56	21.04

during the pre-reform period was more drastic and instable in comparison with that during the post-reform period. Second, within the pre-reform period, the inflationary pressure and the price instability during period IA were higher than those during period IB. It is also worth-noting that the period IA among all sub-periods of the pre and the post-reform period has the highest inflationary pressure as well as the price instability. Third, within the post-reform period, period IIA had higher inflationary pressure as well as price instability in comparison with those during period IIB. It is also surprising that the price situation during period IIA of the post-reform period was much worse than that during period IB of the pre-reform period. It indicates that the benefit of Economic Reform in controlling the inflation was realised just during the period IIB. Fourth, in terms of high inflationary pressure and high price instability, period IA was on the top rank, period IIA on second rank, period IB on third rank and period IIB on fourth rank.

There were some similar and some specific factors which affected the annual rate of inflation during various periods. The period IA as indicated from the above analysis, was the period of the highest inflationary pressure and instability. It was also a period of highly political instability in the history of free India as the imposition of Emergency and the first of all change of the Central Government took place during this particular period. The events of first half of the period were so strong as to keep the average growth in the annual rate of inflation in double digit (10.21 per cent) during whole the period in spite of nearly stable price situation during the second half of the period. The main reasons for the drastic situation of inflation during this period were several like a large influx of refugees from Bangladesh, widespread failure of Kharif crops in 1972-73, the complete failure of the nationalisation of wholesale trade in wheat, rise in crude oil prices effected by the OPEC towards the end of 1973, the world-wide inflation during this period, the depreciation of the external value of rupee *vis-a-vis* many currencies of the world pushing up the cost of imports, etc. To check the inflationary pressure during this period, the Government took a number of fiscal, administrative and monetary measures as the use of compulsory deposit scheme (CDS) to impound a part of the income of people, imposition of limits on declaration of dividends and credit squeeze by the RBI, the use of MISA against smugglers, hoarders and black-marketeers, etc.

The second ranked period in terms of inflationary pressure and instability was the period IIA of the post-reform period. This was also a period of highly political instability as several instable and coalition Governments at Centre were formed during this particular period. However, the main causes for the inflationary pressure and instability during this period were the hike in oil prices due to increase in Gulf-surcharge after Gulf-war, the sharp increase in administered prices of fertilizers and energy items like coal, petroleum products, electricity, etc., the increase in the procurement prices of foodgrains on mere political consideration, increase in indirect taxes, heavy fiscal deficit, sharp rise in reserve money due to large inward remittances and heavy accumulation of net foreign exchange assets with RBI, shortfalls in domestic production of price-sensitive commodities like pulses, edible oils, onions and potatoes, and so on. The steps taken by Government to check the inflationary pressure during this period were the discontinuation of *ad-hoc* treasury bills for financing the budget deficit, check on the issuance of new currency, widening the tax base by introducing Voluntary Disclosure Income Scheme (VDIS) to harness black money and to lessen the fiscal deficit, making available the essential foodgrains and articles through Open General Licence (OGL) import policy, open market sale (especially of rice and wheat) by Food Corporation of India (FCI) and a two-tier subsidised pricing system known as Targeted Public Distribution System (TPDS) especially for poor; using selective credit controls on bank loan against foodgrains, cotton, oil-seeds and oil, sugar and textiles to discourage speculative hoarding; raising the Cash-Reserve Ratio (CRR) to reduce the liquidity in the market, etc. Apart from these measures, good harvest of crops did help to bring inflation rate in the moderate range.

During the third ranked period IB the inflationary situation was by and large, under control. Whatever and whenever the rise in prices took place was controlled partly through credit restraint and partly through increase in the supply of essential goods through the public distribution system. Likewise, the price situation during period IIB has also been under control except in the year 2008. The price situation in 2008 was very drastic due to the reasons like the domestic pass through of international price increase in the prices of petroleum products, coal, cement, steel and some food articles. This situation came under control during that very year on account of adjustment in bank rate (repo rate and reverse repo rate) and cash-reserve ratio (CRR) by RBI, reduction in excise duty on cement and steel and in custom duty on steel only, a rollback in the increase in the international prices of crude oil, etc.

CONCLUSION AND SUGGESTIONS

Inflation in India has been by far of persistent and instable nature for long and consequently, troublesome for the people of every walk. Its pressure and variation during the pre-reform period were relatively high in comparison with those during the post-reform period. However, during overall period, period IA of the pre-reform period and period IIA of the post-reform period were worse in terms of high and instable price situation. Accounts of factors responsible for such situation were numerous. Some were demand-pull factors and some cost-push ones. But the effect of the cost-push factors like hike in international prices of crude oil and global inflation, fluctuations in output and supply of agricultural commodities, increase in indirect taxes, increase in administered and procurement prices of essential commodities, etc. on inflation were much more during both the periods, i.e. period IA and period IIA. These periods were also known for political instability. In this way, a positive correlation between political instability and price instability was observed during the both periods. On the basis of the analysis of this study, it was found that three main factors as the hike in the prices of imported crude oil, shortage of foodgrains due to low production and inefficient distribution system, and political instability have been the main reasons for the rapid rise and instability in the annual rate of inflation. Thus, these three problematic factors should be corrected on the priority basis through the following measures:

(i) Motivating the people to use petroleum products for necessary purposes as to lessen the dependency on imported crude oil;
(ii) Increasing the public and the private investment in the field of infrastructure like irrigation, road, market, etc. to increase the production of foodgrains;
(iii) Making the Head of villages or towns empowered and accountable for efficient functioning of public distribution system; and
(iv) Restoration of political stability through amendment in the constitution for two or three parties-based parliamentary system.

The above mentioned measures will correct automatically all other problematic factors like fiscal deficit, hoarding, adulteration, black-marketing, etc.

References

The Government of India: Economic Survey (various issues).

Pandit, V. (1978), "An Analysis of Inflation in India: 1950-75", *Indian Economic Review*, Vol. 13, pp. 89-115.

Bhattacharya, B.B. and M. Lodhi (1990), "Inflation in India: An Analytical Survey", *Artha Vijnana*, Vol. 32, pp. 69-87.

Nag, A.K. and G.P. Samanta (1994), "Inflation in India During the Eighties : An Analytical Review", *Economic and Political Weekly*, Vol. 29, No. 8, pp. 431-39.

16

An Analysis of Inflationary Trends in India

With Special Reference to Foodgrains Prices

KUMARI REKHA AND VIKASH

INTRODUCTION

In India the impact of rapidly rising prices of food has been felt most sharply by poor people who tend to spend around half of their income on food items. Hence to contain inflation the government should strengthen PDS by universalising it and removing the cuts in supply of foodgrains to states, and inclusion of some other essential oil and sugar in the PDS. We have to effectively manage strategies for supply side management of inflation by increasing the productivity in agricultural sector.

The term 'Inflation' is most conveniently associated with a substantial and persistent rise in the general level of price or what virtually the same thing—a continuously falling value of monetary unit—or a rate of expansion of money income greater than the rate of growth of real output.[1]

This definition of inflation clearly makes it a dynamic process and is sufficiently elastic embrace phenomena such as 'stagflation' and 'creeping inflation' while still remaining simple precise. It represents the state of imbalance or disequilibrium between the value of money in circulation, on one hand, and the available stock of basic goods and services, on the other. Thus, a persistent inflation is a condition where the volume of purchasing power is persistently running ahead of output of goods and services available to consumer and producers, with the result that there is a persistent tendency for prices and wage to raise. That is for the value of money fall. This situation can arise either because of under stimulation of demand because of and over expansion in the volume of money in circulation or because of the failure production of basis consumer's goods to increase fast of meet the growing demand.

In diagnosing, the causes of inflation may separate and group's views have expressed time to time. In the background to gravity and complexity of the phenomenon, which largely consist of excess demand or money supply on the demand side and low degree of productivity of basic consumption goods on the supply side as the major contributory factor in Indian inflation.

The structure of domestic production clearly indicates the built in nature of inflationary pressure in the economy, because the significant changes in the composition of both the agricultural and manufacturing production have gone more in favour on non-consumption items related to consumption item. Unless the primary sector is able to generate adequate supply of food and raw materials needed for expanding industrial development programme, the policies relating to import substitution and export promotion, have been further bringing about such structural change in production which adversely affect the internal price level.

The present articles have been devoted to different dimensions of inflationary trend in Indian economy on behalf of pre and post-reforms era. The present study is divided into five Sections. Section I deals with "Introduction"; Section II bring the emphasis on "Recent Global Inflationary Trends and its Impact on Indian Economy"; Section III elaborates the "Consequences of Inflation"; Section IV focused on "Inflation Control Measures"; in the last Section V we discuss the "Conclusion".

RECENT GLOBAL INFLATIONARY TRENDS AND ITS IMPACT ON INDIAN ECONOMY

In India the impact of rapidly rising process of food has been felt most sharply by poor people who tend to spend around half of their income on food items. Hence to contain inflation the government should strengthen PDS by universalising it and removing the cuts in supply of foodgrains to states, and inclusion of some other essential oil and sugar in the PDS. We have to effectively manage strategies for supply side management of inflation by increasing the productivity in agricultural sector.

The current growth of the world population requires the production of more food. Along with population growth, many countries have shown increased purchasing power causing a demand for more and other food. Now inflation is a worldwide phenomenon, with global food, commodity and oil prices rising. Food shortages and rapidly rising prices of food have adversely affected billions of people, especially the poor in the developing world. According to FAO, food prices have gone up by 75 per cent in dollar terms since 2000.

The price rise was particularly marked during 2007. The increase has been marked in essential foodgrains that are staples for most of the world's population. Global prices of wheat prices increased by nearly 20 per cent, which are some of the most rapid annual increases in the past half century. Since the start of 2008, world rice prices have soared even more, increasing by nearly 150 per cent in the first 100 days of the year. The impact of this has been felt most sharply in poor countries where most people tend to spend around half of their family budgets on food items. Jacques Diouf, Director General of the FAO says, "the world food situation is very serious today with food riots reported from many countries like Egypt, Cameroon, Haiti, Burkina Faso, Senegal and Bangladesh."[2]

A joint report by the FAO and the OECD warned that food prices are expected to high over the next decade even it they ease from their recent peaks. Indian Economy has been experiencing an impressive growth in the recent years. The performance of the Indian economy showed GDP growth of 9.4 per cent during 2006-07 as against 9 per cent during 2005-06 (at 1999-2000 prices). The growth rate in output and employment has put some pressure on the level of inflation. Inflation touched a 13 year high of 11.42 per cent for the week ended June 14, 2008. Inflation is happening primarily because of rising prices of food products, increasing in the price of basic materials like steel and cement price. The inflation has remained at over 7 per cent far above the RBI's target of 5 per cent. Inflation is no stranger to the Indian economy. In fact, till the early nineties Indians were used to double digit inflation, but inflation today is caused more by global rather than by domestic factors.

The present level of India inflation is considered as a challenge to the growing potentiality of the Indian economy. A decline in agricultural, particularly foodgrain output and per capita availability of foodgrains and stagnant public sector investment in this sector have become issues of contemporary debate and concern in India. In this background this paper attempts to analyse the reasons for recent increase in food prices in India.

FOOD AND POPULATION GROWTH

The rate of population growth in India has been slowing down, so total foodgrain demand has been increasing at a slower rate that they were in the previous decade. Between 1979-81 to 1990-92, production of foodgrains increased at an annual rate of 3.2 per cent compared to the population growth rate, which averaged at 2.1 per cent. The scenario, however, changed during the post-economic reforms period between

1990 and 2007 when the rate of growth of foodgrains production fell to 1.2 per cent, which was lower that the average population growth rate of 1.9 per cent (Table 1).

TABLE I
Growth of Food and Population (Average Annual Rate of Change (%))

	1979-81 to 1990-92	*1990-92 to 1995-97*	*1995-97 to 2001-03*	*1990-91 to 2006-07*
Food	3.2	2.2	1.7	1.2
Population	2.1	1.9	1.7	1.9

Source : Food Security Statistics—India, FAO, United Nations, March 2007.

PER CAPITA INCOME AND CONSUMPTION

One of the reasons for the increasing inflation is that the purchasing powers of the people have gone up. This in turn led to shortage of commodities and price increase. The per capita income of Indians has gone up as much as 7.6 per cent in 2006-07, enabling them spend more on nutritional foods, manufactured products like mobiles and health care services.

The per capita income at current prices is estimated at Rs. 29,642 in 2006-07 as against Rs. 25,956 for the previous year, depicting a growth of 7.6 per cent, according to the figures released recently by Central Statistical Organisation (CSO). If adjusted against inflation, the per capital income at current prices rose by 8.1 per cent during the year and was estimated at Rs. 22,553 as against Rs. 20,858 for the previous year.

Per capita private final consumption expenditure has also increased in line with per capita income. The growth of per capita consumption accelearated from an average of 2.2 per cent per during the 12 years from 1980-81 during the next 11 years following the reforms of the 1990s. The growth rate has almost doubled to 5.1 per cent per year during the subsequent five years from 2003-04 to 2007-08, with the current year's growth expected to be 5.3 per cent, marginally higher that the five year average.

CHANGES IN FOOD CONSUMPTION PATTERNS

Consumption patterns reflected the socio-economic progress of countries. Economic development is normally accompanied by improvements in a country's food supply and the gradual elimination of dietary deficiencies, thus improving the overall nutritional status of the country's population. A fast growing middle class is also diversifying its food basket. Eggs poultry, and other forms of animal products are becoming popular. This increases the pressure on foodgrains and large quantities of grains go in to animal feed.

As per capita incomes rise, even though people may spend less of their income on food, the absolute amount of demand still increases. And even when they consume less food grain directly because of change in food consumption patterns, the indirect demand for grain still increases, often more than proportionately, because of more demand for animal products, since live stock also need to fed and some like require even grain than humans.

The most important contributor to shifts in food consumption patterns is the rapid increase in purchasing power of people. As incomes go up, the food basket becomes more diversified. Tenth Plan drawn attention to changes in consumption pattern. It sates that between 1972-73 and 1993-94, the food basket has become much more diversified.

The cereals consumption is higher in the rural areas that in the urban areas during 1972-73, 1993-94 and 2004-05. Consumption of cereals per capita per month has decreased both in rural as well as in urban areas. Cereal consumption per capita in India declined from 13.4 kg per month in 1993-94 to 12.1 kg per month in 2004-05 in rural area. For urban areas the decline was from 10.6 kg per month in 1993-94 to 9.9 kg per month in 204-5. Consumption of milk and meat products as well as vegetables and fruits has increased due to natural outcome of economic development. It is also observed from National Sample Surveys of 27th (1972-73), 43rd (1987-88) and 50th (1993-94) rounds that the consumption expenditure in cereals and cereal substitutes have decreased indicating thereby an overall improvement in income levels of the masses.

EFFECTS OF CLIMATE CHANGE

The effect of climate change on agricultural production is another reason for increase in the price of foodgrains. Australia, a prime wheat producing region, has had droughts for two years in a row. Inclement weather in Ukraine and in Latin America has resulted in low production of staples such as wheat and rice.

HIGH OIL PRICES

Oil is a universal input that directly and indirectly enters into the cost of production of almost every other commodity. In 2006-07, India's consumption of crude oil was around 147 million tonnes, of which only 34 million tonnes was produced domestically. Between the mid-1980 and 2003, the real price of crude oil on the major international trading exchanges was typically less than $ 25 a barrel. The recent rise in the price of oil began in 2004. In the three years between January 2004 and April 2007, the oil price in nominal dollar terms increased by around 2.3 times, to $ 65 a barrel. But in the period between then and early June 2008, that is just 14 months, the price more than doubled again, to reach a peak of $ 139 on June 6 (*Frontline*, June 4, 2008). The rate of inflation in India was 8.75 per cent on June 20, 2008. It has galloped to a 13 year high to 11.42 per cent for the week ended June 14, 2008. This has been caused mainly by the June 5, 2008 increases in fuel prices and its cascading effect on all food commodities and other manufacture items, such as consumer durable goods and steel.

CHANGES IN CROP PATTERN

The impact of both oil prices and government policies in the US, Europe, Brazil has led to significant shifts in acreage to the cultivation of crops that can produce bio-fuels, and diversion of such output to fuel production. For example, in 2006 the US diverted more than 20 per cent of its maize production to the of ethanol: Brazil used half of its sugarcane production to make bio-fuel, and the European Union used the greater part of its vegetable oil seeds production as well as imported vegetable oils, to make bio-fuel.

CONSEQUENCES OF INFLATION

Apart from uncertainties in production, inflation had caused certain serious imbalanees in the Indian economy. Price relationships were badly distorted and production pattern had gone out of line with demand. Besides, capital resources available in the country were often derived from long-term to short-term uses and production had also shifted from essential and controlled goods to non-essential and free goods.

ADVERSE EFFECT ON PRODUCTION

Inflation had led to economic recession in many sections of the Indian economy. As a result of inflation, prices of certain important articles of consumption such as textiles had increased to very high level forcing demand for such goods to decline specially from the poorer sections of the country. With increasing expenditure on essential goods, the expenditure on the other goods had declined. While demand had declined, production too had declined due to shortage of raw materials, transport, power and so on. Production had also been adversely affected by frequent labours troubles such as strikes and lockouts.

ADVERSE EFFECTS ON THE DISTRIBUTION OF INCOME

The really serious effect of inflation are on the distribution of income in India. Inflation has brought about a mal-distribution of incomes. The producers, traders and speculators have gained enormously through ever-rising profit margins and through illegal gains and windfall profits, due to hoarding, speculation and black marketing. On the other hand, people living on past savings, fixed interest and rental income and old age pensioners have been literally ruined due to continuous depreciation in the purchasing power on the rupee. The working class has suffered badly, particularly the unorganized workers—the vast majority of them working in small establishment—whose money wages have remained almost stationary, despite persistent rise in the price level in the country for the last so many years. Inflation has thus brought about shifts in the distribution of income from the poor and the weak to the rich and the powerful.

INFLATION CONTROL MEASURES

The central government has initiated financial, monetary and administrative measures to rein in recent inflation. To douse the anger of the common man, Government adopted 'Fire Fight Approach' to tackle inflation, the following measures were announced[3]:

1. Scrapped import duties on edible oils,
2. Banned export of basmati rice,
3. Reduced duty on maize imports from 15 per cent to zero,
4. Extended ban on export of pulses for one year,
5. Banned export of edible oils, and
6. Withdrew export incentives in steel and cement.

The principal objective of the Government was to make available supply of foodgrains, pulses, edible oils for domestic use and to facilitate the import of these commodities to reduce the impact of supply constraint

In an effort to temper price rises, the government has reduced import duties on edible oils, ghee, butter and banned the export of pulses, wheat and rice except basmati. The RBI first announced 0.50 per cent hike in CRR and again raised the Cash Reserve Ratio by 50 basis points to 8.75 per cent from July 5, 2008 and 8.75 per cent from July 19, 2008 and raised Repo Rate (the rate at which the banks lend from RBI for shortage of short-term funds) from 8 to 8.50 per cent to suck excess liquidity out of the system as well as to reduce the money supply in the market.

It has cut the import duty on steel products and imposed export duty on steel products. To make steel exports less attractive, the central government announced a 15 per cent export duty on specified primary forms and semi finished products and hot rolled coils. The government has also leaned heavily on steel manufactures, pressing them into making "voluntary" price cuts or risk mandatory price caps. It imposed a 12 per cent *ad valorem* duty on bags costing over Rs. 250 a 50 kg against the current specific duty of Rs. 600 a tonne. Unfortunately none of the steps taken by the Government and RBI to check inflation in the last two months have yielded results.

Inflation has been by far the most pressing problem for the common man in India for the last many years. Over the years, the Government has experimented with various anti-inflationary policies at different times and has largely succeeded in controlling inflation. Containment of inflation largely depends upon containing fiscal deficit and checking monetary expansion. Besides these, it would be necessary to promote the expansion of agricultural production, and manage the supply of foodgrains and other essential commodities like edible oils and sugar among the poorer sections of the people.

CONCLUSION

In India the impact of rapidly rising prices of food has been felt most sharply by poor people who tend to spend around half of their income on food items. Hence, to contain inflation the government should strengthen PDS by universalising it and removing the cuts in supply of food grains to states, and inclusion of some other essential items such as pulses, edible oil and sugar in the PDS. We have to effectively management of inflation by increasing the productivity in agricultural sector. A cut in custom and excise duties on oil and reduction in the retail prices of petrol and diesel is required. Action should be taken against hoarding of essential commodities and strengthening of the Essential Commodities Act to empower State governments to deal with hoarding and black marketing.

Notes

1. Das, D.K., "Inflation Trend", (1984), p. 25, 281.
2. Diouf Jacques (Director General of the FAO), Food Security Statistics (2007), p. 7.
3. Datt and Sundharam (2008), p. 450-51.

References

CMIE: Monthly Report on Indian Economy, Dec. 2008.

Economic Survey, 2007-08.

Food Security Statistics—India, Food and Agricultural Organisation of the United Nations, March 2006.

Frontline, June 4, 2008.

The Hindu, June 25, 2008.

17

Global Inflation
Changing Dynamics and its Impact on Indian Economy

SUDHA RANJAN SINGH AND AJIT KUMAR

1. INTRODUCTION

At a time of financial turmoil in advanced countries, emerging economies have provide a welcome measure of resilience, but this has also set the stage for inflation, mainly from rising fuel and food prices. Even as global business activity slows, consumer prices are rising at an annual pace of nearly 5½ per cent, compared with less than 4 per cent in recent years. Much of this pressure is concentrated in emerging economies, where inflation has spiked to 7 per cent after years of moderation.

This development is part of the changing dynamics of the global business cycle. Strong internal growth momentum in emerging and developing economies are providing a valuable global trade shock absorber. The US downturn has further accelerated it by providing its huge pressure on sectors engaged in trading with faster-growing economies found the globe.

But the commodity price shock absorber is no longer working as it did in the past. Moderate demand in advanced economies has not led to the usual softening of commodity process that would boost purchasing power. This is because demand for economies is more energy and commodity-intensive than that in advanced economies. Several emerging economies, including China, India, Indonesia and Malaysia, have recently increased domestic prices. The removal of market-distorting protectionist policies had helped them to reduce pressures on food prices.

2. CHANGING DYNAMICS IN GLOBAL INFLATION AND INDIA

Most of the acceleration inflation in India is due to global inflation which has driven the Indian price upwards. Among the products responsible for the current inflation are food products of different kinds, including cereals, intermediate like metals and the universal intermediate like oil. Underline the buoyancy in prices is the closing gap between global petroleum demand and supply at a time when the spare capacity is more or less fully utilized. The oil market become highly sensitive to new of supply disruption and geopolitical events, pushing oil prices to all time high both in real and nominal terms.

Table 1 shows the recent trends in global inflation of developing and under developed countries. The rate of inflation in developed countries is some what stabilised whereas in developing countries it is moderate and in under developed countries the rate of inflation is very high. It is known that energy market have attracted substantial financial investors interest since 2004. But specially after the recent decline in stock markets and in the value of the dollar, investors are now in search of new investment targets and they have moved into speculative investments in commodities in general and oil in particular. The recent increase in oil prices is the root cause of inflation. I.M.F data shows that except for agricultural raw materials whose prices have increased very

TABLE I

Trends in Global Inflation : A Comparison (Data for Inflation are Annual Percentage Charge for the Year 2000, 2002, 2008)

Sl. No.	*Countries*	*2000 Rate of Inflation in (%)*	*2007 Rate of Inflation in (%)*	*2008 Rate of Inflation in (%)*
		Based on CPI (Index 1993=100)	*Based CPI (Index 2000=100)*	*Based on CPE (Index 2000=100)*
Developed Countries				
1.	Canada	2.3	2.4	2.9
2.	Japan	0.21	0.60	1.8
3.	U.K.	1.9	2.0	4.6
4.	U.S.A.	3.2	4.0	3.1
Developing Countries				
5.	Brazil	7.4	4.4	6.2
6.	China	0.50	6.6	4.5
7.	India	5.5	5.5	9.1
Under Developed Countries				
8	Afghanistan	N.A	20.7	15.5
9.	Kenya	5.1	12	24
10.	Nigeria	5.1	6.5	13

Source : The World Economic Outlook (WEO), 2000, 2007, 2008, International Monetary Fund, Washington, D.C.

little, all other commodity groups have shown sharp rise in prices. The I.M.F. data shows more than 40 per cent increase in world food prices over 2007. It has been observed that these developments are largely demand driven, being the result of several years of rapid global growth and the voracious demand from some fast growing countries like India and China.

3. IMPACT OF GLOBAL INFLATION ON INDIAN ECONOMY

Slowdown in the world economy has given the outlook

for global commodity prices higher even if the world economy slows down in terms of output growth. What does this mean for India? Until the 1990s, both producers and consumers in India were relatively sheltered from the impact of such global tendencies because of a complex system of trade restrictions, public procurement and distribution and policy emphasis on at least food self-sufficiency. The liberalising policies that began in the early 1990s have rendered all of that history, since one explicit aim of the reform strategy was to bring Indian prices closer in line to world prices. Countries like India seeking to manage this effect of global speculation on the prices of a universal intermediate like oil have to decide how important it is to insulate the domestic economy and the domestic consumer from its effect. Increasing pressure to hike oil prices further and aggravate an inflationary tendency that is already proving to be economically and politically damaging. Due to increase in prices of various commodities in the Indian economy, there is a steep rise in inflation which had directly effected our export competitiveness, as a result the exports had became dearer in the international market.

The job outlook has also turned grimmer as, there is a slowdown in the economy. Global inflation had deeply hurt the job prospects in rapidly growing sectors such as, telecommunications, IT services, infrastructure, and the manufacturing and engineering sector, etc. This rising rate of inflation Indian economy is facing the problem of currency appreciation, due to which there is a sharp rise in imports, further enhancing our trade deficit. The extent and impact of global meltdown on the Indian economy and the predictions is that there will be somewhat optimism and pessimism. The fiscal and monetary measures taken had targeted for increase in liquidity for pushing up demand, addressing the concerns of the industries and providing incentives to exporters who have been hit by the reversionary conditions. The RBI has already lowered its key interest rates—the CRR to a 2 year low and the repo and reverse repo rates to an 8 year low.

The FDI flow in the developing nations had generally declined in 2009. The government of India had now started a liberal policy which permits FDI up to 100 per cent on the automatic route, in most of sectors. The other area of concern is that India's industrial growth has declined for the first time in 15 years. Since Industry accounts for about 25 per cent of the country's GDP it is bound to affect the growth rate. Exports declined by 9.9 per cent in November 2008 which is also worrisome. The RBI in its report says there are downsize risks from India's increasing global integration such as the sustained outflow of capital, financial contagion and slowing world growth. The under mentioned Table 2 shows our present situation in foreign trade.

TABLE 2
Foreign Trade

(*US dollar Million*)

Item	*Year*		*Apr.-Dec.*		*Apr.-Dec. (% change)*
	2006-07	*2007-08*	*2007-08*	*2008-09*	*2008-09*
Exports	126361	162907	112737	131990	17.1
Imports	185749	251444	1717118	225809	31.5
Oil	57144	79646	54421	78827	44.8
Non-Oil	128606	171798	117297	146982	25.3
Trade balances	-59388	-88537	-58981	-93891	59.1

Source : Provisional Data for Apr.-Dec., 2008 as per press note of the Ministry of Commerce and Industrty, Govt. of India.

4. RECENT SCENARIO OF INFLATIONARY TRENDS IN INDIA

The silver lining is that since 50 per cent of our GDP comes from the service sector, which is not affected much by this global inflation and recession, growth rate in the current year will end up around 7 per cent. That is what the mid-year economic review estimates. Five years of nearly 4 per cent of agricultural growth and high domestic saving rate of 36 per cent has made this possible. The Government has raised public expenditure by Rs. 20,000 crore through the first stimulus package announced on December 7, 2008. The RBI too injected Rs. 300,000 crore liquidity into the system through a series of cuts in rates. The second package will increase availability of funds with banks and non-banking financial companies by Rs. 75,000 crore. The state governments too have been allowed additional market borrowings of Rs. 30,000 crore. The economic crisis of 1991 which Asia faced and which was "more" serious, but India has overcome it efficiently. With steadfast commitments of all the players in the field we look forward to see India coming out of the present global crisis with minimum bruises.

5. CONCLUSION

The global economy is wedged between slowing growth and rising inflation. While risks of the return to the widespread stagflation of the 1970s appear to be modest for most countries, we could instead be faced by a similarly challenging phenomenon: stagflation or a least low growth in the advanced economies and inflation in the emerging economies. With dynamics of global inflation changing, policy-makers in emerging economies will need to play their part in ensuring that we avoid a repeat of the 1970s—keeping domestic inflation under control, but also ensuring policies for robust demand and supply responses to rising commodity prices.

Financial shock absorbers are working too—through new channels as emerging economies as a group have shifted to being a net source of global savings as sovereign wealth funds are helping to recapitalise ailing banks.

References

Govt. of India, *Economic Survey 2006-07*, Ministry of Finance, Economic Division, Govt. of India, New Delhi (2007).

International Monetary Fund, The World Economic Outlook (WEO) IMF, Washington, D.C. (2000), (2007), (2008).

Kalpana Kochhar and Charles F. Kramer (2009), Indian Managing Financial Globalisation and Growth, B.S. Book, New Delhi.

K.K. Dewett, J.D. Verma and M.L. Sharma (2002), *Indian Economy : A Development-Oriented Study*, S. Chand & Company Ltd., New Delhi.

Suraj, B. Gupta (2006), Monetary Economy, S. Chand & Co. Ltd., New Delhi.

S.S. Tarapore, Y.V. Reddy, S. Ahluwalia (2002), Macroeconomics and Monetary Policy, Oxford University Press, New Delhi (2002).

18

Inflationary Trend in India
During Five Year Plans

SYED ALAY MUJTABA AND PANKAJ PURUSHOTAM

One of the most important characteristics of money is that its value does not remain constant but it very often changes. Due to change in the value of money price-level also changes. As we have seen, there is an inverse relationship between the volume of money and the value of money. When the volume of money increases the value of money declines and when the volume of money decreases its value increases. On a careful analysis we can notice that the value of money changes in a cycle. Usually the term inflation is used to denote rise of prices brought about by an increase in the volume of quantity of money. In other words, inflation is defined as an increase in the price-level due to an increase in the volume of money. There is broad agreement among economists that in the long-run, inflation is essentially a monetary phenomeon. A great deal of economic literature concerns the question of what causes inflation and what effect it has. There are different schools of thought as to what causes inflation. Most can be divided into two broad area: quality theories of inflation and quantity theories of inflation. Many theories of inflation combine the two. The quality theory of inflation rests on the expecatation of a seller accepting currency to be able to exchange that currency at a later time for goods that are desireable as a buyer. The quantity theory of inflation rests on the equating of money supply, its velocity, and exchanges. Basically we can say that there is not one theory for explaining inflationary rise in prices. The old quantity theorists and the present day monetarists define inflation as too much money chasing too few commodities and explain it in terms of expanding money supply in the context of an inelastic supply of commodities and services. At the time India is suffering from a lot of causes for inflation. Those like export, production, feminine, flood, earthquake and other non-violence activities. Inflation may occur due to several causes. Inflationary causes and pressure arise both from the demand side as well as supply side. Demand means demand of money-income for goods and supply means available output on which income-money can be spent. On the demand side, the major factors which causes inflationary pressure are the supply of money, disposable income, business expenditure and foreign demand. During war and post-war periods bank credit expands enormously and becomes at once both a cause and an effect of inflationary pressure.

The present chapter is devoted with a view to examining the trends in the movement of general price in India. Because the persistent rise in the general price level and the undesirable consequences of divergent movement of sectional prices as well as the frequent autonomous decision of the Government to hike administered prices of certain selected commodities have not only been fuelling the fire of inflation but also posing a threat to all our achievements and cherished goal. Against this perspective, the present chapter is divided into three sections to enquire these aspects of the behaviour of prices so as to evaluate the degree of contribution of these factors in accelerating the pace of price behaviour for suggesting a proper policy framework in the light of the causal factors in operations. The analysis presented in this chapter is based on the wholesale commodity price indices regarding the trends in general, drawn from various issues of Economic Survey, Ministry of Finance. Government of India and a discussion paper entitled 'Administered Price Policy' issued by the Ministry of Finance, on the 4th August, 1986. To analyses the trends in general, a number of statistical tables covering the entire period of the study are formulated together and are divided between the periods of successive Five Year Plans with a view to making macro-economic variables more comparable during the period under study. An attempt has been made in this section to analyse the behaviour of general prices in India with reference to important economic events arising out of the process of development over the period 2006 to 2007, i.e. the period from the First Five Year Plan to Tenth Five Year Plan. From the point of view of the overall behaviour of the general price level in India over the period of successive Five Year Plans, the entire planning age, i.e. from First Five Year Plan to the Sixth Five Year Plan may be classified mainly into four phases: The First phase (1951-52 to 1955-56) can be termed as deflationary period because over the period, the prices of almost all commodities came down to a significant extent, as a result, general price level registered a fall to the extent of 14.11 per cent. The Second phase (1956-64) can be termed as moderate rise in prices which include the whole period of Second Five Year Plan and the three successive years of the third Five Year Plan while the annual rate of increase in general price level during the Second Five Year Plan was 7.01 per cent followed by a downward annual trend in the Third Five Year Plan, i.e. by 6.38 per cent per annum. Hence, the period can be considered as moderate rise in prices. The Third phase (1964-68) which covers the two years of Third Five Year Plan and two Annual Plans can be termed as 'Significant the third Five Year Plan was 6.38 per cent while it became 8.52 per cent in the two Annual Plans'. The Fourth phase (1969-40 to 1984-85) which covers one Annual Plan and the entire Fourth, Fifth and Sixth Five Year Plans can be termed as 'high inflationary period' while the accelerated price rise which occurred from the beginning from early 1970s was owing to the inflationary psychology among people generated by various forces like fear of further galloping increase in prices, demonetization and stringement measures to curb black money, price expectations, changes in international monetary situations, etc. It is not out of place to mention that only in single year, i.e. 1974-75, the general price level increased at a galloping rate of 25.19 per cent. Similarly, during the year 1979-80 it was 17.11 per cent followed by a further accenterating annual increase 18.24 per cent in 1980-81, i.e. the first year of the Sixth Plan. Thus over the entire period the rise in general price level was much galloping. As a result, the compound rate of increase in general price level which was 7.9 per cent in the Annual Plans became more pronounced and increased by 9.2 per cent over the period of the Sixth Five Year Plan.

A review of price movement during 1977-78 and 1978-79 brings out the fact that the Janta Party Government was indeed successful in holding the price line and infact a positive achievement of the government's short-term demand and supply management policies. During the first year of the Seventh Plan, there was noticeable reduction of inflationary processes. So the annual rate of inflation had declined to 4.7 per cent as compared to 7 per cent during, 84-85. This was essentially due to comfortable supply position during this period. The average inflation rate as measured by the Wholesale Price Index (WP1) during the 8th Five Year Plan was about 8.7 per cent. In the terminal year of the plan, the inflation rate is expected to be about 6.4 per cent. Thus, the average inflation rate during the Eighth Plan period was about 8.7 per cent, significantly higher than the projected 5 per cent but showed signs of acceleration during the second half, due to a hike in administered prices of petroleum products and coal. The Ninth Plan envisages a reasonable degree of price stability. The average inflation rate measured by changes in Wholesale Price Index (WPI) was 4.8 per cent in 1997-98. This is considerably less than the inflation rate of 6.5 per cent in 1996-97. This moderation in the rate of inflation in 1997-98 was achieved against a relatively high rate of monetary expansion and also increases in the administered prices of certain petroleum products. Tenth Plan annual rate of inflation was around 4 per cent better than last all year five plan too. Above sentence can be drawn from the following data:

Wholesale Price Index, Consumer Price Index and Percentage Charges in Indices (1951-52 to 1984-85) (Base 1970-71 = 100)

First Five Year Plan

Year	*Wholesale Price Index (1970-71=100)*	*Percentage Charge in*
1951-52	50.4	–
1952-53	44.01	-12.5
1953-54	46.2	4.76
1954-55	43.0	-6.93
1955-56	40.8	-5.12
		14.11

Second Five Year Plan

Year	*Wholesale Price Index (1970-71=100)*	*Percentage Charge in*
1956-57	46.5	13.97
1957-58	47.9	2.15
1958-59	49.8	3.97
1959-60	51.7	3.82
1960-61	55.1	6.58
		+ 35.05

Third Five Year Plan

Year	*Wholesale Price Index (1970-71=100)*	*Percentage Charge in*
1961-62	55.2	0.18
1962-63	57.3	3.80
1963-64	60.9	6.28
1964-65	67.5	10.84
1965-66	72.7	7.70

Annual Plan

Year	*Wholesale Price Index (1970-71=100)*	*Percentage Charge in*
1966-67	82.8	13.89
1967-68	92.4	11.59
1968-69	91.3	-1.19
		+25.58

Fourth Five Year Plan

Year	*Wholesale Price Index (1970-71=100)*	*Percentage Charge in*
1969-70	98.8	3.83
1970-71	100.0	5.49
1971-72	105.6	5.6
1972-73	116.2	10.04
1973-74	139.7	20.22

Fifth Five Year Plan

Year	*Wholesale Price Index (1970-71=100)*	*Percentage Charge in*
1974-75	174.9	25.20
1975-76	173.0	-1.09
1976-77	176.6	2.08
1977-78	185.8	5.21

Annual Plan

Year	*Wholesale Price Index (1970-71=100)*	*Percentage Charge in*
1978-79	185.8	0
1979-80	217.6	17.12
		+17.22

Sixth Five Year Plan

Year	*Wholesale Price Index (1970-71=100)*	*Percentage Charge in*
1980-81	257.3	18.24
1981-82	281.3	9.33
1982-83	288.7	2.63
1983-84	316.0	9.46
1984-85	338.4	7.09

Seventh Five Plan
(Price movement during the Fifth Plan)

Year	*Wholesale Price Index (1981– 82=100)*	*Annual rate of Inflation*	*Primary Commodities*
1985-86	125	4.7	5.7
1986-87	133	5.8	5.3
1987-88	144	9.4	7.6
1988-89	154	6.3	—
1989-90	166	8.1	—

Eighth Five Year Plan

Year	*Wholesale Price of Primary Commodities (1993-94=100)*	*Annual rate of Inflation in Percentage (%)*
1992-93	232	7
1993-94	259	10.8
1994-95	121	10.4
1995-96	125	5
1996-97	136	6.9

Ninth Five Year Plan

Year	*Wholesale Price of Primary Commodities (1993-94=100)*	*Annual rate of Inflation in Percentage (%)*
1997-98	142	4.8
1998-99	153	6.9
1999-2000	159	3
2000-01	162	7
2001-02	168	4.9

Tenth Five Year Plan

Year	*Wholesale Price of Primary Commodities (1993-94=100)*	*Primary Commodities*	*Annual rate of Inflation in Percentage (%)*
2002-03	178	3.3	3.4
2003-04	181	4.2	5.4
2004-05	183	3.7	6.4
2005-06	193	2.9	4.4
2006-07	212	11.7	6.5

Broadly speaking, the aggregate demand management consists of those measures which contain growth of excess liquidity in the economy in line with year to year growth in output so that a balance can be maintained between the flow of expenditures and the flow of output. The Committee to Review the working of the Monetary system in India which was set-up in 1982 has emphasized the need for a framework from the angle of aggregate demand management.

The component of demand management which has contain excess liquidity in the economy emerging out of the excess flow of income as well as expenditure consists of the following measures:

(i) Monetary Policy,
(ii) Fiscal Policy, and
(iii) Income Policy Regulations.

Monetary Policy, an indispensible componet of demand management has evolved to a stage of maturity in the sphere of applied policies in India during the era of planned economic development. During this era, as it is well known, both the promotional and regularly objectives came to the equally emphaised. Between the two objectives, emphasis shifts from year to year depending on the circumstances prevailing in a particular year. The Reserve Bank of India has applied a large number of the quantitative and qualitative techniques of monetary policy both the traditional as well as the new ones during the period of study. The applied instruments included: (i) Bank rate, (ii) Open Market Operations (OMO), (iii) Moral Suasion, (iv) Discretionary Control of Refinance from R.B.I., (v) Ceilings on R.B.I. Refinance, (vi) Regulation or interest rates on commercial Banks, deposits and loans and other interest rates, (vii) Cash Reserve Ratio (CRR), (viii) Statutory Liquidity Ratio (SLR), (ix) Quantitative Ceiling on Direct Allocations of the volume and Direction of Bank Credit, (x) Fixation of average and marginal Credit Deposit Ratio, (xi) Selective Credit Controls, (xii) Credit Authorization Scheme, and (xiii) Formulation of Credit Budgets or Plans. It is, thus, obvious that over a period of time a number of innovations in the sphere of monetary policy have been introduced by R.B.I., for the purpose of economic stabilizations. Hence, it is essential here to focus in details the developments, evaluation, and working of all these techniques during the period of successive five years plans so as to bring out the problems such as lags, leakages, loopholes, and range of variation in important tools that have limited the scope of the working of instruments of monetary policy in India.

The active phase of Reserve Bank of India's Policy operations started from 1951 with the beginning of the First Five Year Plan. The measures taken by the R.B.I. to contain unusual price behaviour were three-fold, the bank rate was raised marginally from 3.0 per cent to 3.5 per cent in November, 1951, the open market operation policy was raised and an attempt was made to introduce credit elasticity in the money market by developing a bill market in January 1952. Monetary Policy, thus, played a positive role in providing adequate supply of credit matching with the growing requirements of industry, agriculture and trade. However, the R.B.I. followed a moderately restrictive monetary policy during the First Five Year Plan. The average annual rate of increase in M_3 being of the order of 3.4 per cent. National income at constant prices rose at an annual average of 3.6 per cent and prices declined by 2.7 per cent per annum on the average.

The role of fiscal policy with the growing functions and responsibilities of Government particularly in developing countries like India has undergone vitually a metamorphosis. The static purpose of fiscal policy of the Keynesian days has shifted from the saving investment equilibrium to the dynamics of growth. Whereas in early days taxation was the primary instrument. Now-a-days, non-tax revenues and borrowing from the public have become more and more important. Further, borrowing from the banks through the extension of credit to the government by the banks has impact. Consequently, the measure of forced savings of forced transfers from the civilian sector to the government has grown in size and incidence. Despite this, government receives foreign aid for its projects and channels such as aid to other sectors. Hence, the whole structure of Indian fiscal systems has undergone revolutionary changes in the background of the attainment of the goals of planned development and economic stability. It thus consist of policies and arrangements both for the determination of the scale and the pattern of expenditure of the government and its agencies and of the channels and instruments by means of which financial resources are procured and allocated. During the First period, Government could not strongly exercise its fiscal measures. However, fiscal policy was used for obtaining more savings for increased investment, and to reduce inequality in the distribution of wealth and income. The central budgets which were presented to the nation during the First Plan period, proposed slight adjustments in excise duties and export duties and occasionally announce small tax reliefs. Despites budgetary deficits and increase in money supply, inflationary repercussions could be avoided mainly due to fulfilment of the target of agricultural production.

The main object of an income policy is to reconcile economic growth and price stability through influencing directly the evalution of income and, therefore, the level of aggregate demand in the economy so that a minimum balance can be maintained between any upward revision of wages and salaries with overall increase in prouductivity. In fact the need for such an approach was recognized in India when the Government constituted in 1964 a steering group of income, wage and price policy which reported in 1966. It, therefore, follows that the rate of growth of wage and non-wage money incomes in India should be regulated and held, as a general rule, Below the rate of growth of national productivity. Such an approach does not mean a uniform prescription, but a package of measures consistent with each other and serving common objectives. The experience of the developed countries in the matter of income policy is still not rich enough to facilitate any valid inferences. Their limited experience has, however, shown that income policy is not substitute for credit and fiscal discipline. Income policy can be successfully operated only in an atmosphere of overall stability. In a period of excessive overall demand, an Income Policy, though helpful in restoring equilibrium, can play a role only subordinate to monetary, fiscal and other economic policies. In India, however, the wage and salary sector is much smaller and non-wage incomes constitute a major component. Within the wage and salary sector, the organized portion of the wage sector forms a small fraction of the total working force. In general, therefore, the experience of developed countries would not be of much relevance for us because conditions are radically different.

CONCLUSION

The theoretical as well as empirical study of Price behaviour and related applied policies for containing such an unususal phenomeon has been extensively explored themes of discussions both in the developed and developing nations. While the debate with regards to developed nations has generated a good deal of literature on the controversy between Kenyesianism and Monetraism regarding the more dependable channel exhibhiting the process of excess demand inflation in these economies, in developing nations especially in Latin America, this debate has given birth to so-called structural and monetary schools. The structuralist-monetarist controversy reflects a deep difference of social and political attitudes towards the appropriate means to contain unusual price-beheviour during the process of rapid economic development in developing economies. To structuralists, it is development through which the structural bottlenecks and basic rigidities can be eliminated. Any attempt to achieve complete price stability through monetary or fiscal means will result in unemployment, under utilization of Industrial capacity and will slow down the rate of growth, whereas according to the monetarists there is no necessary conflicts between stability and development. As long-run policy, they do not recognize inflation as serious possibility.

The problem of suitable price policy in the context of the Eleventh Plan arises largely due to the existence of persistent pressure of inflation. Price stability need not mean freezing the price at a given level. Slow and steady rise in the price level and has in addition the power to infuse a good degree momentum to the economy. This type of non-inflationary growth is necessary when the Indian economy is poised at 8 to 9 per cent annual rate of growth of GDP. The Indian Government has sufficient experience in controlling inflations. It is therefore, unnecessary to worry too much about rise in prices of some goods during 2006-07. Chiefly stressing point in 11th Five Year Plan for Railway Infrastructure.

Taking aggregative view of the study, it may be concluded that economy should be capable of absorbing inflationary impact of development of expenditure, should have agricultural growth fast enough to meet the requirements of growing industrial incomes. Hence the monetarist anti-inflationary policy can get support only from an expanded structural stabilization policies because the price behaviour under the Indian conditions call for an attack on both the variables and it may effectively be tackled inflationary situation in the long-run perpespective.

References

Akhtar, M.A., The Inflation Problem in Developing Economics, India and Phillliphines, *I.E.J.*, Vol. 23, No. 2, Oct., Nov., 1975, pp. 144-45.

Anderson and Jordan, Physical and Monetary Action, *Review of Federal Reserve Bank* of St. Louis, Nov., 1968.

Bruton, H.J., Inflation in a Growing India, University of Bombay, 1961.

Chawla, B.K., Inflation in India, Century, June 15, 1964.

Economic Survey, 2006-07.

M.L. Roy, Money and Banking.

Reserve Bank of India Bulletin, April 1968, Price Policy in Developing Economy.

Ruddar Datt and KPM Sundharam, Indian Economy.

Planning Commission, Tenth Five Year Plan (2002-07), Vol. 1, 11th Five Year Plan.

The Government of India, Economic Survey, 2002-03 and 2006-07.

19

Inflation in India and Ways Out

Sadanand Jha and Anil Kumar Jha

Inflation is no stranger to the Indian economy. In fact, till the early nineties Indians were used to double-digit inflation and its attendant consequences. But, since the mid-nineties controlling inflation has become a priority for policy framers. The natural fallout of this has been that we, as a nation, have become virtually intolerant to inflation. While inflation till the early nineties was primarily caused by domestic factors (supply usually was unable to meet demand, resulting in the classical definition of inflation of too much money chasing too few goods), today the situation has changed significantly.

Inflation today is caused more by global rather than by domestic factors. Naturally, as the Indian economy undergoes structural changes, the causes of domestic inflation too have undergone tectonic changes. Needless to emphasise, causes of today's inflation are complicated. However, it is indeed intriguing that the policy response even to this day unfortunately has been fixated on the traditional anti-inflation instruments of the pre-liberalisation era.

To understand the text of the present bout of inflation, let us at the outset understand the context. The functioning of the global economy, which in a state of extreme imbalance. This is simply because developed western economies, particularly the United States, are consuming on a massive scale leading to gargantuan trade deficits. Crucially their extreme levels of consumption and imports are matched by the proclivity, nay fetish, of the developing countries in having an unique economic model. Thus while a set of developing countries produces, exports and also saves the proceeds by investing their forex reserve back in these countries, developed countries are consuming both the production and investment originating from the developing countries. In effect, developing countries are building their foreign exchange reserves while the developed countries are accumulating the corresponding debt. After all, it takes two to a tango. For instance, the US current account deficit is estimated to be 7 per cent of GDP in 2006 and stood at approximately $900 billion. Obviously, current account deficit of the US becomes the current account surplus of other exporting countries, viz. China, Japan and other oil producing and exporting countries.

The reason for this imbalance in the global economy is the fact that after the Asian currency crisis; many countries found the virtues of a weak currency and engaged in 'competitive devaluation.' Under this scenario, many countries simply leveraged their weak currency *vis–a-vis* the US dollar to gain to the global markets. The mercantilist policy to maintain their competitiveness is achieved when their central banks intervenes in the currency markets leading to accumulation of foreign exchange, notably the US dollar, against their own currency.

Implicitly it means that the developing world is subsidising the rich developed world. Put more bluntly, it would mean that the US has outsource even defending the dollar to these countries, as a collapse of the US currency would hurt these countries holding more dollars in reserves than perhaps the US itself! In this connection, commenting on the above phenomenon in the Power and Interest News Report, Jephraim P. Gundzik wrote that the world growth "was hardly sufficient to be behind the further rise of commodity prices in the first five months of this year (i.e. in 2006). Rather than demand pushing the value of commodities higher in the past 18 months, it has been the (impending) dollar's devaluation against commodities has pushed commodity prices to record highs." Naturally, as the players a fall in the value of the dollar and reach out to various assets and commodities, the prices of these commodities assets too will rise.

But as the imbalance shows no sign of correcting, players seek to shift to commodities and assets across continents to hedge against the impending fall in the US dollar. Thus, it is a fight between central banks and the psychology of market players across continents. As a corrective measure, economists are coming to the conclusion that most of the currencies across the globe are highly undervalued *vis-a-vis* the dollar, which, in turn, requires a significant dose of devaluation. For instance, a consensus exists amongst economists and currency trade that the Yen is one of the most highly undervalued currencies (estimated at around 60%) along with the Chinese Yuan (estimated at 50%) for by other countries in Asia. This artificial undervaluation of currencies is another fundamental cause for increasing global liquidity.

To get an idea of the enormity of the aggregation of these two factors on the world's supply of dollars, Jephraim P. Gundzik calculates the dollar value of rising prices of just one commodity—crude oil. In 2004, global demand for crude oil grew by a mere four per cent. Nevertheless higher oil prices advanced by as much as 34 per cent. Consequently, it is this factor that significantly contributed to increase the world's dollar supply by about $ 330 billion in 2005, international crude oil prices gained another 35 per cent and global demand for oil grew by only 1.6 per cent. Nonetheless, the work supply of dollars increased by further $ 460 billion. Naturally, with all currencies refusing to be revalued, this leads to increased global liquidity. While one is not sure as to whether the increase in prices of crude led to the increase of other commodities or *vice versa*, the fact of the matter is that, in the aggregate, increased liquidity has led to the increase in commodity prices as a whole.

Although some of this increase in the world's supply of dollars has been reabsorbed into US economy by the twin American deficits—current well as budgetary—it is estimated that as much as $ 600 billion remains outside the US. What has further compounded the problem is the near-zero interest rate regime in Japan. With almost $ 905 billion forex reserves, it makes dollar to borrow in Japan at such low rates and invest elsewhere for higher returns. Obviously, some of this money—estimated by experts to be approximately $ 200 billion—has undoubtedly found its way into the asset markets of other countries.

Most of it has been parked in alternative investments such as commodities, stocks, real estates and other markets across continents, leverage many times over. Needless to reiterate, the excessive dollar supply too has fuelled the property and commodity boom across markets and continents. The twin causes—excessive liquidity due to undervaluation of various currencies (technical) and fear of the US dollar collapse leading to increased purchase of various commodities to hedge against a fall in US dollar (psychological)—needs to be tackled upfront if inflation has to be confronted globally.

What actually compounds the problem for India is the fact that lower harvest worldwide, specifically in Australia and Brazil, and the overall status of demand *vis-a-vis* supply and low stock positions world over, global wheat prices have continued to rise. Wheat demand is expected to rise, while world production is expected to decline further in the coming months, as a result of which global stood already at historically low levels, may fall further by 20 per cent. These global trends have put upward pressure on domestic prices of wheat which expected to continue to do so during the course of this year. No wonder, despite the government lowering the import tariffs on wheat to zero, there has been no significant quantity of wheat imports as the international prices of wheat are higher than the domestic prices.

Another cause for the increase in the prices of these commodities has been due to the fact that both India and China have been recording excellent growth in recent years. It has to be noted that China and India have a combined population of 2.5 billion people. Given this size of population even a modest $ 100 increase in the per capita income of these two countries would translate into approximately billion in additional demand for commodities. This has put an extraordinary highly demand on various commodities. Surely growth will come at high cost.

The excessive global liquidity as explained above has facilitated buoyant growth of money and credit in 2005-06 and 2006-07. For instance, net accretion to the foreign exchange reserves aggregates to in excess of $ 50 billion (about Rs. 22,500 crore) in 2006-07. Crucially, this incremental flow of foreign exchange into the country has resulted in increased credit flow by our banks. Naturally, this is another fuel for grow and crucially, inflation. This Reserve Bank of India's strategy of dealing with excessive liquidity through the Market Stabilization Scheme (MSS) has its own limitation. Similarly, the increase in repo rates (ostensibly to make credit over-extension costly) and increase in CRR rates (to restrict excessive money supply) are policy interventions with serious limitations in the Indian context with such huge forex inflows.

To conclude, all these are pointers to a need for a different strategy. The current bout of inflation is caused by a multiplicity of factors, mostly and is structural. Monetary as well as trade policy responses, as has been attempted till date, would be inadequate to deal with the extant issue effectively. Crucially, a stock market boom, a real estate boom and a benign inflation in the foodgrains market is an economic impossibility. It has to be noted that the Indian market is structurally suited for leveraging shortages rather effectively. Added to this is the information among various classes of consumers as well as between consumers, on the one hand, and producers and consumers, on the other. Further, the sustained flow of foreign money, thanks to the excessive global liquidity in the world, has fuelled the rise of the stock markets an estate prices in India to unprecedented levels. This boom has naturally led to corresponding boom in various related markets as much as the increased credit flow has in a way resulted in overall inflation. Economic policy rests in the triumvirate of fiscal, monetary and trade policies. Theoretical understanding of economics meant that these policies are interdependent.

Also one needs to understand that growth naturally comes with its attendant costs and consequences. While these policies are usually inerded deed and typically compensatory, one has to understand that the issues with respect to inflation cannot be subjected to conventional wisdom in globalisation. One policy route yet unexamined in the Indian context by the government is the exchange rate policy, especially revaluation of the Rupee as instrument to control inflation. It is time that we think about a revaluation of the Indian Rupee as a policy response to the complex issue of managing inflation, while simultaneously address the constraints on the supply side on food grains through increase in domestic production.

A higher Rupee value *vis-a-vis* the dollar would mean lower purchase price of commodities in Rupee terms. The Indian economy has undergone significant changes in the past decade and a half. With increased linkages to the global economy, it cannot duck the negatives of globalisation. Quite the contrary, it needs to come with appropriate policy responses for the same, which cannot be of the 1960s vintage. Allowing Rupee to appreciate is surely one of them. The time for a rethink on our exchange rate policy to tackle inflation is now.

With the annual rate of inflation in India having touched 7 per cent on a point-to-point basis during the week-ending March 22, 2008, the search for policies to combat the price rise has begun. One factor seen as making that search difficult is the ostensible rule of "imported inflation" in driving the rise in domestic prices. There is an obvious reason why such an argument arises. Among the products primarily responsible for the current inflation are food products of different kinds, including cereals, intermediates like metals and the universal intermediate, oil. Of these, the difficulties that high and rising levels of oil prices pose have been known for some time now. Price movements of the two varieties of crude that enter India's import basket show that since May 2003 international prices have, despite fluctuations, been on a continuous rise. In the event the prices per barrel of these varieties have moved from less than $ 25 in May 2003 to close to or well above $ 100 today.

Underlying the buoyancy in prices is the closing gap between global petroleum demand and supply at a time when the spare capacity is more or less fully utilised. Much of the increase in demand is coming from China, but that is affecting stockpiles everywhere. This trend, combined with the uncertainty in West Asia resulting from the occupation of Iraq and the standoff in Iran, has created a situation where any destabilising influence—such as political uncertainty and attacks on the oil supply chain in Nigeria—triggers a sharp rise in price.

What needs noting, however, is that prices are where they are because speculators have exploited these fundamentals. It is known that energy markets have attracted substantial financial investor interest since 2004, but especially after the recent decline in stock markets and in the value of the dollar. Investors in search of new investment targets have moved into speculative investments in commodities in general and oil in particular. The Organisation of the Petroleum Exporting Countries (OPEC), which is normally held responsible for all oil price increases, has repeatedly asserted that oil has crossed the $100-a-barrel mark not because of a shortage of supply but because of financial speculation.

The FAO food price index, which includes national prices as well as those in cross-border trade, suggests that the average index for 2007 was nearly 25 per cent above the average for 2006. Apart from sugar, nearly every other food crop has shown very significant increases in price in world trade over 2007, and the latest evidence suggests that this trend has continued and even accelerated in the first few months of 2008. The net result is that globally the prices of many basic commodities have been rising faster than they ever did during the last three decades.

It has been argued that these developments are largely demand-driven, being the result of several years of rapid global growth and the voracious demand from some fast-growing countries such as China. Certainly, there is some element of truth in this. And to the extent that this is true, it implies that the world economy is heading back to the late-1960s and early-1970s scenario wherein rapid and prolonged growth came up against an inflationary barrier. Capitalism's success over the last two decades was its ability to prevent such an outcome, political economy processes that restrained the wage and income demands of workers and primary producers. But clearly there are limits to such a process, and these limits are now being reached.

If this were the only cause of the recent commodity price inflation, it would not necessarily be of such concern to policy-makers, because it could then be expected that a slowing down of overall growth would simultaneously reduce inflation. It would also reflect some recovery of the drastically reduced bargaining power of workers and primary producers. But there are other, more worrying tendencies in operation, that suggest that the current global inflationary process has other factors pushing it which will not be so easily controlled.

To understand this, it is necessary to examine the forces behind the price rises for different commodities. In the case of food, there are more than just demand forces at work, although it is certainly true that rising incomes in Asia and other parts of the developing world have led to increased demand for food. Five major aspects affecting supply conditions have been crucial in changing global market conditions for food crops.

First, there is the impact of high oil prices, which affect agricultural costs directly because of the significance of energy as an input in the cultivation process itself (through fertilise and irrigation costs) as well as in transporting food. Across the world, governments have reduced protection and subsidies on agriculture, which means that high costs of energy directly translate into higher costs of cultivation, and therefore higher prices of output.

Second, there is the impact of both oil prices and government policies in the US, Europe, Brazil and elsewhere that have promoted bio-fuels as an alternative to petroleum. This has led to significant shifts in acreage as well as use of certain grains. For example, in 2006 the US diverted more than 20 per cent of its maize production to the production of ethanol Brazil used half of its sugarcane production to make bio-fuel, and the European Union used the greater part of its vegetable oil production as well as imported vegetable oils, to make bio-fuel. This has naturally reduced the available land for producing food.

Third, the impact of policy neglect of agriculture over the past two decades is finally being felt. The prolonged agrarian crisis in many parts of the developing world; the shifts in acreage from food crops to cash crops relying on purchased inputs; the excessive use of groundwater and inadequate attention to preserving or regenerating land and soil quality; the lack of attention to relevant agricultural research and extension; the overuse of chemical inputs that have long-run implications for both safety and productivity; the ecological implications of both pollution and climate change, including desertification and loss of cultivable land: all these are issues that have been highlighted by analysts but largely ignored by policy-makers in most countries. Reversing these processes is possible but will take time and substantial public investment, so until then global supply conditions will remain problematic.

Fourth, there is the impact of changes in market structure, which allow for greater international speculation in commodities. It is often assumed that rising food prices automatically benefit farmers, but this is far from the case, especially as the global food trade has become more concentrated and vertically integrated.

A small number of agribusiness companies worldwide increasingly control all aspects of cultivation and distribution, from supplying inputs to farmers to buying crops and even in some cases to retail food distribution. This means that marketing margins are large and increasing, so that direct producers do not get the benefits of increases expect with a time lag and even then not to the full extent. This concentration also enables greater speculation in food, with more centralised storage.

Finally, primary commodity markets are also attracting financial speculators. As the global financial system remains fragile with the continuing implosion of the US housing finance market, commodity speculation is increasingly emerging as an important alternative investment market. Such speculation by large banks and financial companies is in both agricultural and non-agricultural commodities, and explains at least partly why the very recent period has seen such sharp hikes in price.

Commodity speculation has also affected the minerals and metals sector. For these commodities, it is evident that recent price increases have been largely the result of increased demand, especially from China and other rapidly growing developing countries, but also from the US and European Union. A positive fallout of the recent growth in demand and diversification of sources of demand is that it has allowed primary metals producing countries, especially in Africa, to benefit from competition to extract better prices and conditions for their mind products. But there is also the unfortunate reality that higher mineral prices have rarely if ever translated into better incomes and living conditions of the local people, even if they may benefit the aggregate economy of the county concerned.

At any rate, metal prices are high and likely to remain so because of the growing imbalance between world supply and dĕmand. A reduction in global output growth rates would definitely have some dampening effect on prices from their current highs, but the basic imbalance is likely to continue for some time. This is also because there has been a neglect of investment in this sector as well, so that building up new capacity will take time given the long gestation period involved in investments for metal production. Hence the medium-term outlook for global commodity prices, while uncertain, is that they are likely to remain high even if the world economy slows down in terms of output growth. What does this mean for India? Until the 1990s, both producers and consumers in India were relatively sheltered from the impact of such global tendencies because of a complex system of trade restriction, public procurement and distribution and policy emphasis on at least food self-sufficiency.

The liberalising policies that began in the early 1990s have rendered all of that history, since one explicit aim of the reform strategy was to bring Indian prices closer in line to world prices. Countries like India seeking to manage this effect of global speculation on the prices of a universal intermediate like oil have to decide how important it is to insulate the domestic economy and the domestic consumer from its effect.

Given the huge revenues being derived from duties on oil products, one way this can be done is to forego duty while holding oil prices. This would require compensating for revenue losses with taxes in other areas which a growing economy can contemplate. But the Government appears unwilling to take this route, increasing pressure to hike oil prices further and aggravate an inflationary tendency that is already proving to be economically and politically damaging.

This reticence till recently to proactively insulate the domestic economy has meant, that both producers and consumers are now more or less directly affected adversely by global trends. The Government's response to the domestic price rise, which is already creating panic in official corridors in an election year, has been to reduce or eliminate import duties on several food items such as edible oils, so as to allow imports to bring the price down.

But that is a short-sighted and probably ineffective strategy. It provides direct competition to Indian formers producing oilseeds, even as they suffer rapidly rising costs. It sends confused signals not only to farmers for the next sowing season, but also to consumers, and leaves the field open for domestic speculators as well because the imports are not under public supervision but left to private traders.

Most of all, given the tendency of international commodity prices noted here, it will not solve the basic problem of rising inflation in such commodities. Instead, it will make the Indian economy even more prone to the volatility and inflationary pressure of world markets. In fact, the increases in prices in India have not been as sharp for some commodities largely because of the vestiges of the intervention era. Thus, Prices of some commodities, like rice for example, have gone up less than world prices only because exports have been prohibited. This does suggest that the Indian economy cannot hope to remain insulated from these global trends without much more proactive policies that rely substantially on government intervention in several areas. In the case of food, this essentially requires a more determined effort to increase the viability of food cultivation, to improve the expand and strengthen the public system of procurement and distribution. For other commodities too, it is now evident that a *laissez faire* system is simply no good enough, and public intervention and regulation of markets in essential.

References

FAO Bulletin, 2005-08.

Imported Inflation, C.P. Chandrasekhar and Jayanti, Global Inflation in India: How to Tackle it: http://indiabroad.com/many/2007/mar/21.

The Hindu Business Line, Global Inflation and India.

Macroeconomic and Monetary Developments, Mid-Term Review, 2008-09.

Monetary Policy and Fiscal Policy, Impact Inflation that Effects with a New Keynesian Assignment of Weapons to Targets, Madras, James and Vines, David, 1988.

Polackova, Hana (1997), Inflation in Non-Tradeable and the Macroeconomic Policy Mix: A Model with Policy Application to Transition Economics, Policy Research Working Paper Series.

RBI Annual Report, 2006-07.

20

Inflationary Trends in India Over-all

An Exclusive Truth

Priyatam Kumar

Of the many questions that may be asked on the subject of inflation perhaps of first importance to economists is that of causation. Inflation is a persistent and appreciable rise in the general level of prices. This is the definition with which we will work. But this is no fully satisfactory definition is available. However, this problem is not too serious. What matters is not how fast and how long the price level must rise before the rise is called inflationary, but what causes the price level to rise in the first place and what are the consequences of deferent rates of price level charge for the distribution of income the level of output and employment, the growth rate, and other critical variable used to measure the economy's performance. Recognizing the ambiguities of our terminology, we will define inflation simply as a persistent and appreciable rise in the general level of prices.

Four Measures of inflation that is, The Consumer Price Index (CPI); The Producer Price Index (PPI); The GNP Implicit price deflator and the PCE implicit price dictator. Although some members of society gain from inflation others get hurt; the major measure of how badly they get hurt is the amount of their income and wealth that inflation takes away from them. To investigate this question of who gains and who loses from inflation, we will first examine the way that inflation results in a redistribution of income and wealth among different income classes. In looking at the broad question of the effects of inflation we have gone far enough to see that inflation is a pervasive economic process. Its effects are felt to some degree by every citizen and in every corner of the economy. Some of the effects are quite certain at least when stated as broad generalizations, other are just as much uncertain. We know that inflation causes a redistribution of income and wealth. A rapid rate of inflation that is unanticipated and to which there is therefore no chance to adjust is undoubtedly damaging. When inflation proceeds at a mild rate of not more than a few percentage points per year, there is no ready answer to the question posed. In view of this uncertainly the best policy to many economists appears to be one aimed at achieving and maintains a stable price level or a zero rate of inflation.

Considering the record since the 1990s specially 2008, such an achievement look like a remote possibility but it does not mean that it is not the best ultimate goal toward which policy should aim.

Inflation in India: How to trackle it. It is based on the information of March 21, 2007, Global Inflationary trend.

Inflation is no stranger to the Indian economy. In fact, till the early nineties Indians were used to double-digit inflation and its attendant consequences. But, since the mid-nineties controlling inflation has become a priority for policy framers.

The natural fallout of this has been that we, as a nation, have become virtually intolerant to inflation. While inflation till the early nineties was primarily caused by domestic factors (supply usually was unable to meet demand, resulting in the classical definition of inflation of too much money chasing too few goods), today the situation has changed significantly.

Inflation today is caused more by global rather than by domestic factors. Naturally, as the Indian economy undergoes structural changes, the causes of domestic inflation too have undergone tectonic changes.

Needless to emphasize, causes of today's inflation are complicated. However, it is indeed intriguing that the policy response even to this day unfortunately has been fixated on the traditional anti-inflation instruments of the pre-liberalization era.

CHART I

CPI Inflation

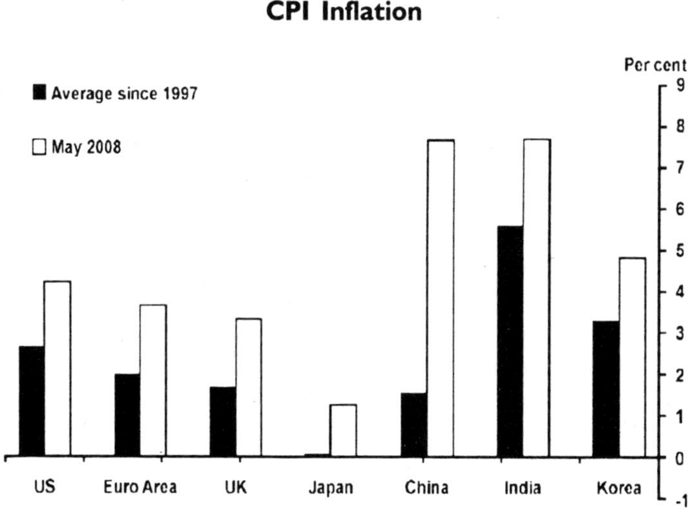

The most striking feature of the recent charge in the global inflation climate has been the upward pressure on oil, food and other commodity prices.

So the main instrument of monetary policy in modern economics with liberalized financial markets is the short-term interest rate.

So far, many of these countries have sought to causation the impact of rising global price rises on their consumers and producers through subsidies. The more important question

CHART 2
Monetary Policy, the Global Economy and Inflation

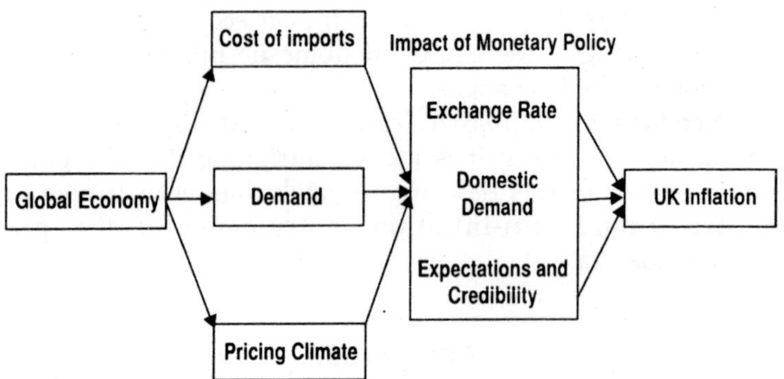

however, for global inflation over the medium term is whether what starts out as a temporary rise in inflation becomes more deeply embedded through its viability.

Despite this, at last but not the least : Rising inflation level is a major issue worrying all the countries. This report is an attempt to just verify the inflation trends in India abroad. The monetary policy by RBI stance also becomes clearer with time and become more preempting 2004 onwards. But in both the cases takes about an year for the effect and again total about an year. It take about an year to lower the inflation but we can't pinpoint a particular measure as there were a series of measures.

As there were a series of measures.
WPI inflation (Findlly sticky or volatility)
Analyzing stickiness in WPI inflation.

Though, the analysis needs to be improved to understand both the stickiness and impact of monetary measures. We would also like to reiterate that past is not a guide to the future and the latter could be completely different from the past. So, we cannot say as this has happened in the past, it is likely to happen in future as well.

References

Average annual inflation shown is from 1997 to May 2008.
Economic Research Paper, IDBI.
Economic Advisor to commerce ministry, RBI, IDBI.
IMF World Economic outlook, April 2008.
Thomson Data Stream.

21

Growth and Inflation

RINA CHAND

Almost fifty years ago economists at the Economic Commission for Latin America (ECLA) had posed the rhetorical question 'economic development or monetary stability?', and had gone on to answer it themselves by asserting that it was a 'false dilemma'! Nothing has occurred in the world of economics that would require us to alter this view as there is no demonstrably stable relationship between inflation and growth across economies and/or over time.

Clearly the relationship is conditional on several other factors, prime examples of which are the degree of openness of an economy, the nature of wage determination and the extent of competition in the product markets. A little more mundanely, it is directly related to two aspects of the growth that takes place, namely its sources and its composition. By 'source' we mean the relative contributions of inputs and productivity growth and by 'composition' we mean the output mix. I shall develop this theme in what follows as it is central to understanding the relationship between growth and inflation including my general proposition that no definite relation exists.

To start with the manner in which the composition of growth matters for inflation, we can see that high GDP growth accompanied by an even more rapid expansion of agricultural growth may actually be less inflationary than low growth with even lower agricultural growth. This has to do with the fact that economic activity in India is occurring in an environment of generally low consumption levels, especially of food. The price of food, a major component of the index of agricultural prices, is highly sensitive to demand and the growth of income, especially in the non-agricultural sectors of the economy, directly increases the demand for food. So there is no basis in economic theory for the view that there is a direct relationship between growth and inflation, even though much discussion takes place having implicitly assumed that one exists. Very likely the inspiration for this comes from macroeconomics where the Phillips Curve, positing an inverse relation between inflation and unemployment is a prominent construct. Apart from the fact that the relation between growth and unemployment is itself nebulous, the Phillips Curve was to more or less vanish within a decade of its having been discovered on the basis of almost a century of data on wage changes and unemployment in the United Kingdom. In the seventies it was demonstrated that no such relationship existed for the UK economy at least, and possibly not for the United States either, these being the economies usually studied in Anglo American economics. Of course, we can think of a reason for the breakdown of any relationship that might have existed between these two variables in the form of the oil price hikes of the seventies. A supply shock was an altogether new macroeconomic phenomenon to be reckoned with in the theory of inflation. The point of the reference to the Phillips Curve is only to suggest that the positing of a stable relationship between inflation and growth could be equally hazardous even if one is empirically demonstrated to hold in some particular period.

While there is recognition that thy economy is today growing rapidly, it is useful to also pin down the nature of this expansion. India is now undergoing an investment boom located in the manufacturing sector. After having been used to over a decade when it was the services sector that had led the growth in GDP we are now currently observing growth rates of manufacturing that have seldom been observed in the past. This is altogether a good thing as we tend to believe that it is only growth of manufacturing that can generate the kind of employment demand for unskilled Indian who constitute the greater part of the labour force. However, the good news of a manufacturing resurgence has been tempered by news of a rising inflation rate, currently averaging around 6 per cent per annum. In the language fashionable in certain circles this is the sign of the economy overheating. We find this characterisation unhelpful both from a theoretical and a policy point of view. Had the manufacturing growth been accompanied by higher agricultural growth we would have had not only higher growth but conceivably less inflation that we find now. The composition of growth matters, and the same rate of GDP growth is compatible with different inflation rates. When this is recognised we see that it cannot be asserted that growth beyond a certain norm is necessarily inflationary. Unlike the boiling point of water we cannot pin-point the rate of growth beyond which the economy will 'overheat'.

We may now proceed directly to the source of the problem in India. Since the nineteen nineties we have had indifferent growth of agriculture. While there have been years of high growth, the average rate of growth appears to have slowed down. Within this general framework, we can point to some specific pathologies. The pattern of the price rise of the past three months or so signals a particular area of weakness in agriculture. The rise in the inflation rate has been led by the price of food and particularly the price of vegetables. Though we have had periodic scares over the price of onions in the past, a sustained increase in the price of vegetables is relatively new for us. Upto about the eighties the trajectory of inflation has been more closely led by the price of foodgrains. This change reflects the trend in purchasing power of the average household and the expansion of the food consumption basket previously dominated by cereals. Before moving on to consider specific policy measures to tackle inflation in general and some that have been implemented in the current context, the following merits being reflected upon. After over fifty years' efforts at planned development we are today still facing shortages on the food front. Generally food is paid scant attention except when a crisis erupts. Over a decade and a half since 1991 we can now safely assume that the trade, industry and macro-economic policy reforms that have been implemented are clearly inadequate to the task. Agricultural growth needs targeted attention.

When it comes to factors that can counter inflation, productivity growth has a somewhat special place. However, while more permanent in its impact productivity increase does take a while. It may be clarified here that the productivity that we are talking about here is labour productivity. The unique implication of a given productivity increase is that it enables an increase in wages and profits without requiring an increase in prices. Indeed a productivity increase can even enable the lowering of prices. This leaves it unique among anti-inflationary measures. In the context of our discussion so far, it may also be pointed out that the possibility of productivity growth renders the suggestion of a necessarily direct relation between growth and inflation—as false. Where growth is entirely due to a productivity increase, as in the steady state of the Solow model, it can actually end up being deflationary. Now growth is the antidote to inflation. It is in this sense that, as I had raised at the beginning, whether growth generates inflation depends also on the source of the growth. Note that in this case, the growth has come about entirely via productivity increase. Deflation, however, is no unalloyed good !

We now come to the role of monetary policy as an anti-inflationary instrument. Though monetary policy aims to slow the rate of increase of money it can do so mainly by raising the rate of interest. (Targeting inflation through fiscal policy is time-consuming and cumbersome.) As the rate of interest is the cost of finance, this must put a brake on investment spending and thus growth. However, in certain instances it does not even succeed in curbing the price rise. This is in the presence of cost-plus pricing by firms and wage resistance by workers. Such a scenario is to be expected in the industrial sector and has been shown to characterise reasonably well India's industrial economy. Now, while the rising cost of finance may curb investment outlay and choke off growth it may not succeed in curbing inflation very much. In the presence of cost-determined prices and wage bargaining monetary policy might generate stagflation. Outside orthodox macroeconomic policy circles it has long been recognized that some form of an 'incomes policy' is more efficient in keeping inflation down. Incomes polley which works by setting limits to rise in wages and prices acts to check the wage-price spiral. It requires a state that is adept at mediating between economic interests. In the presence of demand determined prices, such as that of agricultural goods in general and food in particular, monetary policy works to abate inflation only by further reducing the demand. Where levels of consumption are not uniformly high this can hardly count as an efficient policy from a welfare point of view. I have elsewhere studied the options with respect to monetary policy in the context of inflation, and noted that they are meagre?

In an open economy, trade throws up another option in the management of inflation. That is to augment supply. This is particularly effective in the context of a supply shortfall for a commodity subject to demand determined prices. Something of the sort is being tried by the Government of India today when it cuts the import duty on some crucial goods. There have been episodes in India when imports had a major impact on prices as during the fifties and sixties when PL 480 imports of wheat from the US were sold domestically to ease a shortfall. There is a slight difference in the contexts however between what had occurred then and what is occurring in India today. For private imports of food to have an impact on domestic prices it is necessary that their landed cost is lower than the prevailing domestic price. It is not clear if that is the case with goods that are driving the current inflation. This consideration did not enter the picture in the case of PL 480 imports as they had come here on US government account, and were therefore not subject to the economic calculus. So while imports can help and must be used to combat inflation at every turn the current inflation in India points resolutely to the importance of a more dynamic food sector in India. This is not getting the attention it deserves. The challenges to raising the production of food at a steady price are not inconsiderable but they are not insurmountable either.

22

Review of Inflationary Control Measures

A Micro Analysis

CHANDRA SHEKHAR RAVI AND BADRI NARAYAN SAH

INTRODUCTORY VISION

In ordinary language or sense, inflation means a process of rising prices. Inflation is that situation while the prices or the supply of money are rising, because in practice both will rise together. Inflation is that condition where the total money supply is more than its demand and or a result of this the value of money starts decreasing and the normal price level rises.

In a broad sense, inflation is that state in which the prices of goods and services rise on the one hand and value of money falls on the other. When money circulation exceeds the production of goods and services, the state of inflation takes place in the economy.

Inflation hurts and it hurts common man the most whose income is fixed and more so those who do not have a regular job and steady source of income. It hurts savers and eventually it hurts investments and eventually growth. Growth takes time to trickle down whereas inflation directly affects common people.

Thus inflation is generally associated with an abnormal increase in the quantity of money resulting in abnormal rise in prices. Basically inflation represents a situation whereby the pressure of aggregate demand for goods and services exceeds the available supply of output (both being counted at the prices ruling at the beginning of a period). In such a situation, the rise in price level is a natural consequence.

On the other side, inflation's scenario viewpoint, such inflation is a monetary phenomenon as economists. According to economists, the evidence of growth-inflation trade off in the Indian context is more pronounced in recent times. Till the early 1990s, high inflation was induced by either monsoon failure or oil price shock. The early 1990s saw high inflation and then acceleration in growth. The late 1990s witnessed deceleration in growth as well as lower inflation. Now is the present times, with the growth accelerating to 8-9 per cent, we also have rising inflation rate.

Therefore, a careful look will show that higher inflation rate today is largely driven by fuel prices and food prices both of which are facing supply side pressures. For example, year-on-year wholesale price-based inflation for vegetables stood at 25.3 per cent and 12.3 per cent for edible oils in August 2007. The international crude oil prices have reached $ 74 per barrel. The Reserve Bank of India has projected inflation close to 5 per cent for the current fiscal and 4-4.5 per cent for the medium-term.

TYPES OF INFLATION

There are different types of inflation which are classified on various bases, but only two very important types of inflation which are as under:

1. Demand Pull Inflation

Demand pull inflation is that inflation when prices rise due to higher demand for goods on services over the available supply.

In other words, demand pull inflation takes place when increase in production lags behind the increase in money supply.

This represents a situation where the basic factor at work is the increase in demand for resources either from the government or the entrepreneurs or the households. The result is that the pressure of demand is such that it can not be met by the currently available supply of output.

2. Cost Push Inflation

Cost push inflation is another type of inflation in which prices rise due to increased input costs. In other words, cost push inflation takes place when price level rises due to increase in cost of production.

CAUSES OF INFLATION

The pivotal causes of inflation is created while aggregate demand for output tends to be excessive in relation to the supply of output or production. Inflation arises as a result of imbalance between real income and monetary income. At first hand, monetary income increases because of increase in quantity of money, but on the other hand, the production of goods and services don't increase in that ratio. Consequently, the ratio of quantity of money (monetary income) is higher than the production of goods and services (real income) and price level rises. Thus, the causes of inflation may classified under two main headings;

1. Increase in Monetary Income or Demand

(a) Increase in monetary supply.
(b) Increase in unproductive expenditure.
(c) Increase in disposable income.
(d) Increase in velocity of income.
(e) Governmental policy.

(f) Increase in population.
(g) Credit policy of banks.
(h) Excessive speculation and tendency to hoarding.
(i) Gap between investment and production.
(j) Increase in salaries, wages or dearness allowance.
(k) Relaxation in recovery and Payment of old loans.
(l) Increase in foreign demand and exports.
(m) Excessive public expenditure.
(n) Deficit financing.

2. Causes of Limiting Production

(a) Droughts, famine, floods, earthquake and any other natural calamity.
(b) Decrease in capital equipment.
(c) Application of law of diminishing return.
(d) Speculative hoarding by the producers, traders and middlemen.
(e) Commercial policy.
(f) Production structure.
(g) Scarcity of other complementary factors of production.
(h) Tax policy.
(i) Lack of dynamic entrepreneurs.

Such these causes clarify that when the monetary income of public increases in ratio of production then price-level rises. Not only it, but these factors also operate simultaneously to exert inflationary pressure and, if continued sufficiently long, to create hyper-inflation. Indeed, such situation or condition is called 'inflation'.

MEASURES TO CONTROL INFLATION (OR MEASUREMENT OF INFLATION)

Doubtless, inflation is a very complicated phenomenon. Because uncontrolled inflation produces serous ill-effects on economy as well as it gives rises to many political, economical and also moral malformations. This is why, its control is too much necessitated. But there is no one sovereign remedy to combat it. Despite it, the different measures or measurement to check inflation have to be taken on several fronts, specially monetary and non-monetary. All these measures have one common aim. They aim at reducing aggregate monetary expenditure taking the available output as given. First and foremost we want to discuss about former measures to control inflation which are as:

I. Monetary Measures

Of course monetary measures is the best measures or measurement to control inflation and is to reduce the aggregate spending. Monetary policy can help in reducing the pressure of demand. This policy works by controlling the cost and availability of credit. The main reason of inflation is increased money supply more than required. So during inflation, the Central Bank can raise the cost of borrowing and reduce the credit creating capacity of the commercial banks. This will make borrowing most costly than before and thereby the demand. For funds will be reduced. With respect to reduction in the money supply, the Central Bank can withdraw old money and can issue new currency in place of it. Old money is converted to new quantity of money.

Similarly, with a reduction in their credit creating capacity, the banks will be more cautious in their lending policies. Central bank can control credit by adopting the qualitative and quantitative methods of control, which reduces money supply in the economy and discourage new investment.

- In this way, monetary measures control inflation by consist in fixing.
- Reduction in money supply; or reduction in the volume of spending money supply.
- Increase in the rate of interest/bank rate.
- Higher reserve requirements.
- Higher discount rates.
- By adopting strict note issue policy.
- Open market operation.
- Varying reserve ratios.

By adopting the qualitative and quantitative methods of credit controls or regulation of consumer credit and varying margin requirements.

2. Fiscal Measures

Fiscal measure is the another remedy for fighting or control inflation. For combating inflation there are two important wings of fiscal policy—(a) Government revenues, and (b) Government expenditure which is followed or adopted by the Indian Government. The government's fiscal policy can contribute to the control of inflation either by reducing private spending by increasing the taxes on private sector or by decreasing government expenditure, or combining both the elements. Thus, the following fiscal measures could be adopted by government for combating inflation;

- Increase in tax rates.
- Reduction in government spending.
- Increase in public debts.
- Imposition of new taxes.
- Reduction in government expenditure.
- The encouragement of Savings/Introduction of compulsory saving schemes.
- Check on investment.
- Balance budget.
- Revaluation of money.
- Over-valuing domestic currency in terms of foreign currencies.
- Wages freeze.
- Gold sterilisation or done in the United States.
- Other controls.

3. Non-Monetary Measure or Physical Measures

In lieu of monetary and fiscal measures there are some important non-monetary or physical nature measures which is adopted to control inflation which are as;

- Increase in output/production.
- Increasing imports of goods.

- Decreasing experts of goods.
- Check on profit distribution.
- Check on speculation.
- Check on hoarding.

OTHER METHOD TO MEASUREMENT OF INFLATION

Inflation indicates the rise in the price of a basket of commodities on a point-to-point basis. It basically suggests an increase in the cost of living over a period of time. For example, if you buy 20 essential commodities on 11th February, 2009 for Rs. 200. If the same set of 20 commodities costs Rs. 110 on 11th February, 2010, the inflation rate will be 5 per cent. It means that the prices are rising at 5 per cent per-annum.

Now inflation is measured by monitoring changes in price indices. The purpose of a price index is to be able to quantify the overall increase or decrease in prices of several commodities rather than the increase or decrease in individual commodities. The means through which the price index does this is to measure changes in individual prices and then arrive at a weighted average change for the whole lot. The weights assigned to individual commodities would depend on their relative importance. For instance, how the price of rice, which you might consume everyday changes is obviously more important than say, changes in the price of footwear.

To control inflation is measured by general price index. General price index measures the changes in average price of goods and services. For this first and foremost a base year is selected and its index is assumed as 100 and on this basis price index for the current year is calculated. If the index of the current year is below 100 it indicates the state of deflation and on the contrary, if index of the current year is above 100 it indicates the state of inflation.

Inflation rate and the value of money (or the purchasing power of money) are inversely correlated. Hence the value of money can also be measured with the help of price indices. The value of money declines when price index goes up and *vice-versa*.

1. Wholesale Price Index (WPI)

The former measures changes in wholesale prices, which may be more meaningful. From the producers point of view, while the letter measures changes in retail price, which are obviously more relevant to the consumer. The inflation in India is calculated on the basis of the WPI. For example when the annual inflation rate for a particular week has reached 5.2 per cent, what that means is that the average level of prices of the commodities tracked by the WPI for that week was 5.2 per cent higher than for the corresponding week a year (or 52 weeks to be precise) earlier. It is important to recognise that the inflation rate going down does not mean prices are declining. It only means the rate at which prices are going up has slowed down.

For the WPI, this will mean all categories of goods produced or used in the economy. Each item would be assigned a weight in the overall index proportion to the value of the output of that item in total output of all goods in the case of the WPI. The index reflects nothings but the weighted average of each commodity's price. An appropriate base year is selected, in which the price of each commodity, and hence the overall index, is equated to 100. This base is used as a benchmark for future prices. Thus, if rice costs, say, Rs.15 per kg in the base year and Rs. 20 per kg in a subsequent period, the rice index for the later year would be 300. How much the change in the index of a particular commodity influences the overall index would depend on what its weight is the greater the weight, the more the impact.

2. Cost Inflation Index (CII)

Cost Inflation Index (CII) is a pivotal measures of inflation (for control inflation) that finds application in tax-law, when computing long-term capital gains on sale of assets.

According to the *Section 48 of the Income Tax Act*, "The index as what is notified by the union government every year having regarded to 75 per cent of average rise in the Consumer Price Index (CPI) for urban non-manual employees for the immediately preceding previous year."

In this regard, the Cost Inflation Index (CII) having base as 1981-82, stands at 519 in financial year 2006-07. In the first few years this index grew/increased only by single digits. The latest jump is of 22 points, from 497 in 2005-06 to 519 in 2006-07. The latest cost inflation index (i.e., of 2006-07) shows five-fold growth or increment in 25 years (i.e. 1981-2006).

CURRENT STEPS TAKEN UP PREVENTING INFLATION IN INDIA

To control the inflation rate and to remove inflationary situation or condition in Indian economy, a lot of steps have been taken on both demand and supply side. During recent years, the government has taken a number of steps in this direction which are as under;

1. Steps Related to Supply Side

(a) Open market sale of wheat and rice by Indian Food Corporation.
(b) Wheat and wheat products were brought under the provisions of licensing and storage limit for preventing black marketing of these products.
(c) Import of edible oils on 20 per cent import duty and pulses on 5 per cent import duty under OGL.
(d) Import of wheat to maintain the buffer stocks in the economy.
(e) Import of 2 lakh tonnes Palmolin Oil for the sale under public distribution system.
(f) To ensure the sufficient supply of sugar, edible oil and pulses, liberalised imports were permitted.

2. Steps Related to Demand Side

(a) To curtail fiscal deficit upto 5 per cent of GDP.
(b) To put a check on money supply increase.
(c) Price control and rationing.
(d) Controlling money wages.

These measures are much less practicable than the monetary and fiscal measures, because, due to institutional, technological, psychological and other non-economic causes, hinder the success of the non-monetary measures. Thus full reliance can't be placed on such measures. Therefore, they can only be considered as supplementary to more effective measures.

CONCLUSIVE REMARKS

Indeed, inflation is a complex monetary phenomenon in economy, and it hurts common man or people the most whose income is fixed and more so those who do not have a regular job and steady source of income. Due to high inflation rate, common people directly affected by it. So what should be the policy response to the rise in inflation rate? At political level, protecting the consumption? At political level, protecting the consumption level of poor is a high priority. Fiscal measures provide short-term relief. The monetary policy response is more potent and would be needed if there are no signs of inflation coming down. However, monetary policy measures can only provide temporary solution. We are experiencing inflation a result of "supply side" constrain especially in food sector. So the long-term remedies are in easing supply side constraints.

Though both the phases of trade cycle (i.e. inflation and deflation) are harmful to the economy but a low rate of inflation is an inducing tonic to the developing economy. Slow rise in prices is supposed to induce the producers to increase the production which in turn ensures more and more employment opportunities in the country. But uncontrolled and ever-rising inflation rate disturbs the economy. Hence, it is required for the developing economies to keep a strict control on inflation rate in the economy by former measures as well as new invented measures like CII and WPI.

REFERENCES

Employment News.

Ibid.

Ibid.

Devett, Kewal Krishan and Chand, Adarsh, Modern Economic Theory, S. Chand and Co. Ltd., Ram Nagar, New Delhi.

Kurukshetra, A Rural Development Monthly Journal; Various Issues.

Pratiyogita Darpan, A Monthly Development Excellence Magazine, Various Issues.

Swami, H.R., Gupta, B.P. and Vaishnav, B.L., Economic and Business Environment; Ramesh Book Depot, Jaipur, New Delhi.

www.google.com.

Yojana, A Development Monthly Magazine; Various Issues.

23

Recent Global Inflationary Trends and the Role of Central Banks in Developing Economy (India)

D.K. Bhattacharya and Niyati Chakraborty

Most of the developing countries have been subject during the recent years to inflationary pressures of various degrees of intensity. As a rule, these pressures emanate from attempt by one or more sectors of the economy to secure a larger share of the total product. The primary motivations of such attempts are the desire of other public sector or the private sector, or both, to undertake additional investments and to put the burden of the required additional savings on the other sector. However, the attempts of any one sector, once made effective, tends in terms to induce defensive reactions of other sectors that want to maintain their share in the total product, not only for investment but also, especially on the part of the government and of wage and salary earners, for consumption. These defensive reactions usually intensify the inflationary pressures.

Asian economic growth is slowing as weaker global demands dents exports, but accelerating inflation across the region is expected to pile pressure on Central Banks to tighten policy. China is on track for its sixth straight year of double-digit growth in 2008, but momentum will probably slow down in nearly a decade. Meanwhile, China's consumer prices in 2008 will probably rise at the fastest pace in more than a decade, extending a policy dilemma for Chinese leaders as they try to balance the risks from slower economic growth with higher inflation. "Inflation will remain as a pressing issue", said Wong Jianhui, an analyst at South-west Securities in Beijing. Economists forecast slower gross domestic product growth this year in 11 of the 12 economies in the Asia-Pacific, excluding Japan. Thailand's economic growth is seen bucking the trend, accelerating to 5 per cent from 4.8 per cent in 2007-08 as solid exports under pinned by rice sales—help the economy defy expectations of a slowdown amid political uncertainty.

India's economic growth is expected to slow to 7.6 per cent in 2008-09 (April-March) as inflation forces the central bank to fighten policy, while South Korea's growth could slip to a 3 year low of 4.5 per cent in 2008. The Asian Development Bank has said it expects growth in the region's economies, excluding Japan to ease to 7.6 per cent in 2008 from 8.7 per cent last year as exports slow due to weaker demand from the United States. Bur Asia's exports remain resilient due to rising demand from other emerging markets, reflected in solid trade surplus in such countries as China, Indonesia, Taiwan and Malaysia. Indonesia's annual average inflation this year is seen accelerating sharply to 11.2 per cent from 6.6 per cent in 2007. India's annual inflation is expected to rise to 11 per cent in fiscal year 2007-08. That far exceeds the 6 per cent in a previous poll conducted in March 2007 and now 4 per cent rate recorded in 2009.

Inflation is accelerating across Asia, driven by surging food and oil prices, posing threat to economic growth. Central Banks in Indonesia, the Philippines, Taiwan and Vietnam and India have raised interest rates in last year (2008), but analysts believe they remain behind the curve as inflation expectations rise and firms try to pass on higher costs to consumers.

"Government of India, like other governments all over the world is fighting inflation. We have taken fiscal, monetary and administrative measures and we are willing to take more measures" said Indian Finance Minister. Inflation as measured by the wholesale price index has become a cause of measure concern ever since it crossed 9 per cent in March 2008, and since then it has been steadily rising without respite. Owing to its wide coverage of commodities and frequently available data, the wholesale price index is the most commonly used measure of inflation in India. However, it excludes services and non-tradable commodities. Further it only measures headline inflation.

It is important to distinguish between headline inflation and core inflation. Headline inflation includes the entire set of commodities in the general price index, in this case, the wholesale price index. Core inflation does not take into consideration commodities that have volatile prices, for example, food and fuel. It follows that supply shocks that arise from a poor crop yield or hikes in international prices of fuel while lead to increases in headline inflation. In contrast, core inflation would not be affected by these shocks. In India and most other developing countries, food articles are significantly weighted in the price index. As such, a measure of core inflation may not provide a complete picture of the price scenario. Inflation in 2007-08 and in the current fiscal so far has been driven mostly by price increases of manufactured products followed by primary articles and then the fuel price.

So, the Indian economy has experienced robust growth since 2003-04 to date. However, while the first three years in this period showed moderate inflationary pressures, the last two years have experienced relatively high inflation. In terms of wholesale prices, inflation began to firm up mid-2006-07 mainly due to: (i) an increase in the prices of wheat, pulses and edible oils because of the shortfall in domestic supply relative to demand and firm international prices; and (ii) an increase in prices of international crude. The R.B.I. continued to follow its policy of gradual withdrawal of monetary accommodation in order to be able to stabilize using inflationary expectations. This in addition to an enforcement in the availability of wheat, pulses and edible oils and fiscal and supply-side measures put into place by the government of India helped contain inflation. This declarating trend continued into 2007-08 until Dec. 2007 and increased sharply thereafter.

Increases in prices of food and non-food primary articles as well as manufactured products also affected to the economy and the wholesale price index inflation (in the current fiscal year 2008-09) has consistently been above 7 per cent mark and touched a three and a half year high of 8.24 per cent in the week ending May 24, 2008 on account of increases in food, metal products and industrial fuel. In order to combat the inflationary pressures, the government has taken a number of measures which became successful to control over it in 2009.

There is no easy policy response to the present inflationary crisis but there are critical differences between what should be done for food and for oil and what should be done in short-run and the long. For basic food, there is no alternative to shielding poor consumers from the market price rise. Some experts have remarked how this is all a matter of supply and demand and if Government do not interfere in the market, the price rise will bring a supply response, which will cause inflation to level out. That may be true. But markets pay no heed to grinding poverty. There would be starvation deaths before such a market process fully works itself out. The state needs to intervene even though, in the long-run, the State should invest heavily in agricultural sector to boost productivity and allow for the free flow of food between regions and also in and out of the nation, in response to market incentives.

On oil, continuing to shield consumers from the global price rise is not sustainable policy. It is causing unmanageable fiscal strain and by keeping the demand for fuel artificially high, it is distorting markets which will soon hurt the economies growth. Prices will have to be raised, even though will hurt consumers in visible ways, hurt in itself is unavoidable given the global situation.

While some subsidy for end-use goods, such as basic food, education and health, is unavoidable in a nation of as much poverty as ours, subsidies in general are a bad idea. They distort prices and get subverted by corporations and the rich and seldom reach the needy. In a strange way, this crisis can be an opportunity. Faced with rising costs, corporations in industrialized nations are struggling to protect their profits. India needs to work on a war-footing to our bureaucracy, increase efficiency and attract international business. This will help stave-off the immediate crisis, create unemployment and yield large, long-run benefits.

The central bank attempted some avenues forward impairing the efficiency of the central banking in less developed countries like India. The experience of these countries reviewed suggest that governments are perhaps not as universally the principle source of inflation as often seems to be supposed. Nor is the actual, and much less the potential, scope for an anti-inflationary monetary policy quite so limited as is frequently. The more significant is central bank credit to the private sector as a primary expansion factor, the greater will be the possibility of preventing chronic inflation through monetary measures. It follows that the realization of a stabilizing, or, of the government is the primary expansion source, an atleast partially compensating policy, requires the removal of obstacles. The most important obstacle seems to be unwillingness of the monetary authorities to exercise greater restraint upon the private sector. If monetary authorities are reluctant to exercise a greater measure of restraint in their credit policy because they believe that a highly elastic supply of credit is conductive to an acceleration of economic development, the lessons of experience may gradually tend to induce change in views.

So far as unwillingness to enforce sufficiently serve anti-inflationary measures is due to apprehensions regarding the short-run output effects of a restrictive credit policy, it may be more difficult to induce a greater degree of restraint. For a less developed country in which the foremost policy objective is not only absolute but also relative economic growth, underutilized production capacity will be socially less tolerable than in an advanced economy where the stability of full employment objectives tend to take priority over growth objective. It may, therefore, be difficult to persuade monetary authorities to contract credit or even to freeze it, when, for instance, output and income in the agricultural sector fall on account of exogenous factors, like a crop failure or depressed export markets, since such a policy may result in under utilized capacity.

In their day-to-day decisions on credit policy, specially in respect to rediscounting, central banks are likely to be more concerned with the immediate effects of their decisions on output than with the long-run effects on propensities (to save, to invest, to hold money, etc.) and the structure of the financial system. In less developed countries, those long-run effects will, however, determine the scope for monetary policy in the future. Therefore, an important, although perhaps unorthodox, field of what may be called long-run monetary policy may lie in activities that aim at changing these propensities and the structure of the monetary and financial system. Such attempts may often conflict with short-run policies. Other related measures are the encouragement of specialized saving institutions and the extension of central bank control over the investment policies of non-bank financial intermediaries. If such long-run policies succeed in changing saving, investment and asset holding habits in the "right" direction, some reasons for the reluctance of central banks to apply restrictive measures to commercial banks and to private sector will gradually disappear.

One particular aspect of long-run monetary policy may need special attention. The extent to which credit can be expanded without inflation, other things being equal will be greater when income velocity declines than when it remains constant or even increases long-run policy may, therefore, aim at reducing velocity by, say, lengthening payment periods and encouraging the holding of money. On the other hand, it has also been noted that the efficiency of short-run monetary policy will be raised when the public, including banks, can be induced to hold financial assets and to use means of payment less liquid than money. This will reduce the scope for credit expansion without inflation but it will permit greater credit extension by financial institutions outside the monetary system, i.e. from sources other than the central bank and commercial banks.

In spite of institutional limitations, monetary measures could, as required very recently in India, have succeeded in preventing continuous inflation. Central bank action could have reduced the rate of inflation. The potentially most effective restrictive tool would have been greater restraint in central bank rediscounting for banks and the private sector. The unwillingness of the monetary authorities to use restrictive tools more vigourously is due mostly to apprehensions regarding the output effects of a reduction in the rate of credit expansion and of a reduction in the volume of credit.

There are indications that in most of the countries including India reviewed gradual change in the legal and institutional framework were slowly followed by a more determined implementation and restrictive monetary measures. In addition, further improvements in the efficiency of monetary policy in still predominantly agricultural economies may depend on the extent to which the present inflexibility of credit policy can be reduced. This may require the growth of capital markets and credit institutions outside the monetary system.

CONCLUSION

It has been said that inflation is the most regressive form of taxation as it effects the poor and vulnerable sections of society. In the Indian context, it is the unrecognized, without the benefit of trade union or political patronage, who suffer the worst effects of inflation. Inflation dampens exports by making our products expensive and conversely, makes imports attractive. Inflation leads to recession, as people with fixed income set apart an increasing share of their income to meet the growing costs of essential commodities, leading very little expenditure on non-essential items. The production of such items has to be curtailed leading to shutdowns and recession.

Reserve Bank of India assisting in controlling inflation through monetary measures such as quantitative and selective credit controls and by manipulating the Cash-Reserve Ratio (CRR) and the Statutory Liquidity Ratio (SLR). On the other side, the mechanism of Public Distribution System ensures availability of essential commodities for the poor. This helps to maintain price levels. Foreign inflows need to be sterilised by the R.B.I. by withdrawing from circulation an equivalent amount of rupees either through open market operation or through regulating bank credit. The country's inflation rate fall below 3.7 per cent, the lowest in 13 months raising hopes of further fall in the interest rates as policy-makers group for options to maintain growth amid a sharp slowdown in the world economy. A cut in the repo rate—at which the central bank lends to commercial banks appears a possibility.

References

International Monetary Fund Report; International Financial Statistics, Various Issues of 2006 to 2008.

Reserve Bank of India (2007), Macroeconomic and Monetary Development in 2009-07, *R.B.I. Report*, Bombay.

Satura, Understanding Recent Trends, *Economic and Political Weekly*, Vol. X, No. 2G, pp. 108-111.

Sidharth Shastri, Inflation and Economic Growth in India; *Empirical Investigation—Southern Economist*, May 1, 2008, pp. 57-62.

Srinivasan, T.N., Price Indices and Inflation Rates, *Economic and Political Weekly*, June 23, 2008, pp. 217-23.

Various Newspaper Reports on India's Inflation During 2008-09.

24

Inflationary Trends in India

MINA KUMARI AND MANOJ KUMAR VERMA

Every economy calculates its inflation for efficient administration as the multi-dimensional effects of inflation make it necessary. India calculates its inflation on two price indices, i.e. the wholesale price index (WPI) and the consumer price index (CPI). While the WPI inflation is used at the macro-level policy-making; the CPI-inflation is used for micro-level analysis. The inflation at the WPI is the inflation of economy. Both the point-to-point method and may be shown in points as well as in percentage relative to a particular base year.

Inflation has been a highly sensitive issue in India right since the independence and it has been so during the ongoing reforms process period, too. It has an incessant tendency of resulting into 'double digits', taking politically explosive proportions like government falling at the centre and state levels due to price of the commodities such as edible oil, onion, potato, etc. In such situations the government in general has been taking recourse to tighter money supply to contain the state level disturbances due to rise of the commodities such as edible oil, onion, potato, etc. although it has contained inflation but at the cost of higher growth. Price got rooted in India's political psyche in such a way that the Government did check frequent famines quickly at the cost of long-term endemic hunger and sustained malnutrition. The government did not go to search the fine balance of the trade-off between inflation and growth due to political risk. The present period (2007-08) is almost similar to it when economy required higher money supply for investment but the government's monetary policy proposes to contain inflation below 6 per cent with the help of tighter monetary policy.

Decadal inflation in India looks comparatively normal with references to many developing economies. But it has sporadic incidences of double digit tendencies mainly due to supply side short-falls caused by droughts (monsoon failures), price rise of crude oil in the international market or fund diversions due to wars (the Chinese war of 1962 and the Pakistan wars of 1965-66 and 1971). The decadal inflation in India has been as given below.

1. During 1950s: remained at 1.7 per cent.
2. During 1970s: remained at 6.4 per cent.
3. During 1970s: remained at 9.0 per cent.
4. During 1980s: remained 8.0 per cent.
5. During 1990s: remained at 9.5 per cent. (though it reached 0.5 per cent by the fourth quarter of the fiscal 1998-99)
6. During 2000-01 to 2007-08: remained at 4.7 per cent (upto August 2007) with the fiscal 2002-03 at 3.4 per cent (the lowest) and the fiscal 2004-05 at 6.5 per cent (the highest)
7. During 2008-09 reached at the highest level of about 14 per cent.

The last time inflation went in double digits it was in the fiscal 1991-92, when it was at 13.6 per cent by 1997-98, though it moderated to the level of 3.5 per cent later.

An analysis of inflationary trends in India does not pin-point any one reason behind it. The economists have pointed out all possible reasons (the so-called 'good' and 'pad') behind the inflationary pressure in the economy of which we may have a brief review:

1. Structural Inflation

With few exceptional years, India has been facing the typical problem of bottleneck inflation (i.e. structural inflation) which arise out of shortfalls in the supply of goods; a general crisis of a developing economy; rising demand but lack of invertible capital to produce the required level of goods. Whenever the Government managed to go for higher growth by managing higher investible capital it had inflationary pressures on the economy (seen during 1970s and 1980s, specially) and growth was sacrificed at the altar of lower inflation, which was politically more justified). Thus the supply side mismatch remained a long-drawn problem in India for higher inflation. After some time even if the government managed higher experimental areas which did show low growth with higher inflation signs of a stagnating economy.

2. Cost-Push Inflation

Due to 'inflation tax' the price of goods and services in India have been rising as the Government took alternative recourse to increase its revenue receipts. We see it taking place due to higher import duties on the raw materials also.

The non-value-added (non-VAT) tax structure of India in the past was also having cascading effect on the prices of commodities in the country. The Government needed higher revenues to finance its planned development, thus the above given factors looked inescapable

3. Fiscal Policy

To finance the developmental requirements of the economy the Government became trapped in the cyclical process of over-money supply At first it was done by external barrowings bout by the late 1960s onwards (once deficit financing got acceptance around the world) the governments started taking recourse to heavy internet borrowing is contributed by the Reserve Bank of India (RBI) which leads to price rise. For any government deficit if the Central Bank (RBI) is purchasing primary issues of the Government securities or getting fresh advances to the government the combined effect has to be higher inflation, lower savings rates and lower economic growth—the vices of unsound fiscal policy. The higher fiscal deficit tends to bring about higher interest rates as demand for funds rise, excess demand raises expected inflation and expected depreciation of the currency

Once the foreign exchange (Forex) reserves started increasing with a faster pace by the early 2000-01 fiscal its cost of maintenance has been translated into higher prices, as the RBI purchases the foreign currencies it supplies equivalent rupees into the economy which creates extra demand and prices go up.

The higher revenue deficits (driven by high interest payments, subsidies, salaries and pensions, basically) and fiscal deficit make the government supply more money which push the inflation in the upward direction. Once the fiscal and Budget Management Act came into force in 2003, the scenario improved in the coming times. Though the period from 1999 to 2003 did show high growth with low inflation and the lowest interest rates in India.

RECENT STEPS TO CHECK THE INFLATION

High inflation hurts the poor with their incomes not indexed to prices. It also puts pressure on interest rates, and adversely affects both savings and investment. Because of its implications for the poor and its possible destabilizing effects on macro-economic stability, containment of inflation is high on the government's agenda.

The anti-inflationary policies of the government include strict fiscal and monetary discipline; rationalization of excise and import duties of essential commodities to lighten the burden on the poor; effective supply-demand management of sensitive items through liberal tariff and trade policies; and strengthening the public distribution system

EFFECTS OF INFLATION

There are multi-dimensional effects of inflation on an economy both at the micro and macro-level. It redistributes income; distorts relative prices; destabilizes employment, tax, saving and investment policies and finally it may bring in recession and depression in economy.

After the last government change at the centre there are two periods of inflationary pressures on the economy. First, it was just after the General Elections of 2003 when the inflation crossed 7.5 per cent mark on the vibes of costlier oil prices basically. Second, it was by the late-2006 that inflation had a upward tendency due to mixed reasons. It was at the highest level of about 16-17 per cent. If we consider the whole period as the 'recent times', the major steps taken by the Government/the RBI check inflation may be underlined as under:

1. Exercise (i.e. CENVAT) and custom cuts on oil and petroleum products.
2. Lanching market Stabilisation Scheme (MSS) to siphon out the extra money flowing into economy.
3. Off-loading the excessive foreign currency reserves via pre-payments of external loans (public as well as private); easier access to foreign currency at corporate and individual levels; proposal of special purpose vehicles (SPVS) for infrastructural development, etc.
4. Making foreign currency deposit in the country less attractive (by cutting interest rates).
5. Following tighter credit and monetary policy (by rising CRR, repo rates, basically) to check the money supply into the economy.
6. Cutting down the interest rate on the small saving schemes.
7. Housing sector loans have an upward revision in the interest rate with the twin objective of cooling down inflation and curtailing extra-volatility seen in this sector as well as the loan-vulnerability.

8. Allowing fresh imports of wheat to cool down the rising foodgrain price in the market.

REFRENCES

Agrawal, Anupam Inflation, Causes and Effect.

Credit and Monetary Policy Anounced by RBI on March 3, 2007.

C. Rangarajan, Indian Economy: Essays on Money and Finance.

Economic Survey, 2006-07, p. 80.

Jalan, Bimal, India's Economic Policy.

25

Inflation Trends During Pre and Post-Reform Era

VIVEK KUMAR, MANISH KUMAR AND NIRANJAY KUMAR

INTRODUCTION

A well functioning monetary system is indispensable for strong economic growth. Labour, Capital, Technologies are keys to economics growth and development but these become meaningless and less productive in pushing an economy upwards on the ladder of development if the monetary system is inefficient. "The monetary system is the emergency through which people carry out transactions with each other, whether buying or selling. Saving or investing, borrowing of Lending." Money lies at the heart of monetary system. Money is anything that is generally accepted as mean of payment for goods and services. Anything can serve as money if it enjoys the legal backing of the government/monetary authorities i.e. it is backed by legislation. It acts as a medium of exchange, a unit of account, and a store of value.

MONEY AND THE PROCESS OF ECONOMIC GROWTH : THEORETICAL PERSPECTIVES/PARADIGMS

What role does money plays in stimulating the process of economic growth and development? Does it actually play a role or is it simply natural in its effects on the workings of the real sector of the economy? It's an age old controversy as many economists believe it does while many claim that it does not. In economic literature the role of money has been discussed around low contexts :

The stabilization of economic activity and the promotion of economic growth. Growth with full employment and in price stability has been a major concern of macroeconomic policy.

THE MONEY NEUTRALITY PROPOSITION

The real question is as to how does money influence real sector variables like output, employment. Or do real variable remain unaffected by monetary fluctuations in the economy. When one reviews the various growth theories and models one finds that money does not figure as a key determinant of growth. Growth is supposed to depend upon capital accumulation, population, technology, knowledge, etc. This is money neutrality proposition that money does not influence key real sector variables. But the works of Wicksell (1907), I. Fisher (1920), Keynes (1936), Haberler (1952) and Tobin (1965) has challenged this idea. It has been found that financial system in general and money supply in particular caused sustained, and at times accentuated, business cycles; and second money supply had an influence on interest rates which in term had an impact on capital accumulation.

THE KEYNESIAN REVOLUTION : THE TRADE-OF BETWEEN GROWTH AND PRICE STABILITY

Keynes very successfully challenged the Neutrality proposition, Keynesian accepted the classical position that employment is dependent on real wages, but with an added assumption that nominal wages are more rigid than price that are themselves assumed to be stickey. This means that an increase in money supply will lead to an increase in price level and decrease in real wages, and bring about improvement in real economic activity over the underemployment level.

The Phillips curve, depicting the inverse relationship between unemployment and wage inflation, provided the empirical basis for the non-neutrality proposition of the Keynesian school of thought. The Keynesian revolution also brought about a directional change in the thinking on monetary policy. Emphasis shifted from a rule-based discretionary policy initiatives by central banks to offset specific events causing business fluctuations. The liquidity preference hypothesis implied that monetary policy can affect interest rates and influence investment decision and thus effect real variables.

DEVELOPING COUNTRY CASE— THE INFLATION TAX ARGUMENT

The developing nations lack adequate amount of financial resources to promote investment and capital accumulation and in this way promote economic growth the tax base is low and this forces to look for alternative resources. This generally takes the form of inflation tax, which is a tax imposed by inflation on currency and other non-interest earning money holdings of people. The revenue yields of inflation tax depends on the nature of the demand for real money balances and its sensitivity to changes in price level. While theoretically the effect of inflation tax on revenue is ambiguous, the analysis leads to general inference that higher the elasticity of real money demand to inflation the lower is the potential additional revenue from an increase in the inflation tax.

INFALTION IN INDIA

The basic objective of five year plans were "development along socialist lines to secure repaid economic growth and expansion of employment, reduction in disparities income and wealth, preventions of concentration of economic power and creation of volumes and attitudes of a free and equal society the Mahalanobis model of growth emphasized investment in heavy industry to achieve industrialization which was assumed to be the rapid condition of economic development. A major objective of economic planning has been to promote economic growth in an environment of price stability.

Inflation is described that as situation characterized by sustained increase in the general price level. A rate of inflation of around five per cent is considered normal but anything above it starts affecting the growth negatively. An anticipated inflation is less worrisome than an unanticipated one.

During inflation all costs and prices do not rise together in the same proportion. But it is an increase in the general level of prices measured by price index which is an average of consumer or producer prices.

PRICE SITUATION DURING 1951-71

During the first five year plan the price situation was favourable. At the end of First Plan period, the general price index stood at 99 (with 1952-53=100). During the First Plan deficit financing was on a modest scale. Narrow money supply, that is, M_1, grew at the rate of 2.1 per cent per annum whereas Broad money, M_3, grew at the rate of 3.4 per cent per annum. Since money supply fell short of increase in output, the general price level came down. Throughout the Second Plan period, there was gradual and steady rise in prices and it rose by twenty per cent by 1960-65. The period starting from 1956-57 and continuing upto 1963-64 may be characterized as the period of moderate rise in prices. The WPI (1961-62=100) which stood at 74 in 1955-56 rose to 110-56 rose to 110-15 in 1963-64.

The Chinese invasion of India towards the end of 1962, the Indo Pakistan conflict in 1965 and in consequent increase in defence expenditure and serious famine condition of 1965-66 lead to inflationary pressures. Between 1961-66 the rise in prices of foodstuffs was over 40 per cent. For four years, that is, from 1964-65 to 1967-68 prices rose at an annual rate of @ 11 per cent per annum.

PRICE SITUATION DURING 1970S

The upward movement in prices during the initial year of fourth plan (1969-74) was rather slow. For the first three years the rise in price level ranged between 7 and 9 point. In the fourth final year price level rose by 19 point and 47 points respectively. Large influx of refugees from Bangaldesh, heavy government expenditure, failure of Kharif crops in 1972-73 and the complete failure of take over of wholesale trade in wheat resulted in unprecedented rise in price during 1973-74 will all the characteristics of galloping inflation. Rise in crude oil prices also strengthened inflation and also led to depreciation of rupee. This pushed up the cost of imports. WPI (1961-62 = 100) stood at 331 in Sept. 1974.

During the final years of 1970s the inflation was well under control and price stability was achieved as a result of government's short-term demand and supply management policies.

Price Trend During 1975-76

(1961-62=100)

	WPI of all Commodities
Sept. 1974	331
March 1975	309
March 1976	283

Source : *RBI Bulletin.*

	WPI of all Commodities (1970-71=100)
March 1977	183
Jan. 1978	184
Jan. 1979	185

Source : *RBI Bulletin.*
Economic Surveys, 1981-82

FIVE YEAR AVERAGE INFLATION RATE

Though on an average, inflation based on the WPI remained below the 7 per cent level through the 1950s and 1960s, it accelerated during the first half on the 1970s to touch double figures but decelerated in the second half of 1970s.

(Per cent)

Period	*52 Weeks Annual average*
1956-57 to 1960-61	6.3
1961-62 to 1965-66	5.8
1966-67 to 1970-71	6.7
1971-72 to 1975-76	12.0
1976-77 to 1980-81	8.5

Source : Economic Survey.

PRICE MOVEMENT DURING THE 1980S

The poor agriculture production of 1979-80 and adverse impact on industrial production due to weak demand for consumer and capital goods from agriculture sector, and due to the strengthening of international crude oil prices during 1979-80 led to the development of inflationary tendencies in the economy. Government adopted strong anti-inflation any measures and this helped in checking prices. On the demand side the monetary policy was used to check the growth of liquidity in the system so that excess credit creation didn't take place. On the fiscal front public expenditure was checked. The exercise of monetary and fiscal policy was meant to control the aggregate effective demand in the economy.

On the supply side the government attempted to increase the supply of goods and services through both short-term and long-term measures which included increase in outflow of foodgrains through public distribution system and steps taken to increase production in critical areas.

Price Movement During the Sixth Plan (1970-71=100)

Year	*WPI of all Commodities*	*% variation over the previous year*
1979-80	218	—
1980-81	256	17.4
1981-82	281	9.8
1982-83	289	2.9
1983-84	316	9.4
1984-85	338	7.0

Source : Economic Survey, 1988-89.

During the Seventh Plan period (1985-90), the wholesale prices moved rather steadily. The pressure on prices was due to shortfall in production of essential agricultural commodities. On the monetary side RBI tightened credit outflow and steps were taken to check excess liquidity in the system. Foodgrains, edible oil and pulses, etc. were imported. Food reserves were used through public distribution system to project the poor from the onslaught of inflation.

Price Situation During the Seventh Plan (1985-90)

Year	*Wholesale Price Index*	*Annual Increase %*
1984-85	120	6.0
1985-86	125	4.9
1986-87	133	4.7
1987-88	144	10.7
1988-89	154	5.7
1989-90	166	8.1

PRICE SITUATION DURING THE 1990S

The first half of 1990s saw a sharp increase in rate of inflation largely because of the monetization of fiscal deficits. This was intensified by hike in procurement prices as well as supply demand imbalances in essential commodities like pulses, oilseeds and edible oils, the foreign exchange constraint created problems on import front due to which supply could not be augmented the balance demand pressures in the economy. Increase in fuel prices and other administered items also fed higher inflation. The inflationary pressures continued during 1993-94 and 1994-95 in wake of capital flows and the consequent higher monetary expansion. The economic reforms introduced in the early 1990s brought about policy charges on many fronts and a liberalized external regime and deregulate internal scene led to inflows of foreign capital. The focus of monetary policy shifted to the moderation of money supply

Price Situation after 1990 (Average of 52 weeks)

Year	*Wholesale Price Index*	*Annual rate of inflation*
1981-82=100		
1990-91	182.7	10.3
1991-92	207.8	13.7
1992-93	228.7	10.8
1993-94	247.8	8.4
1993-94=100		
1994-95	112.6	12.6
1995-96	121.6	8.0
1996-97	127.2	4.6
1997-98	132.8	4.4
1998-99	140.7	5.9
1999-2000	145.3	3.3
2000-01	155.7	7.1
2001-02	161.3	3.6
2002-03	166.8	3.4
2003-04	175.9	5.5
2004-05	178.3	5.7
2005-06	180.6	5.9
2006-07	179.2	5.7

Source : Government of India, Economic Survey.

with the objective of continuing inflation to create an enabling environment for the process of structural adjustment.

The second half of the 1990s was marked by a significant turnaround in the inflation outcome. The inflation rate declaimed from an average of 11.0 per cent during the second half of 1990s.

CAUSES BEHIND LOW RATE OF INFLATION SINCE THE SECOND HALF OF 1990s

1. There was deceleration in the growth of M_3 from 17.5 per cent during 1990-95 to 16.2 per cent during 1998-02 even as the real GDP growth accelerated 5.0 per cent to 5.6 per cent over the same period.
2. Food articles halved during the period from 11.9 per cent to 6.0 per cent, led by a deceleration in procurement price increase.
3. External pressure on domestic prices (as measured by unit value index of imports in rupees) was lower than that in the first half of the 1990s.
4. While increased capital flows and higher foreign exchange reserves have inflationary implication through monetary expansion, at the same time, they provide greater flexibility in supply management in the act of supply shocks.
5. The decline in inflation rate since the second half of 1990s reflected a confluence of factors. These included better monetary management facilitated by improved fiscal monetary coordination, how pressures from administered procurement price hikes, weakness of domestic aggregate demand, presence of excess capacities, ample flood stocks and foreign exchange reserves.

NATURE OF INFLATION IN INDIA

According, the Economic Survey of 2007-08, inflation in India is a structural as well as a monetary phenomenon. In the short-term, localized demand supply imbalance in wage goods, often due to seasonal variations in production—coupled with market rigidities and regulatory failures have supported inflationary expectations that have resulted in a more widespread impact on the consumers than the initial inflationary impulse. In the medium to long-term, the movement and outcome of monetary aggregates such as money supply and reference interest rates of the financial systems have influenced aggregated demand and consequently price level changes in the economy.

SEVERAL FACTORS ARE INVOLVED IN THE PHENOMENON OF PRICE RISE

1. Demand-Pull Factors

(a) Inflationary financing of government deficits.
(b) Large supply of Bank Credit.
(c) Large inflow of non-debt foreign capital.
(d) Role of Black economy.
(e) Increasing non-development expenditure.

2. Supply Side Factors, (Cost-Push Factors)

(a) Fluctuations in output and supply.
(b) Rise an administered prices.
(c) Impact of global inflationary pressures like higher commodity prices.

PRICES AND MONETARY MANAGEMENT : LATEST TRENDS

Inflation in terms of wholesale prices started increasing from June 2006. It was largely due to increase in the prices of wheat, pulses and edible oils in the "Primary articles" group and mineral oils in the group "fuel and power." Domestic shortfall in Production was responsible for the former and international hardening of crude oil prices affected domestic price of oil. In case of manufactured products year-on-year inflation as on Jan. 19, 2008, was 3.9 per cent compared to 5.9 per cent in the corresponding period of 2006-07. The manufactured products, with a weight of 63.8 per cent in WPI, contributed 55.2 per cent of the year-on-year inflation which is not significantly higher than their contribution in the previous year.

Year-on-year inflation in the primary articles was highest in April 2007. However, there was a significant deceleration since July 2007 and Jan., 19, 2008, inflation in primary articles declaimed by 655 basic points. With deceleration of inflation in Primary articles, contribution of these articles to overall inflation declined from 51.8 per cent as on July 7, 2007 to 22.0 per cent.

Fuel, power, light and lubricants served to be emerging a make contributor of inflation in 2007-08 well a FY inflation rate of 4.5 per cent and a contribution of 30.4 per cent. Annual inflation has been on rising trend since October because of sharply rising fuel Prices.

ANTI-INFLATIONARY MEASURES

Price instability is neither good for growth nor for the poor who are severally hurt by rising prices. Price control is high on government agenda as rising process can have adverse social and political consequences. Anti-inflationary policy of government includes—monetary tighering and curb and excessive money supply and credit growth, changes on fiscal

Inflation as on Jan. 19, 2008 in Major Groups

(Per cent)

Commodities	*Weight %*	*Variation (Year-on-Year)*			
		Inflation		*Contribution*	
		2007-08	*2006-07*	*2007-08*	*2006-07*
All Commodities	100.00	3.39	6.31	100.00	100.00
Pressers Articles	22.03	3.82	10.22	22.03	35.335
Fuel, Power, Light and Lubricant	14.23	3.92	3.57	21.86	12.73
Manufactured Product	63.75	3.91	5.88	55.20	51.92

Source : Economic Survey, 2007-08.

front which includes tax and pub expenditure management, rationalization of excise and import duties of essential commodities to lighten the burden on poor; effective supply demand management of sensitive items brought liberal tariff and trade policies; Strengthening the public distribution system. The government has increased the import of initial goods through its public agencies like STC, MMTC, PEC.

To maintain price stability, the central issue price for rice and wheat has not been revised since July 2002. Import on edible oil has been reduced.

The customs duty or crude oil and soyabean oil has been reduced. The central government issued a Central order dated Aug. 29, 2006, under Essential Commodities Act, 1955 to enable the state government to invoke stock limits in repeat of wheat and rules for a period of six months.

INTERNATIONAL PRICE MOVEMENT

International prices of commodities hardened because of five factors :

1. Demand for food crops and edible oils increased.
2. Food prices also increased because of low output stocks.
3. Higher cost of cultivation due to increase in prices of fertilizers and flues also raised the price expectation.
4. The increase in prices of metals was largely because of increase in demand from emerging economics, particularly in China.
5. Some economics have blamed futures trading for price rise. They argued that the inflationary tendencies were largely speculative in nature.

In India the international hardening of prices did have an impact. On supply side, shortfalls in domestic availability of wheat, pulses and edible oil in 2006-07 aggravated mismatches. On the demand side, large capital inflow extended pressure on liquidity conditions.

CONCLUDING OBSERVATIONS

Due control avoid inflation altogether but can only minimize its retarding consequence through sound policy mix application in the pre-reform are inflation was largely domestic in nature but since the Indian economy has been steadily integrating with the world economy and therefore the 'import-co-import' of inflation cannot be avoided altogether. Large inflation of foreign capital will make the management of external value of rupee as well as domestic inflation a highly challenging and doubling task. Attempt should be made on enhancement of supplies through higher productions and efficient supply management to avoid wastage. Domestic supply management is therefore critical in stabilizing inflationary expectations, moderating pressures for upward revision of wages and prices, and containing pressures for cost-push inflation through monetary and fiscal accommodation. As the economic Survey 2007-08 says that "inflation in India is a structural as well as a monetary Phenomenon" thus both demand and supply side policies are needed to eliminate its negative fallout.

REFERENCES

Economic Services, 2007-08.
Facts of Indian Economy, Rakesh Mohan, Oxford, 2003.
Indian Economy, Dutta, Sundaram.
Indian Economy, Uma, Kapila.
Indian Economy, Mishra and Puri.
Indian Economy, I.C. Dhingra.
Indian Economy Reforms and Development, I.J. Ahluwalia, IMD Little Oxford 1998.
Macroeconomic and Monetary Policies.
M.S. Ahluwalia etc. at Oxford, 2002.
Monetary Economic, Jagdish Narda, Rontledge, 2000.
Macro Economics, Abel and Perranke.
Previous Issues of Economic Survey.

26

Global Economic Crisis and U.P.A. Government Policy to Counter it

Ravi Ranjan

The utmost symptom and the main fundamental cause responsible for economic recession of the type of which the global economy has been faced with, for nearly a year past, is deceleration in market of purchasing power. To that sequel the uptimum use of the productive capability of the economy remains unutilized, production assumes a decelerating trend, and employed labour begins to be scrutinised and retrenched which, combined together, start a long process of reduction in total effective demand. Once this process begins it assume a chain reaction. The present global crisis is a real portrayal of this process to which inflationary trend in the economy has been contributing heavily.

Now let us examine the case of India as how inflationary trend in the economy has been contributing to deepen the economic crisis. Recession in demand in market is caused mainly due to decrease in purchasing power of people. Besides so many other reasons responsible for reducing the purchasing power of people, one important reason is that of inflation, which reduces the financial capability of people commensurably to the prices hiked. India has been facing a severe price hike problem since the last several years. At the week end 6th December, 2008 there was recorded 6.84 per cent increase in wholesale price index. Inspite of this increase it was treated as a not much harassing one because before it the inflationary move was rampant in double digit. Amidst such an inflationary move as was experienced by India in the week before 6th December, 2008 to equip the market with purchasing power the public sector banks declared that house loan up to Rs. Lakh would be made available for 8.5 per cent interest rate and the loan up to Rs. 20 lakh would be provided for 9.25 per cent interest rate. The economy behind such declaration by banks was that the loans, thus floated, would restrengthen the market by raising demand of various commodities and by giving employment to construction workers. But under the inflationary economy builders were rarely interested to construct houses under scheme of Rs. 20 lakh to be incurred as their total expenses and certain thousand houses to be built by DDA and alike agencies were not enough to give an upward boost to the economy. In stead of putting restriction on price hike and restrengthen the internal market by employment generation such ameliorative steps by banks were causing more injury to the economy. Because allowing more money to operate in market was tantamount to add to the cause which brings inflation speedily.

Furthermore, an indepth analysis of the data related to wholesale price index gives a different story. Among cereals the two items, rice and wheat, which are common food items for all Indian's appear to be absolutely not affected by the lowering down inflationary trend of which government has arrogantly been boasting for last several weeks. On the week ending 8 November, 2008 the wholesale price index for rice was at 210.7 point but in the next week, that was the week ending 15th November, 2008, it increased to 213.2 point. Again there was an increase in it, and on the week ending 22

November, 2008 it touched the hight of 218.6 point, and a further increase in it was experienced at the week ending 29 November, 2008 by 218.9 point and on 6th December, 2008 the wholesale price index for rice was on 219.7 point.[1] This was a period in which, there was said that the wholesale prices of commodities were coming down. But the situation about the wholesale prices of rice falsified as how much arrogant boasting was the side of the authority. In comparison to the beginning of the year 2008, more accurately, comparison to 5th January, 2008, in December, 2008, the wholesale prices of rice increased to 13 per cent—it was an increase in wholesale prices of rice, the increase in the retail prices was much more higher than it.

As regard the prices of wheat, the same story has been repeated. On 8th November, 2008 the wholesale prices of wheat was at 237.7 point but on 6th December 2008 it went to the extent of 238.6 point. The wholesale price index of rice and wheat reveals that even in the period which was claimed by the government to be marked for lowering down inflation the prices of rice and wheat were leaping upwardly.

The position of an another cereal, pulses also witnesses that the check on inflation was a propagated—myth by the government. In comparison to the wholesale prices of pulses on 5th January, 2008 there was 14.42 per cent increase in the wholesale price of pulses on 6th December, 2008. The Price index of *Arhar* pulse was on 228.4 point on 8 November, 2008 which rose to 229.7 point on 8 December, 2008. In summing up the common inferences about rice, wheat and pulses are effective indicators to show that the prices of rice, wheat and pulses have not declined at all.

Just after the presentation of the Central budget for 2008-09 there was started rampant hike in prices of commodities for common use e.g. rice, wheat, edible oil, vegetables, etc. on the next day of the presentation of the central budget in Lok Sabha the price index went beyond the tolerability of R.B.I's, matrix of 5 per cent to 5.11 per cent, and it remained unintermittently increasing in the months thenceforward. On 8th March, 2008 the wholesale price index was on 5.92 per cent, on 15th March, 2008 it reached to 6.68 per cent, on 22nd March, 2008 it approached 7 per cent and on 29th March it leaped to 7.41

per cent[2]. The above inflationary scenario was of the wholesale prices, in retail prices the price hike within a month was 20 per cent.

The above given brief account of the inflationary movement in the Indian economy has been adding much to weaken the internal market of India and creating conditions for the global economic crisis to encompass in its grip the economy. But the World Bank's pension holder Prime Minister of India does not accept this crude fact and escapes the government by arguing price hikes as a world phenomenon. He forgets that the economic crisis has assumed a world wide event and those countries, which are affected, are facing the crisis commensurable to the weak or strong position of their internal market. Without paying a serious heed to the effect of an inflationary move much difficult is to assess the intensity of the economic crash with which the Indian economy is gradually being gripped by the global crisis that has embarrassed the world. The speed with which the graph of the economic growth rate has been decelerating is, in no way, lessor than a terrorist attack. No matter, whether the government accepts this phenomenal economic agony or not, it is a reality in itself that having being infected and contaminated by the crisis-virus the Indian economy has been diseased and its condition has unintermittently been assuming serious position day by day. The very nature of the gravity of this situation can be realized by the fact that right from the Reserve Bank of India (RBI) to the Prime Minister's Economic Advisory Council along with other domestic and foreign think tanks, are forced to calculate the rate of economic growth of India in deceleration. Besides this, no one, irrespective of his location in the economy and administration, is in a position to assure that in coming future there would no need to amend the growth rate of the economy again and to accept its further decline. This scenario is, however, not a simple connotation rather is a clear evidence of the fact about the gravity through which the economy has been passing on to day. The economic symptoms coming from the various sectors signalize that the crisis in the economy has not only been widening and intensifying itself but indicates its longer durability.

Amidst all these economic severities the UPA government and its head, Prime Minister Manmohan Singh are still negating the factual position and in his arrogant boasting, claim that notwithstanding the fact that the economy has been experiencing the odds inflicted upon it by global crisis yet the position of the Indian economy is somewhat better than other countries. In his arguments the Prime Minister is making desperate attempts to convince the nation that in comparison to other countries Indian economy is the fastest growing unit among the comity of nations. Such statements on the part of the UPA government have been directed to achieve two main objectives both being politically tempered, viz. first, to confuse the masses on government's failures in the management of the economy and the second, to dislocate the mass attention from government's ineffective measures for encounter the crisis. The government is fully aware that once the acceptance of the gravity of the crisis is recognized by it the pressure upon the government to initiate measure to ameliorate the crisis would be increased in equal pace. Till now the government has not treated this crisis as a severe one. The non-serious attitude of the UPA government to the crisis the country has been facing today, can be explored by the statement given by the Indian Prime Minister just after his return to India from the G-20 meeting called for exploring devices to meet the crisis and its odd effect on global scale. In his Statement the prime Minister, in his boasting mood, said that Indian government required not to bring separate economic packages to meet the challenges of the economy because the government was aware of the crisis to come and in the budget of the current years financial provisions were made to liquidate the apprehended crisis. Two months earlier than the statement, the government of India and its associated think tanks were arguing that the global economic crisis had no effect on India, because the Indian economy had de-coupled from the American economy. They, thus, had invented their theory of 'de-coupling' to justify their arguments. Hardly one to two months had elapsed that such an arrogant boasting of government disappeared with the severe crash in the Indian share market continued deceleration that gripped the capital market of Indian, threatened the corporate sector to face severe consequences. Under the pressure of the corporate sector the UPA government announced to bring forth an economic package to assist the financial market by adding to its liquidity. Before the announcement for bringing forth such an economic package the government had made disperate efforts to have its control on liquidity by introducing monetary measures e.g reducing CRR, RAPO, reverse Rapo rate and SLR more than once. But all such monetary measures, thus introduced, made it convincingly clear that the intensity of the crisis was more severe not amendable by these measures only. Then, with many ifs and buts the government announced an economic package of Rs. 31,900 crore. In comparison to the gravity of the crisis the package was to meagre to inflict any positive result. Not only that the package was too meagre to leave its ameliorative impacts on the economy, but also its priorities and orientations were much misguided and sectarian in its approach. Through this package attempts were made to extend financial assistances to those sectors and classes which are traditionally anti-welfarism. Of the total amount of the package of Rs. 31,900 crores, one-fourth of the amount was to be met by 4 per cent reduction in the central excise duty. Behind this reduction in the central excise duty there was a hope, which the government had reared, that reduction in excise duty by 4 per cent would bring the prices of commodities, to be purchased by their customers, down, and thus the demand of those commodities in the market would, naturally, increase. This ameliorative steps, as the government of India believed, would assist not only to the producer companies, but would also make the commodities available in the market for lower prices, and the consumers would also be benefited. What in practice this method of package granting has brought about is averse to the intention of the package because the commodity producing corporate sector's companies instead of allowing the benefits of the duty reduction to go to the consumers have been exploiting this occasion for the maintenance of their profit margins. Thus, the UPA government, through such devices has given to the companies, a subsidy of Rs. 87,000 crore to maintain their profit margin.[3] Similarly, a relief of Rs. 200 crores to the exporter through tax reduction is a type of subsidy to them to have their profit margins maintained. Hardly this amount is to be used by the companies to restrict their efforts to wage reduction of their employees and their retrenchment from services. Under such economic packages, the government announced a plan expenditure of Rs. 20,000 crores, but in what plan and where that amount was to be invested was not clear.

All these actions of the government to come out from the perilous economic crisis create suspicion as whether the government is inclined to enhance public investment or in reality adding the corporate sector to maintain its profit margins. Viewing all these facts, it appears that the government of India has its commitment for not transgressing the closed economic clique of neo-liberalism. This is the reason that in granting stimulant economic packages its entire weightage has been guided by the neo-liberal precept of keeping financial deficit but into certain controlled circle. The most funniest is the fact that when the greatest centre of neo-liberalism, America and G-7 countries have opted to expand the areas of public investment the UPA government has still sticked to those devices on which account the crisis has originated and embarrassing more areas in the economy. More serious than any thing else is the negative attitude of the government in sanctioning economic packages for bailing out those economic sectors which are hard hit by the crisis. Among them mentions may be made of agricultural sector, small scale industries and lakhs of workers who have been retrenched by company's managements from their service for keeping up the companies profit intact. Agriculture and SSI are the sectors employing more than 60 per cent of India's total labour force or total persons employed. But when the economy was marching ahead with an accelerated growth rate of 9 per cent these sectors were seething in much awkward condition, and now, when the economy has been gripped by severe crisis no stimulated package is given to these sectors to repair their tortured conditions.

On 7th December[4] 2008 the UPA government hospitably opened the mouth of state exchequer for the economic assistance to the market and by a single stroke of pen near 30 thousand extra money was to be floated within the four months in the market. Of all those amounts 20 thousand crore was made available from extra expenses and 4 per cent reduction in central excise duty and the reduction made on the interest rate of loans given to export activities, combined together, enabled the market to haves Rs. 1000 crores either for investment or consumer expenses. On account of the economic measures initiate by the Reserve Bank of India to encounter the crisis, nearly Rs. 3 lakh crore extra money would be available in the Indian market. Besides it, nearly Rs. One lakh 35 crores has come to the economy through fiscal measure initiated by the government. In the amount thus coming to market there have been included the amount as loan remission, the amount sanctioned for National Rural Employment guarantee schemes and the amount given as wages and salaries to employees on the recommendations of the sixth Pay Commissions along with the subsidy to fertilizers. The amount given as subsidy and remission of loan would hardly yield any liable impacts on market but the amount sanctioned and given under and to the employees employment guarantee and wages and salaries respectively would influence the market to a certain extent, and add to the efforts to encounter the ill-effects of the crisis.

How far all these economic packages are able to restrict the growing menaces of the crisis is a major question which requires an answer. The corporate world, however, is seen not happy with the efforts made by the central government under the aegis of its announcement of 7th December, 2008; as the package, henceforward declared, is very small in comparison to the packages given by the developed countries to their industrial sectors. But it is, undoubtedly, a recognized fact that the intensity of the crisis, India has been facing, is much more less grievious than those faced by the developed comity of nations. India, as such, has been facing the economic constraints of deceleration in its growth but the developed countries, agony and pain are of negative industrial development, their industrial growth going in minus. A comparison between the economic packages given by developed countries and India's package has no sense as there is not comparison between the gravity of crisis in these two economies. But there is an example before India or China a country which has sanctioned an economic package of 586 million dollar for the coming two years but the economic packages sanctioned by India aggregates only 6 million dollar, and the amount is just like a drop in the ocean in comparison to China. If all the amount given earlier to 7th December, 2008 is added to it, even then the total amount would hardly exceed more than 26 million dollar.[5]

An another tragedy with India is that of misappropriation of the amount sanction and not pouring it down to the destination for which it has been directed. A portion of it, a sizeable portion of it, is often misappropriated by the corrupt bureaucracy, which is uncontrolled. Consequently, the 20 thousand crores of Rupees sanctioned for public expense hardly creates any enthusiasm among the people. In its counterpoise the corporate sector, therefore, lays bigger stresses not on the method of public expenses, rather what it is inclined to have is rebate in taxes.

In government's announcement of 7th December, 2008 there are some relief given to sectors like export, housing and infrastructure, but the main trouble in their ways is whether the reliefs reach to their destination. The Commerce Minister assured[6], beside the economic packages given on 7th December, 2008 that the government of India would announce some more packages in near future, which meant that the 7th December packages were not the last but more would be coming to meet the crisis.

Furthermore the greatest constraint for India is un-intermittent decline, in its export e.g. in October 2007 export graph showed 10 per cent decline. The crisis appears not to be ended recently, rather its continuation is expected to remain at least for two years, and the export sector has to prepare for the mitigation of the hardships which are, inevitably, to come in future. The statement of the Commerce Minister about more packages, is an indication that they would given to export sector.

The manner and gravity with which the economic crisis has gripped India no economic packages can be said to have been final one and the comparison between the packages given by developed countries and that of India is not a wise comparison. India has no financial capability to flow in market as much money has been fload by China. For a country like India whose fiscal deficit is 2.8 per cent and is apprehended to be wider in future, there is required certain specific steps to be taken for bailing out the economy. In this regard Arjun Sen Gupta's suggestions, to steer clear the menacing effect of the crisis have much validity. But the UPA government with its pro-corporate sector economic policy does not have, any conscious heed to protect the interest of the common people which is the *sine qua non* to have effective control on the crisis.

Notes

1. Alok Puranik, "Mahagai Se Rahat: Hawai Jyada Hakikat Kam", *Mukti Sangharsha*, Delhi, 28 December-3 January, 2008, p. 6.
2. Anand Pradhan, "Artha Vyavastha Ko Sambhalane Ki Jarurat", *Mukti Sangharsh* 4-10 January, 2009, p. 9.
3. Announcement by U.P.A Government of Economic Package, 7 December, 2008.
4. *Ibid.*, 27 April-3 March, 2008., p. 5.
5. *Ibid*.
6. R.S. Yadav, "Mahagai Mahangi Padegi", Statement by Commerce Minister, December 2008.

27

Pros and Cons of Global Economic Crisis

PUSHPA KUMARI

The two phenomenal events, which attracted the attentions of media the most on global scale in the few months back, were the global economic crisis and the election of the American President. The global economic crisis is, inevitably, a concomitant result of the marketization and the victory of Obama in the Presidential election of America is, besides many other hopes and aspirations of the American public, an expression of the aspiration of the American public to bring on fore more effective measures to restrict the odd affects of the crisis. Inflation, joblessness, the increasing pace of hunger and poverty being the major consequences of the crisis, which have been affecting the globe but their more grievious consequences are realized by the developing countries. U.N interference, world summits of developed nations and economic packages given by the nations to bail out their economies have miserably been failed to give any sort of effective results, as the economies are still showing a decelerating trend in GDP growth rate, capital market, capital investment and to that sequel rapid decline in the standard of living of people *en masse*. Besides all these gruesome facts the economic crisis has sharpened the economic contradiction between the developed and developing nations, which, obviously, demonstrate as how fictitious the concept of a world village, based on the supposed unity of interest among nations. Suffice is a single example to explain how the national economic interests of America and India clashes each other on the ameliorative measures to come out of the crisis. Worth notable is the speech made by the newly elected American president given by him regarding the measures to be initiated to restrict the crisis born constraints. Speaking on the economic crisis he spoke that the American companies should restrict themselves from the outsourcing from other nations. The statement of Obama is contradictory to the economic interest of India as it creates a danger for India's trade specially in IT sector.

However, the government of India is not ready to accept that the inflation, that has gripped the Indian economy, has been contributing abundantly to give the crisis new impetus. All the growing prices of commodities for daily use like rice, wheat, pulses, vegetables, etc. have reduced the real income of the people and they, now, purchase less commodities for the same amount of money which could have purchased greater quantity of goods, had the inflation not affected them adversely. Just after one day later of the presentation of budget for 2008-09 the prices of all necessary commodities like rice, wheat, pulses, sugar, etc. began to hike abruptly. The wholesale price index went beyond the bearing capacity of the RBI, 5 per cent to 5.11 per cent and thesnceforward it continued to increase rapidly. Such a past-march of inflation was seen in the fact that on 8th March, 2008 the wholesale price index was on 5.92 per cent but on 15 March it rose to 6.68 per cent and on 22 March, by further addition in it, the inflation rated 7 per cent and on 29 March it touched the colossal height of 7.41 per cent. The above records of wholesale price index are related to wholesale prices, in retail prices the hike is far more greater than it—within a year the price rise being 20 per cent higher.

The UPA government, and its Prime Minister Manmohan Singh refuse to accept inflation as pros and cons of government policy rather they term it an international phenomenon, what they accept is their denial to restrict the price hike on plea that they do not have any magic stick with which they can put a ban on rising prices. Indian experiences show that the government has allowed all traders, black marketers, hoarders, etc., to play freely for purchasing, hoarding and creating artificial scarcity in marker and extract profit by raising prices of commodities. To restrict all these economic malpractices on the part of trade gamblers the government of India has been defending them by its argument that the price rise has been caused due to inequitably balances in the market between demand and supply.

Manmohan Singh has gone to the extent of proprounding his new theory that high growth rate of the economy has increased the purchasing power of the people who appear in market as purchasers of more commodities and supply has failed to commensurate proportionately. Therefore, the growing prices is not a phenomenon to be bothered about, it will be corrected by market itself. Even the government does not accept that the allowance to *wayada* business in market has been aiding to the forces that are responsible for price hike. Business transacted in crores and crores of Rupees, without monetary transactions, adds to inflation and permits companies to transact business in hundred times more than the actual capital at one's disposal. Artificial scarcity, *wayada* business, and free hand to wholesale traders to hoard and sale commodities on sky touching prices, combined together, have created an awkward economic condition in India in which majority people have been deprived of fulfilling their daily need due to price rise. Under such an economic condition, as inflation has created in India, the internal market of the country has gone synchronized and people are not in a position to purchase even things for daily uses. This has resulted in retrenchment of employees, their wage cuts, closure of lakhs of small and medium scale industrial units which provide jobs to lakhs of people. All these phenomena have created a chain of recession that has been expressing in economic crisis in India under the impacts of global economic crashes.

According to an estimation, the estimated value of work accounts for 63 million dollars in IT and BPO sector and about 90 per cent of total taxes that comes from outsourcing is received by India from America, England and Europe. Nearly 7 lakh Indians are employed in the sector. The attitude of Obama to outsourcing will compulsorily lead India in an awkward trade condition on which account there will commence retrenchment of employees and conditions for weakening of the sector. This type of economic contradiction between the developed and developing nations will have it aftermath political effects. In the economists' assessment the after effects of the economic crisis of 1929-30 were rampant unemployment, price rocketing, starvation, spreading of various types of diseases all the world over, but their intensities were highest in the developing countries. In the present crisis 5 lakh people have been thrown out of their employment in the European Union countries in the September month of 2008, nearly one lakh and 5 thousand people became jobless in America alone. All these unpleasant episodes have been taking place under the menacing effect of marketization, but the government of India, led by Dr. Manmohan Singh, the original initiator of the market economy in India, has not been taking any lesson from this economic tsunami.

There is an apprehension that in 2009 the numerical strength of unemployed people would be increased to 210 million globally, which is the highest in comparison to any year of the last decades. In it there has been included the figure of 20 million employment reduction till the end of 2009.[1] Besides these, construction, communication, tourism, finance and army, real estate, cement and steel would be sectors facing the crisis grieviously. Of 7 crores hunger striken people in the world, 3 crores net belongs to India.[2] In this period the number of those people whose daily income is one dollar and 2 dollar, have gone up to 4 crores and 10 crores respectively. They are those unfortunate people whose 80 per cent income is spent on the compliance of their daily expenses due to high prices of cereals and foodgrains. The American company City Group, has announced to retrench its 59,000 employees, the number of malnutritioned people is expected to reach the colossal height of 967 million due to an addition in it of 40 million more people. The last two decades, economic survey,[3] conducted by an International Economic forum, has inferred that the very growth pattern based on marketization has contributed an ominous result whereby the rich has become richer, the gaps between the richest and the poorest has widened. The Report has estimated that in America the income of the 10 per cent people (the most richest) is 93,000 dollar whereas the same for the 10 per cent of the lowest income group people is 58,000 dollar. This is the income gap between the richest and the poorest in America which entirely boasts to have an ideal economic order for its people and sermonizes the other nations to follow it.

The report has accused that the leaps in trade and technology have given impetus to jobless growth, nations are faced with economic crisis, and the gap between the poor and the rich has become more spacious after 2000. The report has substantiated that barring Maxico and Turkey the rate of poverty and inequality is highest in America.[4] The crisis facing Indian economic scenario compelled the Prime Minister and the Finance Minister to retreat back from their statements that the impact of the crisis on Indian economy is zero. The economic odds arisen due to the withdrawal of their shares by the foreign companies from the Indian capital market there arose the compulsion for the government of India to reduce the import duty and after economic assistances given by the government the banks announced reduction in their interest rate. The crisis of the world capitalism has touched such a colossal height that the most ardent adherents of capitalism have been compelled to amend their opinions about liberalization. The example of Francis Fakuyama is the worthnotable that the person who, in his book *The End of History and the last man,* had once upon a time appraised the American model of economy and polity as the highest manifestation of human history from where the human history had no scope to develop further has changed his entire formulation in an essay by himself.[5] The entire Europe, with its well-meaning economists, is busy to consult K. Marx and F.

Angles, to be acquainted as how these ideologues of socialism forecasted the capitalist crisis as an inherent feature of the system. The sale of Marxist literature has increase three times in Europe to search out a device to come out from the crisis. Inflationary price trend, economic crisis, unemployment, etc. which are the natural consequences of marketized economy, combine together, have affected the Indian economy grieviously. Many giant companies have announced retrenchment of employees or reduction in their wages. The Jet Airways had retrenched their employees on large scale but the agitation launched by the employees the company was pressurised to re-instate 1900 employees. The ASOCHAM has announced to retrench 25 to 30 per cent employees from jobs in its 7 establishments. Among them the sectors included are IT, airlines, steed, finance and services, real estate, cement and construction. In the textile sector nearly 5 lakh workers are being threatened to loose their employment and the handicraft sector has thrown 5 lakh employees out from jobs. On account of recession in demands for vehicle and reduced opportunity for credit facilities the conveyance manufacturing companies have decided to reduce their production and the tractor manufacturing company Scort has closed its production unit in America.

The acceptance by the government of India, the IMF dictated New Economic Policy, the unemployment rate in India grew with greater pace in the year between 1993 and 2004. Nearly 7 lakh employees, either from public sector units or banks, were expelled from their jobs. Non-generation of employment opportunities, expulsion of employed persons from their services, increasing prices, etc. affected the Indian people adversely. Mostly the youths and the poor strata of the Indian population have gone much antagonized by this strategy of growth and bed agitating continuously for its substitution by a pro-people development strategy.[6]

According to U.N Report[6] World Food Insecurity in 2008. nearly 96 crore people are hunger victim in he world owing to high prices of foodgrains. The majority of these hungry people mostly live in developing countries, particularly in 7 countries e.g. India, China, Cango, Bangladesh, Indonesia, Pakistan and Ethiopia. But the government of India is not sensitive to rescue these people from hunger. In these years of economic crisis the UPA government appears to be not so much sensitive to protect the hungry masses as it appears to be sensitive to rescue the share market. With the economic growth the economic hardship of a sizeable section of people in India increases with equal pace and the UPA government's boasting to reduce poverty has been falsified. The menacing effect of economic crisis on the Indian economy can, obviously, be realized by the decleration in production. In the month of October, 2008 the rate of growth in the basic industries in India was at the rate of 3.4 per cent and there was seen deceleration in the production of crude oil and steel. The industrial productivity index (IIP) indicates that in the year 2007 (October) the expansion in 6 core industrial sector was 46 per cent, and from April to October the growth rate of core infrastructural sectors like petroleum, refineries, electrical coal, cement and steel was 6.6 per cent in 2007, which has come down to 3.9 per cent.

The famous economist Arjun Sen Gupta has essessed how India can protect itself against this devastating effects of global crisis emanated as consequences of market economy. In his assessment the paramount importance goes to strengthen and expand India's internal market. This is the most viable method to have the crisis controlled. He has explained it much explicitly that all remedial measures initiated to provide relief to exporters have failed to restrict the crisis even that the heavy devaluation of Indian currency has not enabled the economy to bail it out from the menacing impact of the crisis. He has inferred that unless the economic prosperity of the nation enables itself to have confidence in the future growth of it the outflow of foreign capital can not be stopped. The liquidity position of the investor countries has been synchronized to a great extent and it primarily creates conditions for the withdrawal of capital from India's capital market and its inflow to the investors' countries. Consequently, the share market in India has been crashed and the value of corporate capital would inevitably be diminishing with rapid pace. The corporate sector has been placed in such an ominous financial condition that financial institutions do not have confidence in them and are not ready to extent to them even that much credit which is required to meet daily expenses of the sector. The outflow of dollar from India has assumed a continued process causing less probability of interest rate to come down. In such a condition, as has been prevailed in India, if the economy does not strengthen its internal market and come to the global market with much expanded internal market it can not protect its economy against the global crisis.

Although the Indian economy is much expanded and colossal in size yet during the last 20 years the benefits of its growth has been synchronize to microscopic minority, that constitutes hardly the 23 per cent of the total population of India. The remaining 77 per cent of the population remained untouched by the growth benefit. Therefore, that part of the countries population which was extremely pauperized and compelled to live on the expense of less than 20 rupees a day, after being divorced from the growth benefits mingled themselves to 77 per cent of the population in 2004-05. They are standing still on the same economic stage and look with a compulsion as how the process of growth passes always without touching them. However, that 23 per cent of India's population which has been benefited by the growth process, is numerically 10 crores, a member which is more than the total population of many countries of Europe and America. They themselves create a wider market. But those who are counted in the 77 per cent of India's population are poor, illiterate and resourceless people, victimized by various physical and economic constraints. 84 per cent of India's peasant populations belong to this category, with their agricultural holdings being less than 2 hectares with which they can hardly maintain themselves with their families. They are economically forced to explore some other sources to earn income for their maintenance.

In industrial sector of India there are 5 crore and 40 lakh industrial units employing 10 crore 40 lakh worker. They are working in such industrial units whose total investment is, in emerge, less than Rs. 5 lakh per unit but their contribution to total GDP is at the cresting height of 31 per cent. Scallered from one corner to the another corner of the country, whatever they produce is often consumed by the local people and their 90 per cent products are sold in domestic market. To bail out the economy from the crisis attention must be paid to these small units, and in granting economic packages to extend relief to them. To all these non-agricultural units finance should be made available in greater amount from financial institutions. In total financial credit their shares are only 2.2 per cent which requires to be enhanced.

Arjun Sen Gupta has given many suggestions with which effective encounter can be organized and the economy can be protected. But the UPA government, in its pro-corporate sector policy, is not ready to shift even an inch from the IMF dictated policy and making severe injury to the nation. To have the crisis over-powered, to opt an alternative path of development is a must condition and our patriotism demands from every Indians to fight for replacement of pro-corporate policy.

NOTES

1. *A Report on Economic growth* published by an International Economic Forum (1985-2000).
2. Francis Fakuyama, *"The fall of Americal"* 13 October, 2008.
3. *I.L.O. Report*, 2008.
4. *Ibid.*
5. *Ibid.*
6. U.N. "World Food Insecurity in 2008", *Report of Food and Agriculture Organization.*

28

The Global Economic Crisis and India

SANJAY KUMAR

Dr. Manmohan Singh led UPA government is still not prepared to accept that the inflationary trend in India is a concomitant result of the policy the government of India has been pursuing since the last two decades. He and his government, both, deny that the pace of inflation in India has contributed much to the Indian economy to be indulged in the global economic crisis; rather they argue that price hike has been a world phenomenon and the government of India does not have any magic stick to restrict it. The UPA government accepts the price hike a phenomenon that has been caused due to wide gap between demand and supply. The government has also invented the most funniest argument which propounds that the high growth rate of the economy has added to the demands and market does no comply fully to that demands and result in price hike.

However, Dr. Manmohan Singh and UPA government do not realise as how inflationary move in the American economy has created conditions for such economic tsunami. The Americans made their live pleasant by borrowing of public debt which they collected from length and breadth of the world. On 17th October, 2008 the public debt of American increased to 10.3 trillion dollar. Three years back in 2005 it was 7.9 trillion dollar which was 9 times bigger than what it was in the decade of 1980. The total loan burden of America has expanded to such a colossal range that it has gone to 70 per cent of its total GDA. In one year the Americans spent 800 million dollar more than what they earned. Its domestic loan increased to 14 trillion dollar in 2008 than 7 trillion in the year before 2008. Its loan-based inflationary economy failed to register a growth rate which never exceeded more than 6 per cent, but its employment scenario experienced a heavy jolt; and more than one lakh American were thrown out of their employment. To restrengthen the domestic market the Bush administration had expected that the Indo-American Nuclear deal would creating 2.5 lakh new employment but the delay in it forced the Bush administration to make a gap arrangement by the facilitation of real estate business on basis of providing huge loans. The inflationary move in the economy of America became so strong that more than 40 per cent of the loanees failed to repay the monthly repayment to banks.

Loan-based inflation and reducing purchasing power of American people, combined together, have weakened its internal market, which has given birth to economic crisis.

In India the government has been arguing for several months that inflation is under control, but in real life no symptoms have been visualized to believe this argument. In spite of all boasting on part of government the wholesale prices of rice has increased 13 per cent in December 2008, in comparison to January 2008, the increase in the retail prices of rice is far more greater than its wholesale prices. The same has happened with wheat and pulses the wholesale price index of wheat was on 237.7 point but on 6 December, 2008 it reached 238.6 point. Besides inflation, the *Wayada* business in necessary commodities allowed by the government, has added much to the inflation. The specialities of *Wayada* business are that a company can transact business hundred times more than the actual capital it possesses. The business without transaction of money but only through certain promises, has added much to increase inflation and price hike. Since in conducting *wayada* business there is no need of money, so, they frequently done in crores and crores per day.

The commodities whose prices are getting down, are those which are to be used by higher income group people. The prices in aviation turbine fuel demonstrated nearly 21 per cent decline on 6 December, 2008 in comparison to 5th January, 2008. The wholesale price index of petrol, which was 279.9 point on 8th November, 2008 came down to 252.2 point on 6 December, 2008. In advertisement of a car usually displays that it will be available at the prices of 10 years back, but with more features. But such price decline is not associated with the commodities for common uses, like rice, wheat, pulses, etc.

The reducing purchasing power of people caused due to inflation has affected domestic and international market both and its ultimate consequence is economic crisis. To meet the challenges, based by the crisis, the wages of workers are being reduced, retrenchments are being followed and producing units either have been reducing their production or are being closed. This process has been adding more and more to aggravate the crisis instead of putting restriction on it. This process was started in 1991, when the first budget of Rao's government was placed in the Lok Sabha.

In India, having being it gripped by a severe global economic crisis, every saner mind recapitulates the first budget speech by Manmohan Singh as the Finance Minister in P.V. Narasinha Rao's government. While taking a complete about-turn position from the self-reliant economic growth strategy to the so-called structural re-adjustment dectated by the IMF and the World Bank, the Finance Minister had much arrogantly refused the Nehruvian development policy and had accused its adherents responsible for development stagnancy. In appraisal of his new development strategy under the aegis of globalization he had boasted that in the near future the new development strategy, which he was introducing, was to bring a golden time is each and every man for India and the people of India should bear some temporary hardships, for the attainment of that golden opportunity.[1] Nearly two decades have elapsed, when the speech was made, and what type of golden future the people of India have been experiencing today, has become obviously clear. The economic class for whom there has come golden era, has much strenuously done efforts to place Manmohan Singh on the highest helm of political affair, the post of Prime Minister of India and on the another brink there are the pauperized masses, the underdogs, on whose sacrifices the 'golden era' of Manmohan Singh had glittered for a time being in the profits and dividend earned by the corporate sector but, now, suddenly has collapsed.

Now, it has become evidently clear that capitalism, as a world socio-economic order, has miserably failed to provide to the human being a system of living that is prosperous and of sustainable happiness. The myth about capitalism, being almighty, has been torn and its main citadel, America, has been gripped under a severe economic crisis, more agonizing and harassing than the 1929-30 economic crisis that had disturbed the globe for many years. The gravity of the crisis is so serious that nearly two crores people are apprehended to be thrown out of their employment.[2] In the month of September, 2007, 15,900 people had lost their jobs and in August 2008 a further addition in this figure of 73,000 people being thrown out of their jobs was made.

However, the most surprising is the fact that to restrict the collapse of the system and to protect the corrupt management the public money is being spent much lavishly. It is an accepted fact that in capitalist system entire profits, earned therein go to individuals but the losses incurred upon, come to public. The global crisis is, inevitably, a concomitant result of the unrestricted greed for profit earning activities of the companies under the bourgeois higgledy-piggledy of an economic system that is oriented to accumulation of money by the application of all sorts of mechanisms, fair foul both. Till a few months back the capital market was roaring in such a manner as if it did not have any fear at all. For creation of artificial economic boom, there were furnished fictitious deals which did not have any relationship with the conduct of business and basic economic norms and all sorts of warnings were negated as if they were absured pre-historic things whose relevance had been rejected by the history long ago. The authority, concerned, upon whom the responsibility to restrict the economic irregularities rested, was so much fascinated by the economic boom as they completely forgot to imposed restrictions upon the corrupt economic trustees and their nefarious economic actions on which account the present crisis has emanated. During the second presidential tenure of Clinton and in the 8 years period of the presidential tenure of George W. Bush, the entire legal structures meant for market control, had collapsed fully.

To have a general glance upon the capitalist crisis of today's world one has to give a cursory look on the history of 150 years Lehman Brothers, the financial institution which applied for being it declared bankrupt and accepted that on it there was a loan burden of 600 million dollar of world-wide creditors. Then came the turn of an another financial giant, Meril Linch, which attempted to evade its crisis by selling itself to the Bank of America. Amidst these crisis-oriented situation the investment and insurance company, AIG, of American International group was hard hit by rating down, and then, to save it the federal government came forward to protect it.

The present global crisis and its global impacts, if examined apropos, explain that the basic reason responsible for the generation of the crisis is colossal financial deficit of America. The recent economic data reveal that America, the main fortress of capitalism, was managing its economy be the extraction of 3 trillion or 13,500 million Rupees loan per day. Of all these loaned money two-third was coming from the developing countries. With all these loaned money the American people were leading a more prosperous life than what they could have enjoyed with their own actual resources. In this sense the American economy was, by and large, a bankrupt economy. In particular case of India and China whatever money America has invested in them, the investment of these two countries in America is larger. So, it was not surprising that in a year when the domestic income decelerates one-fifth the job loss automatically increased. In the period between July 2007 and July 2008 nearly 11,000 job liquidation occurred in the New York city alone[3] and the apprehension of job losses in America was of 120,000, which was a grievous injury to the employment scenario of America.

To have a clear understanding of economically fictitious base of the American economy it is not necessary to be an economist rather a lay man can also see that the economic prosperity of the American economy was the result of liberal credit. The profit earned therein was and still is not based on production of commodities but through various types of economic gimmicks which have assumed a form of widely expended trade on papers only. On this account, the economic bases of those developing countries which remained in discouraging position of technology development were severely injured. In doing so America, in fact, surrendered its superiority before the countries such as the south-East Asian countries, which have lower production cost and skilled labour force. After having being surrendered to these countries America continued to have its control on the monetary inflow and assisted its national budget and the conversion of America into a wide market. Such an U-turn position, as was taken by America, became a danger for all those countries which were fully depended on America for market for their produced commodities. The economic crisis, thus emanated gripped in its danger zone not only America but also the majority of countries which have been harassed by the crisis.

The above briefly illustrated fact is the crisis scenario, how it has emanated, widened and gripped the entire glob in its embarrassing fold. Its impact on India—one of the most severe injurious impacts—is frequent injury to labouring masses that has come in the form of speedy retrenchment form employment, as obviously seen in the I.T. sector. In other sectors too, where the companies are inclined to retrench labour for the maintenance of their profit margins, scrutiny and retrenchments have been taking place silently. In an already crisis ridden labour market of India this process has speeded up the pace of crisis.

Regarding its impacts upon India a Corporate Manager has assessed that only the I.T. sector of India, in a period following 6 months from December 2008 onwards, 15,000 to 20,000 employees are apprehended to lose their eimployment.[4]

In an another study the apprehension for total job loss in India has been calculated to be more than 10 lakhs. Under the grievious economic crisis the sensex came down to 11328 points, the institutional investors withdrew crores of dillar from the market. Just before a few days of the commencement of Diwali festival the sensex came down below 10,000 points. The foreign institutional investors, who had invested 17.4 billion dollar in 2007, withdrew 11 million dollars in 2008. In the closing months of 2008 the outflow from India of foreign capital aggregated to 36 million dollar, and the total foreign exchange reserve, which was 309 million dollar on 31 March, 2008 receded to 273 million dollar on 17 October, 2008. Till recently the domestic economic players, who were accustomed of purchasing equity in the share market, are, now, faced with the difficulties arisen out of the withdrawal of capital, as much as is possible, inspite that numerous relaxations have been given to them by SEBI. Notwithstanding that SEBI has relaxed the regulation related to participatory notes yet the vibration of the crisis has obviously realized in the backbone of the Indian economy. Its obvious expression is seen in the growth rate deceleration of the economy, and along with it, in the sky touching prices of the cereals and foodgrains, as the country has been experiencing the bitterest results of stagflation. If the Indian economy has experienced lesser injurious impacts of the global economic crisis, its credit will go to the fact that the country still has a strong public sector set-up. This feature of the economy has made it absolutely necessary that the policy of structural reform not only be reviewed but also be rejected in its entirety. Because the crisis has approved that the development through the de-regularised market is not the appropriate path to be followed.

On 10 October, 2008 the crisis appeared with its seriousness when the Indian sensex experienced a decline of 1000 point. Being in panic the Reserve Bank of India (RBI) hurriedly came to protect the economy by making 1.50 points in CRR on which account the banks received Rs. 60,000 crores extra amount for operation. Again, the government of India sanctioned an amount of Rs. 2000 crores to protect mutual finds, which were in acute paucity of capital due to large scale withdrawal by investors having being feared by the crisis. But all these measures yielded no positive result to bring the economy on correct track. When the industrial production index, which was 10.9 per cent in 2007 suddenly synchronized to 1.3 per cent and government's devices like reduction in CRR, Paporate, dismantling control from participatory notes, etc. failed miserably to extend any relief to the economy. Under the pressure of the corporate sector the government of India, on demand of the corporate sector, reduced interest rate on institutional credit.

The global severeness of the crisis is much more agonizing than what the government of India accepts. The Asian tiger, Singapore, has revised its expected growth rate downwardly, Pakistan sent its emissaries to London and Washington for demanding economic package to encounter the challenges posed on it by the global crisis. In an assessment the losses incurred upon Laxmi Mittal, the richest person in England, was 7 million pound per hour, the Danish Parliament itself bore the guarantee of bank deposits, etc.

The indications from the Indian stock market come of the effect that the investors have gradually been withdrawing from the market and have explored a safe sector, that is, the purchase of gold, to invest their capital. This trend of switching over from capital market investment to investment in gold and precious metal will, inevitably affect the market, productions would decline, and recessionist trend would get impetus. Consequently, the crisis would become more grave causing narrowing down the prospect of employment and reduction in worker's wages. However, all these economic measures, initiated by the government, only can give protection to the share market from the possibility of its complete collapse. What the ameliorative steps require are need to invest heavily in production sector, so as to restrict the growth rate from going it downward, to create large scale employment possibilities and to increase the purchasing capabilities of the people *en-masse*. Besides these ameliorative devices what more are required are to strengthen the economic role of public sector, to amend the role of controlling authorities and make them more effective than their present day position in the economy.

Furthermore, the Indian economy has been pained by

stagflation and the recessionist trends have been appearing for a few years back, which was never realized by the government, neither its signs nor consequences and what the ruling circle in India wants is to cover its failures by branding the crisis as a world phenomenon. In India agriculture has been placed in the position of negative development and the industrial growth rate come to its lowest ebb, construction sector has been victimized by slower pace of growth than even before, because the rate of credit advanced for housing construction has gone lower than the last year and the danger is so grievous as the loans given to real estate has also decelerated, because banks are afraid of the credit, given, not being repaid by the loanees. The service sector, as being the most prosperous sector in the economy, has also been affected adversely and the export rate within the previous 18 months has recorded the lowest figure

While the growth rate is receding, the inflationary trend has its graph much higher and the prices of consumer good have touched the sky. India has taken stand, on policy matter, which is much injurious for the common people and the protecting of the interest of corporate sector can not relieve India from the crisis. Now, the time has come to give a serious thought as whether the present economic policy be continued or India should return back to the pre-1990-91 policy of self-reliant growth with strong public sector as the main player in the economy.

Notes

1. *Budget Speech by Manmohan Singh* as the Finance Minister, 1990-91.
2. Gurudas Das Gupta, "Vishwa Punjivadi Sankath : America Sankath", *Mukti Sangharsha*, 14-20 December, 2008, p. 9.
3. *ILO Report*, 2008.
4. *The New York Times*, July 2008, (Various issues can be seen).

29

Monetary and Fiscal Policy to Control Inflation

RAHUL KUMAR SANTOSH

INTRODUCTION

Inflation is described as situation characterized by sustained increase in the general price level. A rate of inflation of around five percent is considered normal but anything above it starts affecting the growth negatively. An anticipated inflation is less worrisome than an unanticipated one.

During inflation all costs and prices do not rise together in the same proportion. But it is an increase in the general level of prices measured by price index which is an average of consumer or producer prices.

Governments all across the world use mix of fiscal monetary policies to control inflation. Economists share little common ground with regard to their views about policy-making. Nobel Laureate economist says that J. Stiglitz says that, " After all advance in economic science, the unfortunate truth is that economists cannot agree on the best set of policies."

FISCAL POLICY FOR CONTROLLING INFLATION

Fiscal policy involves the use of government spending, taxation and borrowing to influence both the pattern of economic activity and also the level of aggregate demand and aggregate supply in the economy. Traditionally fiscal policy has been used as an instrument of demand management. Right since the time of Keynesian revolution fiscal policy has been seen as a major way of controlling the economy. It was seen to have two major roles. The first was to remove any severe deflationary or inflationary gaps. In other words, expansionary fiscal policy could be used to prevent a recurrence of the mass unemployment and slow down in output growth and a deflationary fiscal policy could be used to prevent inflation. This first role is to prevent the occurrence of fundamental disequilibrium in the economy.

The second role is to smooth out the fluctuations in the economy associated with the business cycle. This would involve reducing government expenditure or raising taxes. This would dampen down the expansion and prevent 'overheating' of the economy with its attendant rising inflation and deteriorating balance of payment.

FISCAL POLICY IS OF TWO KINDS

(A) *Discretionary Fiscal Policy*: It involves deliberate change on part of the government with regard to its expenditure and taxes.

(B) *Automatic Stabilizers*: It includes those changes in tax revenue and government spending that come about automatically as the economy moves though different stages of the business cycle.

FISCAL POLICY TO COMBAT INFLATION KEYNESIAN VIEW

If the government expenditure on goods and services is

reduced, aggregate demand in the economy will fall as a result of the multiplier effect. Once the economy moves above its potential full-employment level, reduction in government expenditure closes the inflationary gap and reduces the inflation.

As an alternative to reduction in government expenditure, the taxes (direct) can be increased to reduce the aggregate demand for goods and services in the economy. The hike in taxes reduces the disposable income and thereby forces people to reduce consumption demand. Also reduction in business expenditure shrinks aggregate demand and therefore reduces inflation.

THE EFFECTIVENESS OF FISCAL POLICIES

The effectiveness of fiscal policies depends upon many factors—

I. *The Accuracy of Forecasting* : Government would obviously like to act as swiftly as possible to prevent a problem of excess demand. The more reliable are the forecasts of what is likely to happen to aggregate demand, the more able government will be to intervene quickly.

II. The extent to which changes in government expenditure and taxation will effect total injections and withdrawals. Will changes in G and T be partly offset by changes in other injection and withdrawals? If so, are these changes predictable?

III. The extent to which changes in injections and withdrawals affect national income. Will it be possible to predict the size of multiplier and accelerator effects?

IV. The extent to which changes in aggregate demand will have desired effects on output, employment, inflation of balance of payment.

FISCAL POLICY AND AGGREGATE SUPPLY

Supply-side policies have the objective of raising the

economy's potential growth per head. Fiscal Policies changes can help to improve the working of markets and raise productivity and consequently output of goods and services. This helps in controlling inflation but the gains are largely in the long-run. Labour market incentives, capital expenditure by government and businesses, investment on infrastructure, expenditure on research and development and human capital formation, etc. can help in raising the productivity of the economy.

MONETARY POLICY FOR CONTROLLING INFLATION

(A) Ultimate Objective

(i) Achieving high and stable output levels.
(ii) Maintaining law inflation and stable prices.

(B) Intermediate Targets

An intermediate target is an economic variable whose value the Central Bank chooses to control because it fees that doing so would help in achieving the ultimate objectives. An intermediate targets is an objective distinguishable from the ultimate target but closely enough should to it. It serves in a "stand-in" or "proxy" for the ultimate objectives.

One possible intermediate target is the nominal interest rate. A key advantage of using nominal interest rate an intermediary monetary policies target is that doing so automatically stabilizer real income and aggregate demand if the demand for money or money multiplier is volatile. Other possible intermediate targets are the spread between long and short-term interest rates commodity price indices and credit aggregates.

(C) Major Instruments

(i) *Open market operation*: Buying and selling of government securities in the open market to influence the level of reserves.
(ii) *Discount rate policy*: Setting the interest rate, called the discount rate, at which commercial bank and

other depository institutions can borrow from Central Bank.

(iii) *Reserve requirement policy*: Setting in changing the legal reserve ratio requirement on deposits with banks and other financial institutions.

(D) Rules versus Discretion in Monetary Policy

(i) *Monetary Policy Rules*: By this we mean a policy strategy to which a Central Bank might bind or commit itself. If the Central Bank adopted monetary policy rule, it would follow that rule to matter what occurs in the economy, such as an economic expansion or an economic contraction.

(ii) *Monetary Policy Discretion*: Monetary Policy actions that the Central Bank makes in response to economic events as they occur, rather than in ways it might hence previously planned in the absence of those events.

MONETARY POLICY TO CONTROL INFLATION : KEYNESIAN APPROACH

According to Keynesian theory contraction in money supply causes the rate of interest to rise. And this raise in rate of interest adversely impacts interest dependent expenditure, generally the consumption expenditure and investment expenditure. Both consumption expenditure and investment are important components of aggregate demand. A fall in both leads to fall in aggregate demand and consequently fall in prices and national output.

MONETARIST APPROACH

According to the monetarists' inflation is always and everywhere a monetary phenomenon.' They say that to control inflation money supply must be controlled in the economy.

There are for proportions that characterizes the monetarist position—

(i) The supply of money is the dominant influence on the nominal income.

(ii) In the long-run the influence of money is primarily on the price level and other nominal magnitudes. In the long-run real variables, such as real output and employment are determined by real, not monetary factors.

(iii) In the short-run, supply of money does not influence real variables.

(iv) The private sector is inherently stable. Instability is primarily the result of government policies.

Milton Friedman has argued in favour of rules over discretion in macroeconomic policy-making. The essence of Friedman's argument is that monetary policy-makers may have very good intention but may still worsen economic performance through discretionary attempts to stabilize the economy. He says that policies-making is plagued by various policy time lags, which when summed together, constitute on interval of time between a need for a countercyclical policy action and the actual effect of that policy action on an economic variable.

One type of time lag in policy is the "recognition lag". This is the interval that passes between the time that the need for a countercyclical policy action arises and the time this need in recognized by a policy-maker.

A second type of policy time lag is the implementation, or "response lag". This is the time between recognition of a need for a countercyclical policy action and actual implementation of the policy action.

Finally, monetary policy is subject to "transmission lag". This is the time that elapses between the implementation of an intended countercyclical policy and its ultimate effects on an economic variable.

Monetarists argue that if the Central Bank could design a perfectly countercyclical rule it would be much more effective than discretionary monetary policy in its impact.

CONCLUDING OBSERVATIONS

In post-WW-II we have witnessed an increasing globalization of national economies. This means that product and factor market are getting integrated. Therefore, in such a situation making policies to contain inflation is not easy as it can have spillover effects. Also in an open economy alongwith inflation management, exchange rate management is also important because exchange rate instability can influence the external sector. This can impact output and employment generation in the short-run. Therefore, it becomes important that right mix of fiscal and monetary policy is used as an anti-inflationary device keeping in mind the open economy implication of the policy.

During recent times when the Indian economy was witnessing inflationary pressures the RBI hiked the key interest rates as an anti-inflationary policy measure. The idea was to raise the cost of capital, which would adversely impact investment and consumer demand and thus the aggregate demand. This in turn would help in cooling the over heated economy. As a policy measure the government must ensure structural reforms and raise the productive potential of the economy to augment the supply of goods and services in the economy.

J.M. Keynes made an observation that, "By a continuing process of inflation, government can confiscate, secretly and unobserved, an important part of wealth of their citizens." The government by controlling inflation must ensure the well-being of its citizens and that of the economy.

References

Abel and Beranke, Macroeconomics.
Economic Survey, 2007-08.
Economics, N. Mankiw, Paul Samuelson.
Jagdish, Narda, Monetary Economic, Rontledge 2000
M.S. Ahluwalia, Macroeconomic and Monetary Polices, etc. at Oxford, 2002.
M. Friedman, Free to Choose.
Previous issues of Economic Survey.
Rakesh, Mohan, Facts of Indian Economy, Oxford, 2003.
R.T. Froyen, Macroeconomics.

30

Impact of Global Economy on Price Movements in India

SURENDRA KUMAR BHAGAT AND D.N. SAH

From the statistics supplied by Central Statistical Organisation, an annual rate of inflation can be derived. The inflation rate can be constructed on point-to-point basis and also on year-on-year basis. Inflation rate can also be calculated on point-to-point basis. The inflation rate for the week ended 16 June, 2007 can be calculated by considering the Wholesale Price Index (WPI) for all commodities which were prevailing on that date. The price index comes to 211.90. Similarly, the year-on-year basis can also be constructed by considering the Wholesale Price Index of 17th June, 2006 and comparing it with the price prevailing a year later, i.e., 16th June, 2007. After considering the trend in inflation it becomes clear that the rate of inflation has been going down from the beginning of the fiscal year 16th June, 2007. Another fact also emerges from the consideration of the available statistics. It becomes clear that the main culprit of the inflation is the rise in prices of food articles. This rise hits every common man who is vitally interested in the prices of the food stuff. There are other factors which operate powerfully and make the prices for vegetables, fruits, milks and other essential agricultural products shoot up. The intention of the RBI is to keep the inflation rate below 5 percent. The medium term objective of the RBI is to reduce the inflation rate to between 4 per cent and 4.50 per cent. The RBI has taken various measures to contain and control the inflation. It has raised the Prime Lending Rate. It has also increased CRR (Cash Reserve Ratio) at the same time Reverse Repo Rate have been augmented. The cumulative result of all these extraordinary means is to neutralise the excess liquidity present in the economic system and drive it out of the bold. The money supply has also been reduced and hence the inflation or price rise is brought under control. The RBI released its Annual Report 2006-07 which points out.

The Reserve Bank released the document "Macro-economic and Monetary Developments Mid-Term Review 2008-09" on 23rd Oct. 2008 to serve as a backdrop to the Mid-Term Review of Annual Policy Statement for 2008-09 announced on October 24, 2008. According to the first quarter estimates of 2008-09 released by the Central Statistical Organisation (CSO) in August 2008, the real GDP growth was placed at 7.9 per cent during the first quarter of 2009 as compared with 9.2 per cent during the corresponding quarter of 2007-08. The deceleration in growth was spread across all the three sectors, viz., agriculture and allied activities, industry and services. The index of industrial production during April-August 2008-09 recorded year-on-year expansion of 4.9 per cent as compared with 10.0 per cent during April-August 2007-08. The manufacturing sector recorded growth of 5.2 per cent during April-August 2008-09 (10.6 per cent during April-August 2007-08) and the electricity sector recorded growth of 2.3 percent (8.3 per cent during April-August 2007-08).

Available information on Central Government finances for 2008-09 (April-August) indicates that gross fiscal deficit and revenue deficit were placed higher than a year ago. Revenue deficit was 177.4 per cent of budget estimates for the 2008-09 as compared with 74.9 per cent a year ago. GFD during the same period was 87.7 per cent of the budget estimates compared with 68.5 per cent in April-August 2007. Tax revenue rose by 26.2 per cent over that during April-August 2007. Aggregate expenditure (adjusted for acquisition cost of Reserve Bank's stake in SBI) increased mainly on account of sharp increase in revenue expenditure, particularly food and fertiliser subsidies, pension and rural development. Gross and net market borrowing during 2008-09 (up to October 22, 2008) amounted to Rs. 1,27,872 crore and Rs 64,808 crore, respectively, accounting for 72.8 per cent and 65.5 per cent of the estimated market borrowings for the year. During the corresponding period of the previous year, gross net borrowings accounted for 66.5 per cent and 68.1 per cent, respectively, of the estimated market borrowings for that year. Growth in broad money (M3), year-on-year (y-o-y), moderated to 20.3 per cent (Rs. 7,29,338 crore) on October 10, 2008 as compared with 21.9 per cent (Rs. 6,43,963 crore) a year ago. Growth in bank credit continued to expand at a strong pace. Non-food credit by scheduled commercial banks (SCBs) increased by 29.3 per cent (Rs. 5,80,060 crore) y-o-y, as on October 10, 2008 as compared with 23.3 per cent (Rs. 3,74,054 crore) a year ago. The higher credit growth relative to the deposit growth resulted in an increase in the incremental credit-deposit ratio (y-o-y) of SCBs to 96.2 per cent as on October 10, 2008 from 66.8 per cent a year ago. During the financial year 2008-09 (up to October 10, 2008), non-food credit expanded by 10.4 per cent (Rs. 2,40,995 crore) as compared with 5.0 per cent (Rs. 93,781 crore) during the corresponding period of the previous year.

Reserve money growth at 17.6 per cent, y-o-y, as on October 17, 2008 was lower than that of 24.4 per cent a year after. The Reserve Bank continued with its policy of active management of liquidity during the current financial year through appropriate use of the CRR, and OMO, including MSS and LAF, and other policy instruments at its disposal flexibly. Developments on both international and domestic fronts, particularly from mid-September 2008, have impacted domestic liquidity conditions. Nonetheless, liquidity modulation through a flexible use of combination instruments has, to a significant extent, cushioned the impact of international financial turbulences on domestic financial market by absorbing excessive market pressure and ensuring orderly conditions.

INDIAN SCENARIO

Headline inflation has remained firm in major economies during 2008-09 so far. However, there are signs of moderation in inflationary pressure reflecting marked decline in prices of food, fuel and other commodities, as we as augmentation of downward risks to growth from the intensification of global financial market crisis. The monetary policy responses of different countries, which were initially somewhat independent in view of inflation concerns, became more coordinated in terms of simultaneous easing of monetary conditions during the period July-October 2008 in view of the increasing downside risks to growth and the consequent diminishing upside risks to per stability. Global commodity prices have eased somewhat during the second quarter of 2008-09 led by a decline in the prices crude oil, metals and food. After touching a historical high of US $ 145.3 a barrel level on July 3, 2008, international crude oil prices, represented by the West Texas Intermediate (WTI), have eased reflecting decline in demand in OPEC countries and improved near-term supply prospects in non-OPEC countries. WTI crude oil price was at around US $66 a barrel on October 22, 2008. Metal prices eased further during the second quarter of 2008-09, reflecting weak construction demand in OECD countries and some improvement in supply, especially in China. Food prices, which had increased sharply up to the first quarter of 2008-09, reflecting higher demand and low stocks, eased somewhat during the second quarter of the year on the back of improved supply prospects, particularly for oilseeds and grains in major producing countries.

Mirroring global trends, inflation in India increased during 2008-09 so far, albeit with some recent easing. Inflation measured as year-on-year (y-o-y) variation in the wholesale price index (WPI), increased to 11.1 per cent on October 11, 2008 from 3.1 per cent a year ago and 7.7 per cent at end-March 2008, reflecting the impact of some pass-through of international crude oil Prices to domestic prices as well as elevated levels of prices of iron and steel, basic heavy inorganic chemicals, machinery and machinery tools, oilseeds, sugar raw cotton and textiles on account of strong demand as well as international commodity price pressures. However, there has been some moderation in the price of freely priced petroleum products and edible oils/oil cakes over end-June 2008.

Primary articles inflation, y-o-y, increased to 11.5 per cent on October 11, 2008 from 4.6 per cent a year ago and 11 per cent at end-June 2008 (9.7 per cent at end-March 2008) mainly reflecting the increase in the prices of food articles, especially of wheat, rice, fruits and vegetables, milk, and eggs, fish and meat as well as non-food articles such as oilseeds and raw cotton.

Fuel group inflation increased to 14.5 per cent on October 11, 2008 from a decline of 1.5 per cent a year ago and an increase of 6.8 per cent at end-March 2008 (it was 16.3 per cent at end-June 2008) mainly due to increase in the price of minerals oil by 14.1 per cent over end-March 2008. However, in response to easing in international crude oil prices from the peak of early-July 2008, domestic prices of freely priced minerals oil items such as naphtha, furnace oil and aviation turbine fuel have decline in the range of 12-22 per cent beginning from August 2008.

Manufactured products inflation, year-on-year, was 9.5 per cent as on October 11, 2008 as compared with 4.3 per cent a year ago and 10.9 per cent at end-June 2008 (it was 7.3 per cent at end-March 2008). The year-on-year increase in manufactured products prices was driven mainly by sugar, edible oils/oil cakes, textiles, chemicals, iron and steel, machinery and machine tools. Prices of edible oils and grain mill products, however, eased somewhat over end-March 2008.

Consumer price inflation increased further during August/September 2008 mainly due to increase in the price of food, fuel and services (represented by the 'miscellaneous' group). Consumer price inflation for industrial workers increased to 9.0 per cent in August 2008 from 7.7 per cent in June 2008 and 7.3 per cent a year ago. Consumer price inflation for agricultural labourers increased to 11.0 per cent in September 2008 from 8.8 per cent in June 2008 and 7.9 per cent a year ago. Consumer price inflation for rural labourers was 11.0 per cent in September 2008 as compared with 8.7 per cent in June 2008 and 7.6 per cent a year ago.

India's balance of payments position during the first quarter of 2008-09 (April-June) reflected a widening of the current account deficit and moderation in capital flows. The merchandise trade deficit, on balance of payments basis increased from US $ 20.7 billion in April-June 2007 to US $ 31.6 billion in April-June 2008. Net surplus under invisibles remained buoyant, led by increase in software exports and private transfers and financed 66.0 per cent of the merchandise trade deficit during April-June 2008.

The large increase in merchandise trade deficit during April-June 2008 led to a significant increase in the current account deficit over its level during April-June 2007. The current account deficit was financed by capital flows which have, however, remained volatile during 2008-09 so far. Net capital flows during 2008-09 so far have been lower than those in the corresponding period of 2007-08, mainly account of outflows by foreign institutional investors (US $ 7.3 billion) during 2008-09 (up to October 10, 2008) in contrast to net FII inflows (US $ 18.9 billion) during the corresponding period of 2007-08. On the other hand, net flows into India were higher at US $ 16.7 billion during April-August 2008 as compared with US $ 8.5 billion during April-August 2007. NRI deposits recorded a net inflow (US $ 273 million) during April-August 2008 as against a outflow (US $ 168) during April-August 2007.

According to the data released by the Directorate General of Commercial Intelligence and Statistics (DGCI&S) during 2008-09 (April-August), merchandise exports recorded a growth of 35.3 per cent, which was higher than that of 19.3 per cent during April-August 2007. Imports during April-August 2008 grew by 38.0 per cent, as compared with the growth of 34.2 per cent recorded a year ago. Petroleum, oil and lubricants (POL) imports grew significant by 60.0 per cent during April-August 2008 as against 17.9 per cent during April-August 2007 largely due to the escalation in international crude oil prices. Non-oil imports showed a moderation in growth to 28.3 per cent from 4 per cent a year ago. Merchandise trade deficit during April-August 2008 increased to US $ 49.3 billion from US $ 34.6 billion during April-August 2007. India's foreign exchange reserves at US $ 273.9 billion as on October 17, 2008 were lower by US $ 35.8 billion over end-March 2008.

REFERENCES

FAO Bulletin, 2005-08.

Imported Inflation, C.P. Chandrasekhar and Jayanti, Global Inflation in India: How to Tackle it: http://indiabroad.com/manv/2007/mar/21

RBI, Annual Report, 2006-07.

Macroeconomic and Monetary Developments, *Mid-Term Review*, 2008-09.

Monetary Policy and Fiscal Policy: Impact Inflation Effects with a New Keynesian Assignment of Weapons to Targets, Madras, James and Vines, David, 1988.

Polackova, Hana, 1997, Inflation in Non-Tradeables and the Macroeconomic Policy Mix: A Model with Policy Application to Transition Economics; Policy Research Working Paper Series.

The Hindu Business Line, Global Inflation and India.

31

Recent Global Inflationary Trends and its Impact on Indian Economy

CHITRANJAN OJHA AND UMA SHANKAR SINGH

After a long absence inflation seems to be reappearing even if mildly. This is so in the USA; this is so in India and many other countries, largely on account of the sharp increase in oil prices, for more than a year now. Whether oil prices have touched the peak and we can look for gradually diminishing prices is difficult to say; this is possible. We must thank the heavens that the impact on world economy, in particular on commodity prices, has been very much less severe than in 1970s.

Some countries have been taking anti-inflationary measures, in particular monetary measures, tor quite sometime now, not so true: account of the rise in oil prices but on the fast recovery of the economy after a 2-3 year period of sluggish and slump conditions of the economy. In the U.S.A, interest rates were raised frequently on several occasions even as they had been earlier brought down on many occasions subsequently, to record low levels.

In India, the last 3-4 years have witnessed a substantial reduction interest rates by government and the central bank, quasi-government saving Institutions from the giddy heights to which they went, unreasonably as it looks clearly now. But, in recent months there has been a feeling that on account the oil prices showing no indication of a significant decline the substantial and rapid growth of the industrial sector. In the stock market, and the substantial expansion of credit, monetary action was justified, especially through an increase in the bank rate. This will be known towards the end of this month (October) when the usual monetary review is made by the Reserve Bank Governor.

If there is some tightening of credit, it may not be a bad idea, but this must refer mainly to short-term credit, so that investment is not affected adversely. It is not clear if saving rates should be raised. I would say this should wait for sometime, depending upon the judgment of monetary authority, and the Government too, as to how long the increase: in interest rate raise will have to remain and whether these will have to a further dose of rise of the rates. The behaviour of the stock market should also be considered in this decision. The market went to heights: in the last month or two, a significant decline has set in. Anyway, the primary purpose of this article is to discuss the subject generally, with reference to the relative roles, that is to say responsibilities of the central bank and the government in the matter keeping close watch on inflationary movements and taking appropriate action. Till about 20-25 years back, the subject was not prominent, it being assumed, presumably, that both the bank and government had responsibility and had to take action, on the part of both or the bank only, depending upon the circumstances.

Later the view developed that action to deal with inflation was primarily the responsibility of the central bank. And, the central banks, by and large, seemed to accept this position, feeling happy at receiving an important power in economic management, and so-called autonomy too. In fact, in some countries, the arrangements were formalized in this behalf. The maximum rate of permissible (tolerable) inflation rate was fixed by mutual consent and any rate above this brought penalty on the bank. I have been out of touch with developments in these matters, on account of age (88), but my impression is that such rigid arrangements failed.

Therefore, while the central bank has major responsibility in the matter of inflation management, government should not abdicate some role in this task. Inflation is predominantly a monetary phenomenon, but there are other forces influencing prices. Very important among these is fiscal management. Tax changes and varying the features of saving instruments, tightening measures of control to reduce speculation in the share, commodity and bullion markets, will also help check inflation. Inflation is not the exclusive show of one party. It should also be noted that government is answerable to parliament. The Prime Minister or the Finance Minister may say that inflation control is under the charge of the central bank and try to wash off its responsibility. But this will also well to note that inflation is not a phenomenon easy to control even with the joint effort of the central bank and the government. We cannot, for instance, control inflationary causes coming from outside the country such as the price of oil.

Another reason for the close working together government and the central bank on inflation control is that the measures taken by either should not be so draconian as to upset the economy and lead to slump and unemployment. It is desirable to nip inflation win the bud, be cautious, observe carefully and take action at the very early stages, rather than act in panic when inflation has reached serious dimensions. But this is not do so in most countries. The general tendency on the part of the central bank and the government is today the presence of inflation and admit only when the situation has taken a bad shape. This is far from good governance.

In these matters, some rules can be worked out for rough guidance, but there should not be rigid rules. There is need to rely a lot on intuition, judgment and discretion. No blind set of rules or formulae should be relied upon. Commodity prices, consumer prices, money supply, bank credit expansion, money rates, share and bullion prices and exchange rates should all be taken into account.

For some years in the eighties and the nineties, there was a widespread tendency for central banks to rely largely or even solely on money supply figure. It was the practice to fix money supply targets, taking into account the estimates of GDP growth. If the expansion of money supply was more than the target, monetary and credit policies were to be tightened; if it was less, the policies were to be tightened.

Money supply targets were known to the public and so money supply data were awaited with anxiety by the money and exchange markets, which became more restless than the central bank itself! This led to all kinds of speculation, in the country and abroad. Before long, it was realised that money supply variations were not a sure guide to policy. It was important but not all important. So, country after country gave up the practice of money supply being the sole criterion for initiating policy changes.

All said and done, the two really important elements in the inflationary phenomenon are: (1) bank credit to industry, trade and other growing sources of demand, such as trading in shares, and bullion, and (2) credit to government. Experience has shown that barring relatively few countries, where credit to industry and trade predominate, credit to government by the central bank and the commercial banks constitute the primary cause of inflation. Also, taking into account the fact that most central banks lack real autonomy and the selection of the Governor of the bank is, by governmental nomination, there is a built-in tendency for governments to resort to bank credit, especially central bank credit for meeting their needs, which also tend to be flexible! This is the real problem, which is rarely talked with courage and determination. On paper there may be safeguards against excessive borrowing from the banking system on the part of the government.

It is not said that government borrowing alone constitutes the import cause for inflation. Now and then there are other causes, in particular external ones like sharp oil price hikes, which never go back wholly to the old levels. A substantial portion remains on a permanent basis.

We must also take note of the important fact that in general, rarely is parliamentary opinion strong against inflation, either on account of lethargy or the fear of hurting their vote bank sections. In the developing countries, with large illiteracy and the predominance of rural population the general public too remains indifferent, until inflation is very severe and is allowed to last long. The white collar workers and organized labourer are mostly compensated against inflation through "dearness" allowances. It is the vast majority of the poor that suffers.

Enough has been said that inflation control is a very difficult job. We do not have the requisite courage, doggedness, sense of moral values and dedication to true public welfare to avoid inflation and control it when it occurs owing unforeseen causes. Total control is beyond the power of anyone, however much he may brag!

Fortunately, there is a hope, why, more than a hope that there may be a way out of the situation mentioned above. It is our friend globalisation. Whatever may be harmful effects, at least in the short and medium-term, of globalization, it has the power to check inflation, to a suitable extent, especially against inflationary domestic fiscal and monetary policies. Even in respect of external causes, such as oil price rises, recent experience has shown that the harmful impact may not be very severe on the world economy in general, in contrast to what we experienced in the 1970s and early 1980s. Globalization compels the government and the central bank, before long, to refrain from pursuing in inflationary policies as far as possible and check it fairly expeditiously and effectively when inflation does occur. So, there are checks and balances in the economic world, even as there are in nature. The unseen hand is active here too.

References

Economic Survey 2006-07.

E.P.W., Nov. 2007.

RBI Bulletin, 2005.

Tenth Five Year Plan, 2000-07.

32

Agflation in India

A Paradoxical Situation

Shyam Sunder Singh Chauhan,
Ravi Kant and Manish Dev

The global economy faced severe price rise of agricultural commodities during 2006-08 because of natural disasters such as droughts and cyclone, speculative activities in financial markets, failure of governments to maintain required buffer stocks, changing consumption habits of consumers in major developing countries—China and India. Since agricultural commodities are from the group of commodities of mass consumption so any increase in agricultural commodities hits directly common men. The phenomenon of price rise of agricultural commodities has given a new term—"Agflation".

The present paper deals with the situation of Agflation in India in the context of decrease in inflation in general.

AGFLATION : MEANING AND CONCEPTS

Agflation, a term coined in early 2007 by analysts at Merril Lynch, describes generalized inflation led by rises in agricultural commodity prices. In many countries (as in United States), agricultural prices are not generally factored into core inflation figures. The term describes a situation in which "external (i.e. Agricultural) prices drive up core inflation rates.

In general terms agflation means "an increase in the price of food that occures as a result of increased demand from human consumption and use as an alternate source of energy. While the competitive nature of retail supermarkets allows some of the effects of agflation to be absorbed, the price increases that agflation causes are largely passed on to end consumers. The term is derived a combination of the word 'Agriculture' and 'Inflation'.

In countries like India, agflation occurs mainly from supply side. Prices of agricultural commodities show on increasing trends when the supply of foodgrains and other agricultural commodities are in short. Supply of agricultural commodities suffers greatly because of decrease in production because of poor monsoon and some other climatic conditions. Middlemen working in agriculture marketing chain make the situation worst by hoarding and black-marketing.

In recent times the level of buffer stocks of foodgrains in the country also played a crucial role in the price movements of foodgrains. High levels of stocks in FCI godowns forced middlemen not to resort hoarding because it would not be going to fruitful to them because the government would release additional quantity of foodgrains into the market and prices would automatically comes down. On the contrary, the low level of buffer stocks creates a psychological stimulus to increase prices of foodgrains.

Internationally, agflation is also a result of use of foodgrains for alternative purposes such as energy source. Interest in alternative energies contributes to inflation. In order to produce bio-fuel (such as bio-diesel and ethanol), manufactures need to use food products such as soybean and corn. This creates more demand for these products, which causes their prices to increases.

Another factor that causes agflation worldwide, is the decision of developing countries like India to purchase food grains from international market so as to compensate shortage in domestic production. International suppliers take full advantage of weaknesses of developing countries in maintaining balance in demand and supply of foodgrains.

Unfortunately, these price increases spread to other non-fuel related grains (such as rice and wheat) as consumers switch to less expansive substitutes for consumption. Further, more, agflation also affects non-vegetable food (eggs, meat and dairy) as the price increases for grain make livestock feed more expansive as well.

MOVEMENT IN WORLD FOOD PRICES

Green revolution in India and in most of the developing countries resulted in sharp increase in production of majority of agricultural commodities. Increase in production resulted in decline in prices of these commodities. In 1974-2005 food prices on world markets fell by three quarters in real terms. Food articles were so cheap during 2005 that the West was battling gluttony even as it scrap piles of half-eaten leftovers into the bin.

The situation took unwarranted turn in the late 2005 when the prices of almost all food commodities increased extraordinarily. Wheat prices doubled and prices of almost every crop under sun-maize, milk, oilseeds, pulses were at or near peak in real terms. The Economists food price index was higher significantly than at any time since it was created in 1845. Even in real terms prices had jumped by 75 per cent in just 6 months. The prices for commodities in general, and agricultural commodities in particular, had reached all sorts high. Wheat prices hit 11 year high in June 2007.

Food prices were rising, putting upward pressure on producer and consumer inflation. Agflation occurred, given the expanding constraints on food supply, the changing demand for food, and the entrance of energy business as mass consumers of food products. It was not surprising to see food prices worldwide rapidly putting upward pressure on overall inflation.

The situation on price rise of agricultural commodities took ugly turn between the beginnings of 2007 to early 2008. The prices of some of the most basic international commodities increased on international market. Prices of wheat in international market doubled from February 2007 to February 2008 hitting a record high over US $10 a bushel. The BBC predicted that world wheat stocks were expected to fall to a 30 years low in 2008, because of severe droughts in Australia. Paradoxically, agflation erupted at time when global economy was in the grip of recession. Rice prices also reached ten year highs. In some countries, as in India, milk and meat prices more than doubled, and soy which hit a 34 year high price in December 2007: and maize prices have increased dramatically. In more specific terms, between the start of 2006 and 2008, the average world price for rice rose by 217 per cent, wheat by 136 per cent, maize by 125 per cent and soybeans by 107 per cent. In late April 2008, rice prices hit 24 cents a pound, twice the price that it was seven months earlier.

CAUSES OF AGFLATION

Initially unreasonable droughts in grain producing countries and rising oil prices were treated as the main causes of price rise of food products. Oil prices further increased the costs of fertilizers, transportation costs of food articles and production costs of agriculture. Secondary cause of agflation is cited as the increasing use of bio-fuels in developed countries, and an increasing demand for more varied diets across the expanding middle class populations of Asia. These factors, coupled with decreasing global food stockpiles have all contributed to the price rise of food articles.

In more specific terms *British New Statesman Magazine* (2008) declared in an article entitled, "The trading Frenzy that sent prices soaring" noted that besides increase in global population and the switch to bio-fuels speculative activities in commodity futures played an important role in price escalation of food articles. The article states that the food crises has developed over "An incredibly short space of time—essentially over the past 18 months". It continues, "the reason for food 'shortages' is speculation in commodity futures following the collapse of the financial derivatives markets". Desperate for quick returns, dealer withdraws trillions of dollars out of equities and mortgage bonds and ploughed them into food and raw material.

Apart from droughts in wheat producing areas of Australia and Cyclone 'Nargis' hit badly the drawaddy delta and other key rice-growing areas in Myanmar.

Simon Johnson (2008), Chief economist at the IMF pointed to three factors as responsible for the spike in prices.

1. Increased demand from emerging economies like India and China, where consumers are demanding more calories in their diet,
2. *The weather* : Draughts have had an adverse impact in some parts of the world, and
3. Continuous relationship between food and fuel. "Corn was used to be fuel for cars".

In generalized form, analysts enlisted following factors responsible for global price rise:

1. World population growth in absolute terms;
2. Increased demand for resource intensive food;
3. Increase in petroleum prices leads to increase in cost of production and transportation;
4. Declining food buffer stocks;
5. Commodity future markets and financial speculation;
6. Impact of trade liberalization has made many countries food independent to net food importing countries;
7. Use of food crops such as corn for bio-fuels;
8. US government and alike pay farmers to idle their cropland under a conservation programme;
9. Distorted global rice market;
10. Several distinct weather and climate-related disaster caused disruption in crop production;
11. Soil erosion, urbanization and increasing uses of farm land for non-agricultural purposes led to decrease in food production.

12. Loss of agricultural production due to water depletion.

AGFLATION IN INDIA : A PARADOXICAL SITUATION

Inflation in India shows a volatile trends during 2003-09 (Table 1).

TABLE I

Trends in WPI-based Inflation Rates

Year	*Inflationary Trends*
2003	Inflation increased from 3.5 per cent in Jan. 2003 to 6.5 per cent in April 2003. It then declined to 3.5 per cent in Aug. 2003 and rose further to 5.86 per cent in Dec. 2003.
2004	Volatility persisted in 2004 too. Inflation declined from 6.5 per cent in Jan. 2004 to 4.3 per cent in April 2004. It reaches at its peak in Aug. 2004 with 8.7 per cent level and then declined to 6.5 per cent in December 2004.
2005	Inflation declined from 6 per cent in Jan. 2005 to 3.6 per cent in Aug. 2005 and increased by one percentage point in Dec. 2005 (4.6 per cent).
2006	Inflation declined to 3.7 per cent in April 2006 but rose persistently to touch 6 per cent level in Dec. 2006
2007	Inflation increased in early 2007 and reached to 6.5 per cent in March 2007. It declined continuously in subsequent months and touched 3.8 per cent in Dec. 2007.
2008	Inflation surged substantially from 3.8 per cent in Jan. 2008 to 11.6 per cent in June 2008.
2009	Anti-inflationary measures mixed with recessionary forces brought down inflation to (-) 1.78 per cent in June 2009 it happened for the first time since 1975.

Source : Various reports of RBI and Ministry of Finance, Government of India.

Thus, India became the first country in the world which has witnessed the negative inflation rate in June 2009. It should be taken not as a sign of recession in Indian economy, but a decline in inflation rate from a high base in June 2008.

Table 2 shows that the declining trends in WPI-based inflation rate ever since Dec. 2008, but the inflation is still high for primary products. Not even this, inflation rates based on all the three CPIs are still significantly higher, offering little respite declining trend in the headline inflation, while the dip has largely been driven by low fuel group inflation and slowing manufacture products inflation levels. The data released on March 12, 2009 shows that year-on-year inflation in case of primary products, led by mass consumption food items continued to stay near double digit levels. Beside, the sequential inflation in some of these items is also high; the week-on-week inflation in vegetables recorded an alarming 4 per cent.

As per data released on March 12, 2009, WPI-based inflation rose 2.43 per cent in Feb. 2009 lower than the first week of Jan. 2009. Items such as cereals (11 per cent), pulses (13 per cent) and sugar (23 per cent) showed a year-on-year inflation well over the double digits. Besides, inflation levels in case of milk and fruits (both 7 per cent) and vegetables and

TABLE 2

Inflation Rates (Year-on-Year) in India

(Per cent)

Base	*Reference Month*	*For All Commodities*	*Primary Articles*	*Fuel power lights and lubricants*	*Manu-factured products*
	Weights	100	22.02	14.23	63.75
WPI	Jan. 2007	6.38	11.52	3.62	6.08
	Dec. 2007	3.83	4.47	2.9	3.92
	Jan. 2008	4.43	4.83	3.86	4.54
	Dec. 2008	6.16	11.16	(-) 0.22	6.62
	Jan. 2009	5.27	10.86	(-) 1.76	5.74
CPI-IW	Jan. 2009	10.45			
CPI-AL	Jan. 2009	11.62			
CPI-RL	Jan. 2009	11.35			

Source : RBI and Labour Bureau, Shimla.

TABLE 3
Costlier Food in India (Wholesale Price Index)

	Feb. 28, 2009	*1 March 2008*	*(%) change*
Primary Articles (weight: 22.02)	248.1	234.4	5.8
Food articles (weight: 15.40)	244.2	225.5	8.3
Cereals	241.8	218.0	10.9
Pulses	272.1	240.6	13
Fruits and Vegetables	252.2	233.7	7.9
Eggs/meat/fish	250.3	242.3	3.3
Condiments and spices	263.8	241.8	9.09
Manufactured food products	212.8	200.8	5.9
Dairy products	249.1	241.3	3.2
Tea and Coffee processing	196.3	193.9	1.2
Sugar	179.1	144.5	23
Milk	233.7	218.2	7
Edible oils	177.2	193.1	(-) 8.2

Source : *The Business Line*, New Delhi, March 13, 2009.

spices (both 9 per cent) were within touching distance on double digits marks.

There is no doubt that continuing food-based inflation is a worrying sign, though there has been a bit of declining trend in overall inflation rate. It is of great significance that food inflation (i.e. agflation) tends to hit the poor.

WPI-based inflation in India turned negative in June 2009 but it gives no respite to common men as consumer prices of almost all commodities of mass consumption are still high significantly.

CONCLUSION

The current trends of inflation in India has created a situation of paradox under which WPI-based inflation has turned negative, while the inflation rates based on CPIs are still on higher side. The government as well as RBI might feel happy and give credit to their policies and packages for this achievement, but common men still feel the heat of rising prices.

It will be wrong to presume, in the light of negative inflation rate, that economy is in severe recession. What the result show that the negative trend in inflation in June 2009 must be read with higher base of WPI in June 2008, it is therefore suggested that more cautious policies are required to deal with the current situation particularly of agflation.

References

Brooks, Adan (2007), 'Corn's Key Role as Food and Fuel', *The BBC News*, London, Dec. 17.

Global Research (2009), "Financial Speculators Reap Profits from Global Hunger", Centre for Research in Globalization, June 27.

http://en.wikipedia.org/wiki/agflation

http://www.bigpicture.typepad.com

http://www.innestopedia.com/......

http://www.investopedia.com/term/a/agflation.asp

http://www.investopedia.com/term/a/agflation.asp

Steinberg, Stefan (2008), "Financial Speculators Reap Profits from Global Hunger", Global Research, Centre of Research on Globalization, April 24.

The BBC News (2007), "Cyclone Fuels Rice Price Increase", May 7.

The BBC News (2008), "The Cost of Food: Facts and Figures", London, Oct. 16).

Lewis Leo (2008), "Fear of Rice Riots as Surge in Demand hits Across the Far East", *Times Online*, April 8.

The BBC News (2008), Cyclone Fuels Rice Price Increase; London May 8.

The BBC News, 17 Dec. (2007).

The Economist (2007), Dec. 6

The Economist (2007), Dec. 6.

33

Price Inflation and its Economic Effects

D.C. Mishra, Md. Tahir Hussain
and Uma Shankar Bharati

Inflation is defined as a sustained increase in the general level of prices for goods and services. It is measured as an annual percentage increase. As inflation rises, the value of currency goes down. Thus the purchasing power of the currency, i.e. the goods and services that can be bought in a unit of currency, too goes down.

In economics, inflation is a rise in the general level of prices of goods and services in an economy over a period of time. The term *inflation* once referred to increases in the money supply (monetary inflation); however, economic debates about the relationship between money supply and price levels have led to its primary use today in describing *price inflation*. Inflation can also be described as a decline in the real value of money—a loss of purchasing power in the medium of exchange which is also the monetary unit of account. When the general price level rises, each unit of currency buys fewer goods and services. A chief measure of general price-level inflation is the general inflation rate, which is the percentage change in a general price index, normally the Consumer Price Index, over time.

Inflation can cause adverse effects on the economy. For example, uncertainty about future inflation may discourage investment and saving. High inflation may lead to shortages of goods in consumers begin hoarding out of concern that prices will increase in the future.

Economists generally agree that high rates of inflation and hyperinflation are caused by an excessive growth of the money supply. Views on which factors determine low to moderate rates of inflation are more varied. Low or moderate inflation may be attributed to fluctuations in real demand for goods and services, or changes in available supplies such as during scarcities, as well as to growth in the money supply. However, the consensus view is that a long sustained period of inflation is caused by money supply growing faster than the rate of economic growth. Today, most economists favour a low steady rate of inflation. Low (as opposed to zero or negative) inflation may reduce the severity of economic recessions by enabling the labour market to adjust more quickly in a downturn, and reducing the risk that a liquidity trap prevents monetary policy from stabilizing the economy. The task of keeping the rate of inflation low and stable is usually given to monetary authorities. Generally, these monetary authorities are the central banks that control the size of the money supply through the setting of interest rates, through open market operations, and through the setting of banking reserve requirements.

Inflation originally referred to the debasement of the currency. When gold was used as currency, gold coins could be collected by the government (e.g. the king or the ruler of the region), melted down, mixed with other metals such as silver, copper or lead, and reissued at the same nominal value. By diluting the gold with other metals, the government could increase the total number of coins issued without also needing to government could increase the total number of coins issued without also needing to increase the amount of gold used to make them. When the cost of each coin is lowered in this way, the government profits from an increase in seigniorage. This practice would increase the money supply but at the same time lower the relative value of each coin. As the relative value of the coins decrease, consumers would need more coins to exchange for the same goods and services. These goods and services would experience a price increase as the value of each coin is reduced.

Inflation is usually measured by calculating the inflation rate of a price index, usually the Consumer Price Index. The Consumer Price Index measures prices of a selection of goods and services purchased by a "typical consumer". The inflation rate is the percentage rate of change of a price index over time. For example, in January 2007, the U.S. Consumer Price Index was 202.416, and in January 2008 it was 211.080. The formula for calculation the annual percentage rate inflation in the Consumer Price Index over the course of 2007 is = 211.08 – 41/ 202.41 = 4.28 percent. The resulting inflation rate for the Consumer Price Index in this one year period is 4.28%, meaning the general level of prices for typical U.S. consumers rose by approximately four percent in 2007.

Other widely used price indices for calculating price inflation include the following:

1. *Cost-of-living indices (COLI)* are indices similar to the Consumer Price Index which are often used to adjust fixed incomes and contractual incomes to maintain real value of those incomes.
2. *Producer price indices (PPIs)* which measures average changes in prices received by domestic producers for their output. This differs from the Consumer Price Index in that price subsidization, profits, and taxes may cause the amount received by the producer to differ from what the consumer paid. There is also typically a delay between an increase in the PPI and any eventual increase in the Consumer Price Index. Producer price index measures the pressure being put on producers by the costs of their raw materials. This could be "passed on" to consumers, or it could be absorbed by profits, or offset by increasing

productivity. In India and the United States, an earlier version of the PPI was called the Wholesale Price Index.

3. *Commodity price indices,* which measure the price of a selection of commodities. In the present commodity price indices are weighted by the relative importance of the components to the "all in" cost of an employee.
4. *Core price indices:* because food and oil prices can change quickly due to changes in supply and demand conditions in the food and oil markets, it can be difficult to detect the long-run trend in price levels when those prices are included. Therefore, most statistical agencies also report a measure of 'core inflation', which removes the most volatile components (such as food and oil) from a broad price index like the CPI. Because core inflation is less affected by short-run supply and demand conditions in specific markets, central banks rely on it to better measure the inflationary impact of current monetary policy.

Inflation measures are often modified over time, either for the relative weight of goods in the basket, or in the way in which goods and services from the present are compared with goods and services from the past. Over time adjustments are made to the type of goods and services selected in order to reflect changes in the sorts of goods and services purchased by 'typical consumers'. New products may be introduced, older products disappear, the quality of existing products may change, and consumer preferences can shift. Both the sorts of goods and services which are included in the "basket" and the weighted price used in inflation measures will be changed over time in order to keep pace with the changing marketplace.

Inflation numbers are often seasonally adjusted in order to differentiate expected cyclical cost shifts. For example, home heating costs are expected to rise in colder months, and seasonal adjustments are often used when measuring for inflation to compensate for cyclical spikes in energy or fuel demand. Inflation numbers may be averaged or otherwise subjected to statistical techniques in order to remove statistical nose and volatility of individual prices.

When looking at inflation economic institutions may focus only on certain kinds of prices, or *special indices,* such as the core inflation index which is used by central banks to formulate monetary policy.

NEGATIVE EFFECTS OF INFLATION

An increase in the general level of prices implies a decrease in the purchasing power of the currency. That is, when the general level of prices rises, each monetary unit buys fewer goods and services. The effect of inflation is not distributed evenly, and as a consequence there are hidden costs to some and benefits to others from this decrease in purchasing power. For example, with inflation lenders or depositors who are paid a fixed rate of interest on loans or deposits will lose purchasing power from their interest earnings, while their borrowers benefit. Individuals or institutions with cash assets will experience a decline in the purchasing power of their holdings. Increases in payments to workers and pensioners often lag behind inflation, especially for those with fixed payments.

High or unpredictable inflation rates are regarded as harmful to an overall economy. They add inefficiencies in the market, and make it difficult for companies to budget or plan long-term. Inflation can act as a drag on productivity as companies are forced to shift resources away from products and services in order to focus on profits and losses from currency inflation. Uncertainty about the future purchasing power of money discourages investment and saving. And inflation can impose hidden tax increases, as inflated earnings push taxpayers into higher income tax rates.

With high inflation, purchasing power is redistributed from those on fixed incomes such as pensioners towards those with variable incomes whose earnings may better keep pace with the inflation. This redistribution of purchasing power will also occur between international trading partners. Where fixed exchange rates are imposed, rising inflation in one economy will cause its exports to become more expensive and affect the balance of trade. There can also be negative impacts to trade from an increased instability in currency exchange prices caused by unpredictable inflation.

COST-PUSH INFLATION

Rising inflation can prompt employees to demand higher wages, to keep up with consumer prices, rising wages in turn can help fuel inflation. In the case of collective bargaining, wages will be set as a factor of price expectations, which will be higher when inflation has an upward trend. This can cause a wage spiral. In a sense, inflation begets further inflationary expectations.

HOARDING

People buy consumer durables as stores of wealth in the absence of viable alternative as a means of getting rid of excess cash before it is devalued, creating shortages of the hoarded objects.

HYPERINFLATION

If inflation gets totally out of control (in the upward direction), it can grossly interfere with the normal working of the economy, hurting its ability to supply.

ALLOCATIVE EFFICIENCY

A change in the supply or demand for a good will normally cause its price to change, signalling to buyers and sellers that they should re-allocate resources in response to the new market conditions. But when prices are constantly changing due to inflation, genuine price signals get lost in the noise, so agents are slow to respond to them. The result is a loss of allocative efficiency.

SHOE LEATHER COST

High inflation increases the opportunity cost of holding cash balances and can induce people to hold a greater portion of their assets in interest paying accounts. However, since cash is still needed in order to carry out transactions this means that more "trips to the bank" are necessary in order to make withdrawals, proverbially wearing out the "shoe leather" with each trip.

MENU COSTS

With high inflation, firms must change their prices often in order to keep up with economy-wide changes. But often changing prices is itself a costly activity whether explicitly, as with the need to print new menus, or implicitly.

BUSINESS CYCLES

According to the Austrian Business Cycle Theory, inflation sets-off the business cycle. Austrian economists hold this to be the most damaging effect of inflation. According to Austrian theory, artificially low interest rates and the associated increase in the money supply lead to reckless, speculative borrowing, resulting in clusters of malinvestments, which eventually have to be liquidated as they become unsustainable.

POSITIVE EFFECTS

Labour-market Adjustments

Keynesians believe that nominal wages are slow to adjust downwards. This can lead to prolonged disequilibrium and high unemployment in the labour market. Since inflation would lower the real wage if nominal wages are kept constant. Keynesian argue that some inflation is good for the economy, as it would allow labour markets to reach equilibrium faster.

Debt Relief

Debtors who have debts with a fixed nominal rate of

interest will see a reduction in the "real" interest rate as the inflation rate rise. The "real" interest on a loan is the nominal rate minus the inflation rate (R=n–i). For example, if you take a loan where the stated interest rate is 6% and the inflation rate is at 3%, the real interest rate that you are paying for the loan is 3%. It would also hold true that if you had a loan at a fixed interest rate of 6% and the inflation rate jumped to 20% you would have a real interest rate of -14%. Banks and other lenders adjust for this inflation risk either by including a inflation premium in the costs of lending the money by creating a higher initial stated interest rate or by setting the interest at a variable rate.

Room to Maneuver

The primary tools for controlling the money supply are the ability to set the discount rate, the rate at which banks can borrow from the central bank, and open market operations which are the central bank's interventions into the bonds market with the aim of affecting the nominal interest rate. If an economy finds itself in a recession with already low, or even zero, nominal interest rates, then the bank cannot cut these rates further (since negative nominal interest rates are impossible) in order to stimulate the economy—this situation is known as a liquidity trap. A moderate level of inflation tends to ensure that nominal interest rates stay sufficiently above zero so that if the need arises the bank can cut the nominal interest rate.

Tobin Effect

The Nobel prize winning economist James Tobin at one point had argued that a moderate level of inflation can increase investment in an economy leading to faster growth or at least higher steady state level of income. This is due to the fact that inflation lowers the return on monetary assets relative to real assets, such as physical capital. To avoid inflation, investors would switch from holding their assets as money (or a similar, susceptible to inflation, form) to investing in real capital projects.

References

FAO Bulletin, 2005-08.

Imported Inflation, C.P. Chandrasekhar and Jayanti, Global Inflation in India: How to Tackle it: http://indiabroad.com/many/2007/mar/21

Macroeconomic and Monetary Developments, *Mid-term Review*, 2008-09.

Monetary Policy and Fiscal Policy: Impact of Inflation and Effects with a New Keynesian Assignment of Weapons to Targets, Madras, James and Vines, David, 1988.

Polackova, Hana, 1997 : Inflation in Non-tradeable and the Macroeconomic Policy Mix : A Model with Policy Application to Transition Economics, Policy Research Working Paper Series.

RBI Annual Report, 2006-07.

The Hindu Business Line, Global Inflation and India.

Index

Administrated Price, 192
Adverse Effects on:
  Production, 224
  Distribution of Income, 224
Agflation in India, 360
Agflation:
  Meaning and Concepts, 356
Aggregate Supply and Fiscal Policy, 338
Allocative Efficiency, 369
Angles, F., 323
Automatic Stabilizers, 337
Average Annual Inflation Rate, 140

Banking System:
  Pumping of Liquidity, 150
Bharati, Uma Shankar, 364
Bhattacharya, D.K., 281
Brooman, F. S., 14
Bush, George W., 31
Business Cycles, 370

Causes of Agflation, 358
Chakraborty, Niyati, 281
Chakravarty Committee, 104
Chand, Rina, 264
Changes in:
  Money and Wealth, 92
Chauhan, Shyam Sunder Singh, 355
CII (Cost Inflation Index), 277
Climate Change:
  Effects, 223
COLI (Cost of Living Indices), 366
Concepts of Inflation, 98
Consequences of Inflation, 224
Consumer Price Index for Agricultural Labour, 80
Controlling Inflation, 114
Control of Inflation, 85
Cost-push Factors, 191
Cost-push Inflation, 9, 18, 291, 369
Commodity Prices and Inflation, 13, 34
Consumer Price Index, 80
Consumer Price Index for Industrial Works, 80
Control Inflation:
  Remedial Measures, 2
Control Inflation:
  Role of Fiscal and Monetary Policies, 88
Creeping Inflation, 15
Crop Pattern:
  Changes, 223

Current Price Rise:
  Reasons, 194

Debtors and Creditors, 77
Debt Relief, 370
Deficit Financing, 189
Demand Management, 195
Demand-pull Factors, 188
Demand-pull Inflation, 9, 17
Demand-side Measures, 10
  Fiscal Measures, 10
  Monetary Measures, 11
Determinants of:
  Inflation in India, 157
Dev, Manish, 355
Discretionary Fiscal Policy, 337

Effectiveness of Fiscal Policies, 338
Effects on:
  Production, 76
  Distribution, 77
Effects of Inflation, 76, 293
Einzig, Paul, 75
Estimation Procedure, 166

Fiscal Dividend, 90
Fiscal Drag, 90
Fiscal Measures, 195, 207, 275
Fiscal Policy, 25, 86, 291
Fiscal Policy for:
  Controlling Inflation, 374
Fiscal Policy:
  Kinds, 337
Five Year Average Inflation Rate, 300
Fixation of Maximum Prices, 196
Fixed Income Groups, 78
Flexibility of Fiscal Policy, 90
Food and Population Growth, 220
Food Consumption Patterns:
  Changes, 222
Food Situation, 177
Fuel, Power, Light and Lubricants, 129
Full and Partial Inflation, 65

GDP and Money Supply, 71
Global Crisis and Inflations, 174
Global Economic Crisis:
  U.P.A. Government Policy to Counter It, 308
  Pros and Cons, 318
Global Inflation, 228
Global Inflation and India:
  Changing Dynamics, 229
Government and Inflation, 70
Government's Fruitless Strategies, 205
Growth and Inflation, 264
Gupta, Arjun Sen, 324
Gupta, Rajendra Pd., 1

Harming the Poor, 72
High Oil Prices, 223
Hike in Oil Prices, 193
Hoarding, 369
Hoda, Sharful, 157
How Does Inflation Affect our Investments, 206
How Does Monetary Policy Work? 91
Hussain, Tahir, 364
Hyperinflation, 369

Improving Poor Infrastructure, 177
Increase in Monetary Income, 272
Inflationary Control Measures, 270
Inflationary Trends and Measures Taken to Curb, 173
Inflationary Trends in India, 217
  Issues and Policy Options, 144
Inflation Control Measures, 225
Inflation in India, 181
Inflation:
  Causes, 22
  Good Effects, 22
  Threshold Level, 33

Recession, Financial Meltdown and the Indian Economy, 44
Definition, 14
Measurement, 100
Strikes After 20 Years, 135
Causes, 272
India and Ways Out, 247
Types, 271
India Since-1947, 65
Measurement, 79
In India, 94, 297
And Growth, 103
Rate-based on CPI (IW) Consumer Inflation, 122
Recent Steps to Check, 292
Argument, 297
Theoretical Foundation, 158, 182
International Price Movement, 306
Indian Economy:
Nature of Inflationary Trends, 147
Recent Global Inflationary Trends and its Impact, 351
Impact of Global Inflation, 320
Situation and the Crisis, 58
Prices Position, 31
India:
Unrelenting Inflation, 6
Inflationary Trends, 75, 106, 201, 234, 289
Global Economic Crisis, 327
Trends of Price, 183
Control of Inflation, 195
An Analysis of Inflationary Trends, 209
Nature of Inflation, 303

Jani, B.M., 144
Jha, Anil Kumar, 247
Jha, Raghbendra, 99
Jha, Sadanand, 247
Johnson, H.G., 14
Jumping Inflation, 16

Kant, Ravi, 355
Keynesian Revolution, 296
Keynes, J.M., 15
Kumar, Ajit, 228
Kumar, Dalip, 118
Kumari, Bharti, 118
Kumar, Manish, 295
Kumar, Niranjay, 295
Kumari, Pushpa, 318
Kumar, Priyatam, 259
Kumar, Ratnesh, 181
Kumar, Sanjay, 327
Kumar, Shailesh, 181
Kumar, Sunil, 209
Kumar, Vivek, 201, 295

Labour-Market Adjustments, 370
Limiting Production:
Causes, 273
Low Rate of Inflation:
Causes Behind, 303

Manufacturing Products, 127
Manufacturing Sector:
Foreign Investment, 177
Marjit, Sugata, 106
Marx, K., 322
Md. Quddus, 1
Measurement of Inflation, 79
Measures to Beat Inflation, 176
Measures to Control Inflation, 273
Mishra, D.C., 364
Monetary and Fiscal Policy to Control Inflation, 336
Monetary Measures, 195, 207
Monetary Money and Prices, 304
Monetary Policy for Controlling Inflation, 339
Monetary Policy to Control Inflation, 340
Money and the Process of Economic Growth, 296
Money Neutralitry Proposition, 296

Monetary Measures, 274
Monetary Policy, 85
Monetary Policy and Control of Inflation, 24
Money Output and Prices, 94
Mounting Government Expenditure, 188
Movement in World Food Prices, 357
Mujtaba, Syed Alay, 234

Negative Effects of Inflation, 368
Non-food Articles, 126

Oil Bears and Inflation, 175
Ojha, Chitranjan, 351
Open Market Operation, 339

PDS (Public Distribution System), 198
Policy Options to Arrest Current Inflation, 153
Population Planning, 207
Portfolio Adjustment Process, 91
Prabha, Kanchan, 201
Pre and Post-Reform Era:
Inflation Trends, 295
Preventing Inflation in India, 278
Price Movements in India:
Impact of Global Economy, 343
Price Situation during 1970s, 299
Price Situation after 1990, 302
Price Situation during the 1990s, 301
Price Situation during 1951-71, 298
Price Stability, 30
Private Trade in Foodgrains:
Control, 198
Problem of Oilseeds and Edible Oils, 197
Purushotam, Pankaj, 234

Raj, Dev, 13
Rani, Rekha, 118
Ranjan, Ravi, 308
Ravi, Chandra Shekhar, 270
Realistic Measures, 207
Recent Global Inflationary Trends, 219 281
Recession in America, 53
Reddy, Venugopal, 104
Reddy, Y.V., 97
Rekha, Kumari, 217
Remedies to Control Inflation, 21
Rise in Price in India:
Causes, 187
Roy, Bishnu, 173
Rules *v.* Discretion in Monetary Policy, 340
Running Inflation, 15

Saha, S.P., 173
Sah, D.N., 343
Santosh, Rahul Kumar, 336
Seventh Five Year:
Price Situation, 301
Shah, Badri Narayan, 270
Shaprio, Edward, 14
Sharma, Brijesh, 88
Sharma, C.B., 64
Sharma, Jagdish, 201
Sharma, V.D., 88
Shoe Leather Cost, 370
Singh, Manmohan, 312, 329
Singh, Paramanand, 44
Singh, Shashi Bhushan, 44
Singh, Shrawan Kumar, 94
Singh, Sudha Ranjan, 228
Singh, Uma Shankar, 351
Sixth Five Year Plan:
Price Movement, 301
Speculation in Commodities, 177
Stagflation:
How to Control, 19
Stickiness in Inflation Trends, 205
Stimulus Package and Inflation, 178
Structural Inflation, 291

Sultan, Zafar Ahmad, 157
Supply Measures, 196
Supply Side Measures, 10
Sustainability among Assets, 92
System of Dual Prices, 197

To Control Inflation:
  Monetary and Fiscal Policy, 373
Treasury Inflation Protected Securities, 151
Trends of Inflation, 7
Trends of Wholesale Prices since Independence, 120

UNME (Urban Non-Manual Employees), 122
U.S. Economy:
  Growth of the Financial Sectors, 56

Vikash, 217

Wageflation:
  Misconception, 152
Wages and Salary Earners, 78
Walking Inflation, 15
What Drives Inflation Lower? 111
Who is Price-maker, 152
Wholesale Price Index, 79
Wholesale Price Index, 79
Why India Should Adopt Inflation Targeting?, 37
World Price Volatility, 36
Worldwide Oil Price:
  Phenomenal Rise, 176
WPI (Wholesale Price Index), 108, 277